GROWING
UP BLACK

GROWING UP BLACK

From slave days to the present — 25 African-Americans reveal the trials and triumphs of their childhoods

EDITED BY

JAY DAVID

AVON BOOKS ◆ NEW YORK

My sincere thanks to my research assistant,
Beth Pratt-Dewey
and to my editor at Avon Books,
Gwen Montgomery

Additional copyright notices appear on the Acknowledgments pages, which serve as an extension of this Copyright page.

GROWING UP BLACK is an original publication of Avon Books. This work has never before appeared in book form.

AVON BOOKS
A division of
The Hearst Corporation
1350 Avenue of the Americas
New York, New York 10019

Original Copyright © 1968 by William Morrow and Company, Inc.
Revised Compilation Copyright © 1992 by Jay David
Published by arrangement with William Morrow and Company and Jay David
ISBN: 0-380-76632-9

First Avon Books Trade Printing: February 1992

AVON TRADEMARK REG. U.S. PAT. OFF. AND IN OTHER COUNTRIES, MARCA REGISTRADA, HECHO EN U.S.A.

Printed in the U.S.A.

OPM   10   9   8

Acknowledgments

Grateful acknowledgment is made to:

(Original Edition)

The Viking Press, Inc., for permission to reprint material from *A Man Called White* by Walter White. Copyright © 1948 by Walter White.

Harper & Row, Publishers, for permission to reprint material from *Black Boy* by Richard Wright. Copyright © 1937, 1942, 1944, 1945 by Richard Wright.

Sheed & Ward Inc. for permission to reprint material from *Dark Symphony* by Elizabeth Laura Adams. Copyright © 1942 by Sheed & Ward Inc.

Harper & Row, Publishers, for permission to reprint material from *A Choice of Weapons* by Gordon Parks. Copyright © 1965, 1966 by Gordon Parks.

Alderman Library, University of Virginia, for permission to reprint material from *Memoirs of a Monticello Slave: The Life of Isaac Jefferson*. (Original manuscript in The Tracy W. McGregor Library, University of Virginia.)

David McKay Company, Inc., for permission to reprint material from *The Long Shadow of Little Rock* by Daisy Bates. Copyright © 1962 by Daisy Bates.

Grove Press, Inc., for permission to reprint material from *The Autobiography of Malcolm X*. Copyright © 1964 by Alex Haley and Malcolm X. Copyright © 1965 by Alex Haley and Betty Shabazz.

Warner Brothers, Inc. and Soverign Music Co. for permission to reprint lyrics from "Blueberry Hill"—words and music by Noel Coward. Copyright 1929 (renewed) by Warner Brothers, Inc.

Unichappell Music, Inc. and Elvis Presley Music for permission to reprint lyrics from "Sixteen Tons"—words and music by Merle Travis. All rights on behalf of Elvis Presley Music administered by Unichappell Music, Inc. Copyright 1947 by Unichappell Music, Inc.

PolyGram International Publishing, Inc. for permission to reprint lyrics from "The Wayward Wind"—written by Stan Lebowsky and Herbert Newman. Copyright 1955 by PolyGram International Publishing, Inc.

International Publishers for permission to reprint material from *Angela Davis: An Autobiography* by Angela Davis. Copyright © 1988 by Angela Davis.

The Putnam Publishing Group for permission to reprint material from *Sweet Summer* by Bebe Moore Campbell. Copyright © 1989 by Bebe Moore Campbell.

Doubleday, a division of Bantam, Doubleday, Dell Publishing Group, Inc., for permission to reprint material from *Coming of Age in Mississippi* by Anne Moody. Copyright © 1968 by Anne Moody.

The Charlotte Sheedy Literary Agency for permission to reprint material from *Zami, Another Spelling of My Name* by Audre Lorde. Copyright © 1982 by Audre Lorde.

Henry Holt & Company, Inc., for permission to reprint material from *Brothers and Keepers* by John Edgar Wideman. Copyright © 1984 by John Edgar Wideman.

The Washington Post for permission to reprint material from *Dispatches from a Dying Generation* by Nathan McCall. Copyright © 1991 by The Washington Post.

Jobete Music Company Inc. and Stone Diamond Music Corporation for permission to reprint lyrics from "Inner City Blues"—words and music by Marvin Gaye. Copyright 1971 by Jobete Music Company.

Contents

Introduction   1

I Growing Up Black   3

  1. From *A Man Called White* by
     Walter White   5

  2. From *Black Boy* by Richard Wright   10

  3. From *Dark Symphony* by
     Elizabeth Adams   18

  4. From *A Choice of Weapons* by
     Gordon Parks   26

  5. From *I Know Why the Caged Bird Sings*
     by Maya Angelou   32

  6. From *Anger and Beyond: The Negro
     Writer in the U.S.*—The Afternoon of a
     Young Poet by M. Carl Holman   43

  7. From *Black Ice* by Lorene Cary   55

II The Nineteenth Century   63

8. *Memoirs of a Monticello Slave:*
The Life of Isaac Jefferson   65

9. From *Narrative of the Life of Frederick Douglass, An American Slave* by
Frederick Douglass   82

10. From *Up from Slavery* by
Booker T. Washington   94

11. From *The Black Man's Burden* by
William H. Holtzclaw   106

III The Twentieth Century: The First 50 Years   121

12. From *Breaking Barriers* by Carl T. Rowan   123

13. From *The Autobiography of LeRoi Jones* by Imamu Amiri Baraka   135

14. From *And the Walls Came Tumbling Down* by Ralph David Abernathy   150

15. From *Manchild in the Promised Land* by Claude Brown   157

16. From *The Long Shadow of Little Rock* by Daisy Bates   170

17. From *The Autobiography of Malcolm X* with the assistance of Alex Haley   182

18. From *No Day of Triumph* by J. Saunders Redding   188

IV The Twentieth Century: 1951 to the Present   193

19. From *The Long Shadow of Little Rock* by Elizabeth Eckford as told to Daisy Bates   195

20. From *Every Good-bye Ain't Gone* by
    Itabari Njeri   198
21. From *Angela Davis: An Autobiography*
    by Angela Davis   208
22. From *Sweet Summer* by
    Bebe Moore Campbell   224
23. From *Coming of Age in Mississippi* by
    Anne Moody   231
24. From *Zami: A New Spelling of My Name*
    by Audre Lorde   248
25. From *Brothers and Keepers* by
    John Edgar Wideman and
    Robert Douglas Wideman   256
26. *Dispatches from a Dying Generation* by
    Nathan McCall   269

Introduction

Everybody loves stories of childhood. We cherish these tales because they give insight into the character of the adult and an intimate perspective on history.

Growing Up Black gives you that and more—a perspective on what childhood has been like for twenty-five blacks through American history. And even if the title didn't give away the thread that links all the stories, you'd know it just by reading a page or two. Whether it's a racial epithet, a mention of slavery, or a description of the neighborhood, sooner or later the authors mention their race. And whether the piece comes from the early nineteenth or the late twentieth century, the fact of racial minority—with all its implications—drives the plot.

How did a slave learn to read? How can a young girl live with the knowledge that her mother was raped and murdered by white men who were never charged with a crime? What opportunities existed for a young, poor child in Tennessee during the Second World War? Why did a student on scholarship at a prestigious private school have to struggle with feelings of inadequacy?

The pieces presented allow you to measure the authors with that most basic tool, comparison to self. The life-size figures invite empathy, and by the time you finish the book, you'll carry with you the hopeless drudgery of slavery, the tenacity of a shareholder, the anger of a revolutionary, the pride of a child in 1940 singing the Negro national anthem, "Lift E'vry Voice and Sing," and the unfocused rage of a teen in 1968.

—Jay David, Editor, 1992

1

I

Growing Up Black

PROBABLY THE SINGLE MOST IMPORTANT EVENT IN THE LIFE OF ANY AFRICAN-American child is his recognition of his own coloredness, with all the implications of that fact. The realization can come as mild awareness that is taken in stride, or it can come as a rude shock that results in a trauma; but whatever the circumstances, a new understanding of the self influences the child's every thought and emotion from that day forth. Truly, he sees the world through different eyes, from a different perspective, with somewhat less of the innocence of his earlier years.

WALTER WHITE

(1893–1955)

From *A Man Called White*

Born a few years before the turn of the twentieth century, Walter White grew up in Atlanta, Georgia. His skin, like that of his parents, was so light that he could easily have passed for white. He never attempted to do so, even after the violent and bloody rioting in Atlanta in the fall of 1906 demonstrated what he had to look forward to as an African-American.

A college-educated journalist and civil rights leader, White spent most of his life trying to destroy racial prejudice.

There were nine light-skinned Negroes in my family: mother, father, five sisters, an older brother, George, and myself. The house in which I discovered what it meant to be a Negro was located on Houston Street, three blocks from the Candler Building, Atlanta's first sky-scraper, which bore the name of the ex-drug clerk who had become a millionaire from the sale of Coca-Cola. Below us lived none but Negroes; toward town all but a very few were white. Ours was an eight-room, two-story frame house which stood out in its surroundings not because of its opulence but by contrast with the drabness and unpaintedness of the other dwellings in a deteriorating neighborhood.

Only Father kept his house painted, the picket fence repaired, the board fence separating our place from those on either side white-washed, the grass neatly trimmed, and flower beds abloom. Mother's passion for neatness was even more pronounced and it seemed to me that I was always the victim of her determination to see no single blade of grass longer than the others or any one of the pickets in the front fence less shiny with paint than its mates. This spic-andspanness became increasingly apparent as the rest of the neighborhood became more down-at-heel, and resulted, as we were to learn, in sullen envy among some of our white neighbors. It was the violent expression of that resentment against a Negro family neater than themselves which set the pattern of our lives.

On a day in September 1906, when I was thirteen, we were taught that there is no isolation from life. The unseasonably oppressive heat of an Indian summer day hung like a steaming blanket over Atlanta. My sisters and I had casually commented upon the unusual quietness. It seemed to stay Mother's volubility and reduced Father, who was more taciturn, to monosyllables. But, as I remember it, no other sense of impending trouble impinged upon our consciousness.

I had read the inflammatory headlines in the *Atlanta News* and the more restrained one in the *Atlanta Constitution* which reported alleged rapes and other crimes committed by Negroes. But these were so standard and familiar that they made—as I look back on it now—little impression. The stories were more frequent, however, and consisted of eight-column streamers instead of the usual two- or four-column ones.

Father was a mail collector. His tour of duty was from three to eleven P.M. He made his rounds in a little cart into which one climbed from a step in the rear. I used to drive the cart for him from two until seven, leaving him at the point nearest our home on Houston Street, to return home either for study or sleep. That day Father decided that I should not go with him. I appealed to Mother, who thought it might be all right, provided Father sent me home before dark because, she said, "I don't think they would dare start anything before nightfall." Father told me as we made the rounds that ominous rumors of a race riot that night were sweeping the town....

During the afternoon preceding the riot little bands of sullen evil-looking men talked excitedly on street corners all over downtown Atlanta. Around seven o'clock my father and I were driving toward a mail box at the corner of Peachtree and Houston Streets when there came from near-by Pryor Street a roar the like of which I had never heard before, but which sent a sensation of mingled fear and excitement coursing through my body. I asked permission of Father to go and see what the trouble was. He bluntly ordered me to stay in the cart. A little later we drove down Atlanta's main business thoroughfare, Peachtree Street. Again we heard the terrifying cries, this time near at hand and coming toward us. We saw a lame Negro bootblack from Herndon's barber shop pathetically trying to outrun a mob of whites. Less than a hundred yards from us the chase ended. We saw clubs and fists descending to the accompaniment of savage shouting and cursing. Suddenly a voice cried, "There goes another nigger!" Its work done, the mob went after new prey. The body with the withered foot lay dead in a pool of blood on the street.

Father's apprehension and mine steadily increased during the evening, although the fact that our skins were white kept us from attack. Another circumstance favored us—the mob had not yet grown violent enough to attack United States government property. But I could see Father's relief when he punched the time clock at eleven P.M. and got into the cart to go home. He wanted to go the back way down Forsyth Street, but I begged him, in my childish excitement and ignorance, to drive down Marietta to Five Points, the heart of Atlanta's business district, where the crowds were densest and the yells loudest. No sooner had we turned into Marietta Street, however, than we saw careening toward us an undertaker's barouche. Crouched in the rear of the vehicle were three Negroes clinging to the sides of the carriage as it lunged and swerved. On the driver's seat crouched a white man, the reins held taut in his left hand. A huge whip was gripped in his right. Alternately he lashed the horses and, without looking backward, swung the whip in savage swoops in the faces of members of the mob as they lunged at the carriage determined to seize the three Negroes.

There was no time for us to get out of its path, so sudden and swift was the appearance of the vehicle. The hub cap of the right rear wheel of the barouche hit the right side of our much lighter wagon. Father and I instinctively threw our weight and kept the cart from turning completely over. Our mare was a Texas mustang which, frightened by the sudden blow, lunged in the air as Father clung to the reins. Good fortune was with us. The cart settled back on its four wheels as Father said in a voice which brooked no dissent, "We are going home the back way and not down Marietta."

But again on Pryor Street we heard the cry of the mob. Close to us and in our direction ran a stout and elderly woman who cooked at a downtown white hotel. Fifty yards behind, a mob which filled the street from curb to curb was closing in. Father handed the reins to me and, though he was of slight stature, reached down and lifted the woman into the cart. I did not need to be told to lash the mare to the fastest speed she could muster.

The church bells tolled the next morning for Sunday service. But no one in Atlanta believed for a moment that the hatred and lust for blood had been appeased. Like skulls on a cannibal's hut the hats and caps of victims of the mob the night before had been hung on the iron hooks of telegraph poles. None could tell whether each hat represented a dead Negro. But we knew that some of those who had worn hats would never again wear any.

Late in the afternoon friends of my father's came to warn of more trouble that night. They told us that plans had been perfected for a mob to form on Peachtree Street just after nightfall to march down Houston Street to what the white people called "Darktown," three blocks or so below our house, to "clean out the niggers." There had never been a firearm in our house before that day. Father was reluctant even in those circumstances to violate the law, but he at last gave in at Mother's insistence.

We turned out the lights, as did all our neighbors. No one removed his clothes or thought of sleep. Apprehension was tangible. We could almost touch its cold and clammy surface. Toward midnight the unnatural quiet was broken by a roar that grew steadily in volume. Even today I grow tense in remembering it.

Father told Mother to take my sisters, the youngest of them only six, to the rear of the house, which offered more protection from stones and bullets. My brother George was away, so Father and I, the only males in the house, took our places at the front windows. The windows opened on a porch along the front side of the house, which in turn gave onto a narrow lawn that sloped down to the street and a picket fence. There was a crash as Negroes smashed the street lamp at the corner of Houston and Piedmont Avenue down the street. In a very few minutes the vanguard of the mob, some of them bearing torches, appeared. A voice which we recognized as that of the son of the grocer with whom we had traded for many years yelled, "That's where that nigger mail carrier lives! Let's burn it down! It's too nice for a nigger to live in!" In the eerie light Father turned his drawn face toward me. In a voice as quiet as though he were asking me to pass him the sugar at the breakfast table, he said, "Son, don't shoot until the first man puts his foot on the lawn and then—don't you miss!"

In the flickering light the mob swayed, paused, and began to flow toward us. In that instant there opened within me a great awareness; I knew then who I was. I was a Negro, a human being with an invisible pigmentation which marked me a person to be hunted, hanged, abused, discriminated against, kept in poverty and ignorance, in order that those whose skin was white would have readily at hand a proof of their superiority, a proof patent and inclusive, accessible to the moron and the idiot as well as to the wise man and the genius. No matter how low a white man fell, he could always hold fast to the smug conviction that he was superior to two-thirds of the world's population, for those two-thirds were not white.

It made no difference how intelligent or talented my millions of brothers and I were, or how virtuously we lived. A curse like that of Judas was upon us, a mark of degradation fashioned with heavenly authority. There were white men who said Negroes had no souls, and who proved it by the Bible. Some of these now were approaching us, intent upon burning our house.

Theirs was a world of contrasts in values: superior and inferior, profit and loss, cooperative and noncooperative, civilized and aboriginal, white and black. If you were on the wrong end of the comparison, if you were inferior, if you were noncooperative, if you were aboriginal, if you were black, then you were marked for excision, expulsion, or extinction. I was a Negro; I was therefore that part of history which opposed the good, the just, and the enlightened. I was a Persian, falling before the hordes of Alexander. I was a Carthaginian, extinguished by the Legions of Rome. I was a Frenchman at Waterloo, an Anglo-Saxon at Hastings, a Confederate at Vicksburg. I was defeated, wherever and whenever there was a defeat.

Yet as a boy there in the darkness amid the tightening fright, I knew the inexplicable thing—that my skin was as white as the skin of those who were coming at me.

The mob moved toward the lawn. I tried to aim my gun, wondering what it would feel like to kill a man. Suddenly there was a volley of shots. The mob hesitated, stopped. Some friends of my father's had barricaded themselves in a two-story brick building just below our house. It was they who had fired. Some of the mobsmen, still bloodthirsty, shouted, "Let's go get the nigger." Others, afraid now for their safety, held back. Our friends, noting the hesitation, fired another volley. The mob broke and retreated up Houston Street.

In the quiet that followed I put my gun aside and tried to relax. But a tension different from anything I had ever known possessed me. I was gripped by the knowledge of my identity, and in the depths of my soul I was vaguely aware that I was glad of it. I was sick with loathing for the hatred which had flared before me that night and come so close to making me a killer; but I was glad I was not one of those who hated; I was glad I was not one of those made sick and murderous by pride. I was glad I was not one of those whose story is in the history of the world, a record of bloodshed, raping, and pillage. I was glad my mind and spirit were part of the races that had not fully awakened, and who therefore still had before them the opportunity to write a record of virtue as a memorandum to Armageddon.

It was all just a feeling then, inarticulate and melancholy, yet reassuring in the way that death and sleep are reassuring, and I have clung to it now for nearly half a century.

RICHARD WRIGHT
(1909–1960)

From *Black Boy*

A child's curiosity can be terribly embarrassing; when that child is a black, and when the object of his curiosity is the baffling question of race, then that child can be even more frustrating to his parents. Richard Wright was such a boy, trying to come to grips with the complexities of issues too difficult—or perhaps too simple—for his parents to solve.

Born in 1909, playwright, fiction writer, and journalist, Richard Wright is best known for his brilliant novel, Native Son, *and for a book of four novellas,* Uncle Tom's Children. *For the last fifteen years of his life he lived in Paris because he felt there was less discrimination there than in his homeland. He died in France in 1960.*

At last we were at the railroad station with our bags, waiting for the train that would take us to Arkansas; and for the first time I noticed that there were two lines of people at the ticket window, a "white" line and a "black" line. During my visit at Granny's a sense of the two races had been born in me with a sharp concreteness that would never die until I died. When I boarded the train I was aware that we Negroes were in one part of the train and that the whites were in another. Naïvely I wanted to go and see how the whites looked while sitting in their part of the train.

"Can I go and peep at the white folks?" I asked my mother.

"You keep quiet," she said.

"But that wouldn't be wrong, would it?"

"Will you keep still?"

"But why can't I?"

"Quit talking foolishness!"

I had begun to notice that my mother became irritated when I questioned her about whites and blacks, and I could not quite understand it. I wanted to understand these two sets of people who lived side by side and never touched, it seemed, except in violence. Now, there was my grandmother...Was she white? Just how white was she? What did the whites think of her whiteness?

"Mama, is Granny white?" I asked as the train rolled through the darkness.

"If you've got eyes, you can see what color she is," my mother said.

"I mean, do the white folks think she's white?"

"Why don't you ask the white folks that?" she countered.

"But you know," I insisted.

"Why should I know?" she asked. "I'm not white."

"Granny looks white," I said, hoping to establish one fact, at least. "Then why is she living with us colored folks?"

"Don't you want Granny to live with us?" she asked, blunting my question.

"Yes."

"Then why are you asking?"

"I want to *know*."

"Doesn't Granny live with us?"

"Yes."

"Isn't that enough?"

"But does she *want* to live with us?"

"Why don't you ask Granny that?" my mother evaded me again in a taunting voice.

"Did Granny become colored when she married Grandpa?"

"Will you stop asking silly questions!"

"But did she?"

"Granny didn't *become* colored," my mother said angrily. "She was *born* the color she is now."

Again I was being shut out of the secret, the thing, the reality I felt somewhere beneath all the words and silences.

"Why didn't Granny marry a white man?" I asked.

"Because she didn't want to," my mother said peevishly.

"Why don't you want to talk to me?" I asked.

She slapped me and I cried. Later, grudgingly, she told me that Granny came of Irish, Scotch, and French stock in which Negro blood had somewhere and somehow been infused. She explained it all in a matter-of-fact, offhand, neutral way; her emotions were not involved at all.

"What was Granny's name before she married Grandpa?"

"Bolden."

"Who gave her that name?"

"The white man who owned her."

"She was a slave?"

"Yes."

"And Bolden was the name of Granny's father?"

"Granny doesn't know who her father was."

"So they just gave her any name?"

"They gave her a name; that's all I know."

"Couldn't Granny find out who her father was?"

"For what, silly?"

"So she could know."

"Know for what?"

"Just to know."

"But for *what*?"

I could not say. I could not get anywhere.

"Mama, where did Father get his name?"

"Like Granny got hers. From a white man."

"Do they know who he is?"

"I don't know."

"Why don't they find out?"

"For what?" my mother demanded harshly.

And I could think of no rational or practical reason why my father should try to find out who his father's father was.

"What has Papa got in him?" I asked.

"Some white and some red and some black," she said.

"Indian, white, and Negro?"

"Yes."

"Then what am I?"

"They'll call you a colored man when you grow up," she said. Then she turned to me and smiled mockingly and asked: "Do you mind, Mr. Wright?"

I was angry and I did not answer. I did not object to being called colored, but I knew that there was something my mother was holding back. She was not concealing facts, but feelings, attitudes, convictions which she did not want me to know; and she became angry when I prodded her. All right, I would find out someday. Just wait. All right, I was colored. It was fine. I did not know enough to be afraid or to anticipate in a concrete manner. True, I had heard that colored people were killed and beaten, but so far it all had seemed remote. There was, of course, a vague uneasiness about it all, but I would be able to handle that when I came to it. It would be simple. If anybody tried to kill me, then I would kill them first.

When we arrived in Elaine I saw that Aunt Maggie lived in a bungalow that had a fence around it. It looked like home and I was glad. I had no suspicion that I was to live here for but a short time and that the manner of my leaving would be my first baptism of racial emotion.

A wide dusty road ran past the house and on each side of the road wild flowers grew. It was summer and the smell of clay dust was everywhere, day and night. I would get up early every morning to wade with my bare feet through the dust of the road, reveling in the strange mixture of the cold dew-wet crust on top of the road and the warm, sun-baked dust beneath.

After sunrise the bees would come out and I discovered that by slapping two palms together smartly, I could kill a bee. My mother warned me to stop, telling me that bees made honey, that it was not good to kill things that made food, that I would eventually be stung. But I felt confident of outwitting any bee. One morning I slapped an enormous bee between my hands just as it lit upon a flower and it stung me in the tender center of my left palm. I ran home screaming.

"Good enough for you," my mother commented dryly.

I never crushed any more bees.

Aunt Maggie's husband, Uncle Hoskins, owned a saloon that catered to the hundreds of Negroes who worked in the surrounding sawmills. Remembering the saloon of my Memphis days, I begged Uncle Hoskins to take me to see it and he promised; but my mother said no; she was afraid that I would grow up to be a drunkard if I went inside a saloon again while still a child. Well, if I could not see the saloon, at least I could eat. And at mealtime Aunt Maggie's table was so loaded with food that I could scarcely believe it was real. It took me some time to get used to the idea of there being enough to eat; I felt that if I ate enough there would not be anything left for another time. When I first sat down at Aunt Maggie's table, I could not eat until I had asked:

"Can I eat all I want?"

"Eat as much as you like," Uncle Hoskins said.

I did not believe him. I ate until my stomach hurt, but even then I did not want to get up from the table.

"Your eyes are bigger than your stomach," my mother said.

"Let him eat all he wants to and get used to food," Uncle Hoskins said.

When supper was over I saw that there were many biscuits piled high upon the bread platter, an astonishing and unbelievable sight to me. Though the biscuits were right before my eyes, and though there was more flour in the kitchen, I was apprehensive lest there be no bread for breakfast in the morning. I was afraid that somehow the biscuits might disappear during the night, while I was sleeping. I did not want to wake up in the morning, as I had so often in the past, feeling hungry and knowing that there was no food in the house. So, surreptitiously, I took some of the biscuits from the platter and slipped them into my pocket, not to eat, but to keep as a bulwark against any possible attack of hunger. Even after I had got used to seeing the table loaded with food at each meal, I still stole bread and put it into my pockets. In washing my clothes my mother found the gummy wads and scolded me to break me of the habit; I stopped hiding the bread in my pockets, and hid it about the house, in corners, behind dressers. I did not break the habit of stealing and hoarding bread until my faith that food would be forthcoming at each meal had been somewhat established.

Uncle Hoskins had a horse and buggy and sometimes he used to take me with him to Helena, where he traded. One day when I was riding with him he said:

"Richard, would you like to see this horse drink water out of the middle of the river?"

"Yes," I said, laughing. "But this horse can't do that."

"Yes, he can," Uncle Hoskins said. "Just wait and see."

He lashed the horse and headed the buggy straight for the Mississippi River.

"Where're you going?" I asked, alarm mounting in me.

"We're going to the middle of the river so the horse can drink," he said.

He drove over the levee and down the long slope of cobblestones to the river's edge and the horse plunged wildly in. I looked at the mile stretch of water that lay ahead and leaped up in terror.

"Naw!" I screamed.

"This horse has to drink," Uncle Hoskins said grimly.

"The river's deep!" I shouted.

"The horse can't drink here," Uncle Hoskins said, lashing the back of the struggling animal.

The buggy went farther. The horse slowed a little and tossed his head above the current. I grabbed the sides of the buggy, ready to jump, even though I could not swim.

"Sit down or you'll fall out!" Uncle Hoskins shouted.

"Let me out!" I screamed.

The water now came up to the hubs of the wheels of the buggy. I tried to leap into the river and he caught hold of my leg. We were now surrounded by water.

"Let me out!" I continued to scream.

The buggy rolled on and the water rose higher. The horse wagged his head, arched his neck, flung his tail about, walled his eyes, and snorted. I gripped the sides of the buggy with all the strength I had, ready to wrench free and leap if the buggy slipped deeper into the river. Uncle Hoskins and I tussled.

"Whoa!" he yelled at last to the horse.

The horse stopped and neighed. The swirling yellow water was so close that I could have touched the surface of the river. Uncle Hoskins looked at me and laughed.

"Did you really think that I was going to drive this buggy into the middle of the river?" he asked.

I was too scared to answer; my muscles were so taut that they ached.

"It's all right," he said soothingly.

He turned the buggy around and started back toward the levee. I was still clutching the sides of the buggy so tightly that I could not turn them loose.

"We're safe now," he said.

The buggy rolled onto dry land and, as my fear ebbed, I felt that I was dropping from a great height. It seemed that I could smell a sharp, fresh odor. My forehead was damp and my heart thumped heavily.

"I want to get out," I said.

"What's the matter?" he asked.

"I want to get out!"

"We're back on land now, boy."

"Naw! Stop! I want to get out!"

He did not stop the buggy; he did not even turn his head to look at me; he did not understand. I wrenched my leg free with a lunge and leaped headlong out of the buggy, landing in the dust of the road, unhurt. He stopped the buggy.

"Are you really that scared?" he asked softly.

I did not answer; I could not speak. My fear was gone now and he loomed before me like a stranger, like a man with whom I could never share a moment of intimate living.

"Come on, Richard, and get back into the buggy," he said. "I'll take you home now."

I shook my head and began to cry.

"Listen, son, don't you trust me?" he asked. "I was born on that old river. I know that river. There's stone and brick way down under that water. You could wade out for half a mile and it would not come over your head."

His words meant nothing and I would not re-enter the buggy.

"I'd better take you home," he said soberly.

I started down the dusty road. He got out of the buggy and walked beside me. He did not do his shopping that day and when he tried to explain to me what he had been trying to do in frightening me I would not listen or speak to him. I never trusted him after that. Whenever I saw his face the memory of my own terror upon the river would come back, vivid and strong, and it stood as a barrier between us.

Each day Uncle Hoskins went to his saloon in the evening and did not return home until the early hours of the morning. Like my father, he slept in the daytime, but noise never seemed to bother Uncle Hoskins. My brother and I shouted and banged as much as we liked. Often I would creep into his room while he slept and stare at the big shining revolver that lay near his head, within quick reach of his hand.

I asked Aunt Maggie why he kept the gun so close to him and she told me that men had threatened to kill him, white men...

One morning I awakened to learn that Uncle Hoskins had not come home from the saloon. Aunt Maggie fretted and worried. She wanted to visit the saloon and find out what had happened, but Uncle Hoskins had forbidden her to come to the place. The day wore on and dinnertime came.

"I'm going to find out if anything's happened," Aunt Maggie said.

"Maybe you oughtn't," my mother said. "Maybe it's dangerous."

The food was kept hot on the stove and Aunt Maggie stood on the front porch staring into the deepening dusk. Again she declared that she was going to the saloon, but my mother dissuaded her once more. It grew dark and still he had not come. Aunt Maggie was silent and restless.

"I hope to God the white people didn't bother him," she said.

Later she went into the bedroom and when she came out she whimpered:

"He didn't take his gun. I wonder what could have happened?"

We ate in silence. An hour later there was the sound of heavy footsteps on the front porch and a loud knock came. Aunt Maggie ran to the door and flung it open. A tall black boy stood sweating, panting, and shaking his head. He pulled off his cap.

"Mr. Hoskins...he done been shot. Done been shot by a white man," the boy gasped. "Mr. Hoskins, he dead."

Aunt Maggie screamed and rushed off the porch and down the dusty road into the night.

"Maggie!" my mother screamed.

"Don't you-all go to that saloon," the boy called.

"Maggie!" my mother called, running after Aunt Maggie.

"They'll kill you if you go there!" the boy yelled. "White folks say they'll kill all his kinfolks!"

My mother pulled Aunt Maggie back to the house. Fear drowned our grief and that night we packed clothes and dishes and loaded them into a farmer's wagon. Before dawn we were rolling away, fleeing for our lives. I learned afterwards that Uncle Hoskins had been killed by whites who had long coveted his flourishing liquor business. He had been threatened with death and warned many times to leave, but he had wanted to hold on a while longer to amass more money. We got rooms in West Helena, and Aunt Maggie and my mother kept huddled in the house all day and night, afraid to be seen on the streets. Finally Aunt Maggie defied her fear and made frequent trips back to Elaine, but she went in secret and at night and would tell no one save my mother when she was going.

There was no funeral. There was no music. There was no period of mourning. There were no flowers. There were only silence, quiet weeping, whispers, and fear. I did not know when or where Uncle

Hoskins was buried. Aunt Maggie was not even allowed to see his body nor was she able to claim any of his assets. Uncle Hoskins had simply been plucked from our midst and we, figuratively, had fallen on our faces to avoid looking into that white-hot face of terror that we knew loomed somewhere above us. This was as close as white terror had ever come to me and my mind reeled. Why had we not fought back, I asked my mother, and the fear that was in her made her slap me into silence.

Shocked, frightened, alone without their husbands or friends, my mother and Aunt Maggie lost faith in themselves and, after much debate and hesitation, they decided to return home to Granny and rest, think, map out new plans for living. I had grown used to moving suddenly and the prospects of another trip did not excite me. I had learned to leave old places without regret and accept new ones for what they looked like. Though I was nearly nine years of age, I had not had a single, unbroken year of school, and I was not conscious of it. I could read and count and that was about as much as most of the people I met could do, grownups or children. Again our household was torn apart; belongings were sold, given away, or simply left behind, and we were off for another long train ride....

ELIZABETH ADAMS

(1910?–)

From *Dark Symphony*

When a child is hurt either physically or emotionally by someone outside his family, he will, in all likelihood, turn to his parents for aid and comfort. This is true for children of any race, but the problem takes on added significance if the child is black. While all parents have the option of advising the child to follow the adage "an eye for an eye," or admonishing him to "forgive and forget," it is only the white child who can seek revenge with impunity. If the black child retaliates, he risks incurring the wrath of the entire white community.

Elizabeth Adams' parents had faith in the course of nonviolence. It is the harder of the two courses for a child to understand, and certainly the more frustrating, but Adams finally came to believe her mother's words: "A lady never strikes back."

Adams was born a Protestant about 1910 in Santa Barbara, California. After graduating from high school she converted to Catholicism and hoped to enter a convent. The Depression thwarted her plans, however, and she turned her talents toward a literary and dramatic career.

In the following selection she tells of her early school days in California.

One day a stranger arrived at school. We called her the "new girl" because we had never seen her before. When Mary asked her to join our game she shook her head and refused. Pointing in my direction she declared: "I won't play with her because—*she's a nigger.*"

That was the first time that I had ever heard—the word.

I was a very small child when this happened, but I can remember

18

the queer expressions that passed over the countenances of my playmates. A few backed away, a frightened look in their eyes. Others gazed at me—then at one another.

I think every Colored person in the world can recall the first time he or she was called by this uncomplimentary title. Countee Cullen, Negro poet, wrote a poem about it. He called the poem INCIDENT. The poet says:

> *Once riding in old Baltimore*
> *Heart-filled, head-filled with glee,*
> *I saw a Baltimorean*
> *Keep looking straight at me.*
>
> *Now I was eight and very small,*
> *And he was no whit bigger,*
> *And so I smiled, but he poked out*
> *His tongue, and called me, "Nigger."*
>
> *I saw the whole of Baltimore*
> *From May until December;*
> *Of all the things that happened there*
> *That's all that I remember.*

In my case I wondered what had happened to change me so unexpectedly that my playmates would stare wild-eyed.

Mary Carty patted my hand and said, "Never mind, Elizabeth. I love you."

After school hours I marched home (yes, I say *marched*, because I usually hummed something like a tune to step to) and ran into the house and asked:

"Mamma, what am I?"

Mother was busy and replied nonchalantly. "You're Mamma's little girl."

I shook my head. This was the wrong answer.

She then informed me that I was Mamma's and Papa's little girl if it would make me any happier to have both parents included.

I shook my head again.

I asked: "Mamma—what's a 'nigger'?"

My mother was very tactful. She inquired first where I had heard the word. I told her. She suggested that we have a "little talk": and so we went into an adjoining room.

I remember that Mamma became very busy with her sewing as she began the conversation. She kept biting off bits of thread and seemed unable to find the eye in the needle. She told me that the word "nigger" was not a "nice" word. It was not complimentary. Next she hastened to add that perhaps the little white girl who called me that did not know any better. Then followed the admonition to love the little girl just the same, even though she refused to join a game in which I was playing.

Yes, Mamma wanted me to think kindly of her. No matter how many times she called me "nigger" I was not to strike her, it seemed.

"I do not want you to strike her," my mother said. "It is not that she is better than you that I ask this; but you must not strike at people. A lady never strikes back."

Then I was told that if any difficulties came up I was to tell Mother; and she would see my school teacher. She next requested that I reveal the little girl's name. It was Lillian. How could I forget, when it involved so much explanation!

That night when I said my prayers before retiring, Mother demanded that I ask God to "bless Lillian." I did so because I had to obey. Of my own volition I would not have bothered to have told God anything about her. I did not hate the child. I was rather dazed over the affair; because for the first time the fact that my skin was dark had been brought to my attention. I had thought of myself as "Elizabeth" because my parents said that was my name. Mary Carty was "Mary Carty" because she said that was her name. I had never thought of her being different in color to myself.

"Don't worry about it any more," Mamma said as she tucked me in bed that night.

Of course I had no intention of worrying. I did not know what it meant to worry. After I had asked God to bless my parents, grandparents, my school teacher and everybody else far and near including my dolls and "Rags" (the pet who slept in a dog-house out in the back yard) there was nothing else to do but go to sleep. . . .

The awakening of race consciousness wrought a series of bewildering revelations in my life.

I discovered (to my surprise) that Lillian's contempt for dark people influenced several playmates, which resulted in my loss of their friendship. Nevertheless, there were other white children who (like little Mary Carty) remained ever faithful and tried to amend the wrongs of the easily-persuaded-to-become-prejudiced of their own group by engaging in fierce word-battles with them; and who imparted to Colored children petty ways and means of revenge. Thus it was that while my mother saw to it that I implored the Omnipotent to bless Lillian, Mary Carty conscientiously instructed me as to the proper procedure of turning up one's nose at an enemy.

"Doncha be scared a-her," Mary consoled whenever we talked of Lillian. "I'm with you!"

Hence there were mornings when we two (silhouettes in black and white) strutted hand-in-hand past my adversary. And Mary (to whom had been bequeathed an aquiline nose by right of inheritance from Anglo-Saxon ancestors) sniffed and turned up her nose as a gesture of indignation. I tried to imitate her. But alas, I (to whom had been bequeathed a short, stubby, button-like covering for the anterior part of the nasal fossae by right of inheritance from African ancestors) could only sniff disdainfully—my nose (being not of stream-line design) proved a blunt weapon in snooty combat. But I sniffed. I could not strike Lillian without having upon my conscience the guilt of disobedience to my parents. But I could sniff.

It worried my little white companion considerably that my nose (unlike hers) could not be upturned. She was puzzled. So was I. But there was nothing we could do about it. So after numerous disheartening lessons, Mary, exasperated, lost hope and ceased coaching.

"You'll just be happy sniffin' at everybody what makes you mad," she concluded.

Unfortunately, Lillian addressed a few of the other Colored children by the word and they made plans for her to be torn limb from limb. Then extremely troublesome times ensued for me when the dark group *demanded* that I join their ranks.

"We're goin' to beat her up!" they informed me.

The idea astounded and stunned. Helplessly I sought to evade the issue.

"I can't fight," I told the ring-leader, a very pretty Colored child with the face of a cherub and the fists of a Goliath.

"Why not?" she wanted to know.

"Because my mother says I can't. My father says I can't," I replied.

"Beat her up and don't tell them," she suggested.

Fully awakened to the realization that the word was specially devised to carry degrading implications, a conflict began within. If being called "nigger" was supposed to make a person fight, then I wanted to fight. But my hands were tied by the invisible cords of obedience: for my parents having told me that all things done in secret would be witnessed by God, I imagined the Deity peering down at me through the fleecy clouds; and presumed there was some secret method of direct communication between God and my elders so that He could let them know at once if I disobeyed.

The ring-leader threatened to "beat me up" if I failed to comply with her wishes.

That night when I began the recitation of bed-time prayers I decided not to mention Lillian. This white child was a burden on my soul. So I avoided asking that she be showered with toys and made a good girl.

My mother, noticing the omission, demanded a repetition of the prayers. Repeated they were. But again she heard no audible plea for Lillian's share of blessings. Then in no uncertain terms Mother commanded that I incorporate in my heavenly petitions the name of this child who humiliated me. Reluctantly I acquiesced.

Every night my mother led the forgive-thine-enemy campaign.

Once or twice I wondered how God would like it if someone called Him "nigger"; then remembered that according to my Sunday-school teacher no one dared to question or wonder about the Creator.

Finally, owing to Mother's blessed patience, I ceased battling. Of my own volition I asked the Great Unseen Giver of Gifts to give my enemy bountiful treasures from His storehouse of supplies.

I now look back on this part of my life with mingled emotions—mostly smiles. Whenever there is reason to refer to it in the presence of Caucasian friends someone invariably asks with solemn hesitant voice:

"Isn't it difficult for a Colored child to be really happy after finding out that he or she is a victim of racial prejudice for life?"

But in fact the child-victim of racial prejudice, though shocked on becoming aware of the disreputable intention of the word "nigger," regards it merely as a strange happening, a baffling mystery and in time something to fight over; he is too young to have the slightest perception of the many complexities that make up the problem of Negro life.

I particularly recall how my curiosity became aroused as I began to notice the racial differences in my schoolmates. Some were white, red, yellow, brown, black. There were marked distinctions in features and texture of hair. Wondering about these things led me to seek knowledge from the oracle of oracles—Mother.

How did it happen, I wanted to know, that I was born Colored instead of Chinese, Indian or another race? Why had I not been given stringy, taffy-yellow hair like Mary Carty's? Why were my eyes brown instead of blue? Why did I have round eyes instead of slant ones like Kim, my little Japanese playmate? Why? Why? Why? Oh, yes: why was I born anyway? Where had I come from? Where did everybody come from?

Mother volunteered information: and that was how I first heard of the stork.

"An' th' stork brought me as a present to you and Papa?" I queried.

"That's right," Mother responded.

"An' flew right over our house an' dropped me down the *chimmbly*?"

"That's what I have just said," remarked Mother-Oracle. "But the word is chimney, dear, chimney."

The stork-story held me spell-bound. With the vivid imagination with which the majority of normal children are endowed, I visualized the white bird circling over our housetop. According to Mother I slumbered peacefully in a large black satchel which the Bird of Travel held securely in his bill. Then he placed satchel and me right into a cradle.

The idea fascinated me. But if my Mother thought the telling of the story thus far would suffice she was mistaken. My mind was bit hazy concerning a few items which I considered important.

"Where did the stork get me?" I asked.

"From heaven," remarked Mother with an air of intense conviction. "There are trillions, billions and millions of little babies there," she went on as though answering my thought. "And God, being busy, sends them to earth by the stork."

She next proceeded to describe the sales-tag on the satchel in which I reclined, saying that it read:

> Please Deliver To—
> Mr. and Mrs. Daniel Henderson Adams,
> Santa Barbara, California
> One baby-girl to be named,
> Elizabeth Laura.

"Why didn't the stork leave me at Mary Carty's house or Kim's house instead of giving me to you and Papa?" I demanded suspiciously.

Ah—that was a brain wrecker for Mother! All she had to do was to explain to me in simplified language why I, a Colored child, had not been presented as a gift of joy to our white neighbors, the Cartys, or to Kim's family, our Japanese neighbors.

Mother coughed a couple of times and then continued.

"The stork is very wise," she said in a low voice as though sharing a secret. "He has a wonderful eye for color. Likes to see everything match. So he gives white babies to white mothers and fathers and red babies to red mothers and fathers and so on and so on until all the different colors of parents have babies to match. Isn't that wonderful?"

I mused. Smiled. Grinned. Yes, it was wonderful! That explained everything—why Mary Carty was white, Kim Japanese, and I Colored. God had painted us different colors—then the stork selected us to blend harmoniously with the bodily color-scheme of our respective families.

I was almost convinced when one other thought popped into my mind.

"But," I faltered, "how does the stork know Mammas and Papas want the babies?"

Mother cleared her throat and coughed again.

"They pray to God, asking Him for their children," she said. "Then He orders the stork to deliver them to earth."

Then with the dramatic air of an actress, Mother leaned back in her chair and a sad, sad look crept into her eyes.

"All children should love their parents, dear," she sighed. "For they have to work hard, save their money and have a nice home all ready for the little baby when it arrives. And the poor stork," she said pathetically, "goes from house to house, country to country—all over the world. As soon as he delivers one baby he has to fly right back to heaven for another to take to some other family."

That explanation settled all doubts. I needed to hear no more. My sympathy rested with the stork. I pictured the poor bird weary and hungry—his wings rain-drenched one day and scorched and sagging from the heat of the sun on a bright day.

I threw my arms around my mother's neck: glad, glad indeed, that the over-worked bird had remained constant in his fidelity to duties of transportation and had not collapsed from exhaustion while en route to our house.

Even as a very small child I believed that good news and the meritorious achievements of others should be shared, that was why I started for the door to pass the word along to Mary Carty and Kim.

"Where are you going?" Mother demanded.

When I told her she caught me quickly and set me down.

"Now listen," she said positively. "You must never, never tell others the story about the stork. It's our secret!"

A secret! I looked at her.

"Maybe—maybe Mary an' Kim don' know about the stork," I murmured regretfully as my mother's restraining hand continued to rest upon my shoulder, and indications of my opportunity to be a publicity-agent for the stork began to fade.

"Their mothers will tell them," came the response. "Listen, dear—" Mother's tone softened. I looked at her and she whispered:

"We must keep this a family secret. The stork wants all families to keep the story of his coming to themselves. He wants to surprise everybody."

Surprise! I understood that word. A surprise meant something one did not expect and it always brought happiness (so I believed)—unexpected happiness such as rice pudding for dinner, a new doll, a new dress.

I had one more request to make.

"What now?" Mother inquired.

I whispered loudly:

"May I tell Papa when he comes home?"

A few weeks later, there stood in my mother's room a dainty basket-shaped bed decorated with pretty blue and white ribbons, and in it was a baby. A real, live baby!

"It's your Baby-Brother," the lady in the white uniform told me.

I did not like the lady in the white uniform. She was Colored, but even that did not make us congenial. I thought her impatient and very, very cross when she slapped my fingers as I slyly started to poke them into Baby-Brother's eyes to see if he would squeal. Another grievance held against her was that she would not let me see Mother until late in the afternoon, and then for only a short time. And she always spoiled my visits by beginning to speak as soon as I crossed the threshold of Mother's room, saying: "*We* haven't long to stay, Mother. *We* must hurry along."

I did not like the idea of her calling my mother "Mother"—and I did want to stay a long time in Mother's room. I wondered: what right did she have anyway, trying to talk for both of us?

Then something strange happened about the third day after I first saw Baby-Brother. I went over to the fireplace. No fire burned, and no one was looking. I tried to catch a glimpse of the stork.

Alas! Only the black, sooty channel of the chimney was visible.

I sought the lady in the white uniform, knowing that Mother-Oracle was not available.

"Where's the stork?" I asked.

She snapped at me.

"Stork? What are you talking about?"

"The stork that brought Baby-Brother!"

"Questions! Questions! Don't you ever think of anything else but questions?" she snapped again.

"Please, ma'am," I persisted. "Where is he?"

"He's flown!" she said and walked out of the room.

And though it is true that I disliked the lady in the white uniform (and seldom had one confidence in a believed-to-be-enemy) nevertheless Baby-Brother's existence being a visible sign of the stork's arrival—could I do aught else but believe she spoke the truth?

GORDON PARKS

(1912–)

From *A Choice of Weapons*

The youth of Gordon Parks provides a good example of how a childhood of violence and hatred can in turn breed more anger and violence within the child. But Parks' early upbringing also instilled in him a desire to try to "beat the system," to grow up and succeed in spite of the apparent futility of the struggle. The significance of the title of his book, then, is that Parks was presented with a choice of how to wage his personal fight: whether to lash out bitterly and violently, without reason and direction, or to channel his energies into a meaningful, positive effort. It is a choice that, at one time or another, every African-American faces today.

Brought up in a small Kansas town in the early 1900s, Gordon Parks was sent to live with his sister and brother-in-law after his mother died. His premonition that living with them was an impermanent state proved to be correct. He left after a bitter argument. What followed was a succession of temporary jobs—piano player, bellhop, waiter, basketball player—until he began his career as a professional photographer by buying a cheap camera and taking pictures of anything and everything he saw.

Parks has been a staff photographer for Life *magazine since 1949. He has written and photographed award-winning stories on subjects such as the Black Muslims and the plight of an underprivileged boy named Flavio. He is also a composer whose music has been performed in major cities.*

In the following selection he recalls the fears and hopes of his childhood in Kansas during the second decade of the twentieth century.

26

* * *

The full meaning of my mother's death had settled over me before
they lowered her into the grave. They buried her at two-thirty in the
afternoon; now, at nightfall, our big family was starting to break up.
Once there had been fifteen of us and, at sixteen, I was the youngest.
There was never much money, so now my older brothers and sisters
were scraping up enough for my coach ticket north. I would live in
St. Paul, Minnesota, with my sister Maggie Lee, as my mother had
requested a few minutes before she died.

Poppa, a good quiet man, spent the last hours before our parting
moving aimlessly about the yard, keeping to himself and avoiding
me. A sigh now and then belied his outer calm. Several times I wanted
to say that I was sorry to be going, and that I would miss him very
much. But the silence that had always lain between us prevented this.
Now I realized that probably he hadn't spoken more than a few thousand words to me during my entire childhood. It was always: "Mornin',
boy"; "Git you chores done, boy"; "Goodnight, boy." If I asked for a
dime or nickel, he would look beyond me for a moment, grunt, then
dig through the nuts and bolts in his blue jeans and hand me the
money. I loved him in spite of his silence.

For his own reasons Poppa didn't go to the depot, but as my sister
and I were leaving he came up, a cob pipe jutting from his mouth,
and stood sideways, looking over the misty Kansas countryside. I
stood awkwardly waiting for him to say something. He just grunted—
three short grunts. "Well," Maggie Lee said nervously, "won't you be
kissin' your poppa goodbye?" I picked up my cardboard suitcase,
turned and kissed his stubby cheek and started climbing into the
taxicab. I was halfway in when his hand touched my shoulder. "Boy,
remember your momma's teachin'.... You'll be all right. Just you
remember her teachin'...." I promised, then sat back in the Model T
taxi. As we rounded the corner, Poppa was already headed for the
hog pens. It was feeding time.

Our parents had filled us with love and a staunch Methodist religion.
We were poor, though I did not know it at the time; the rich soil
surrounding our clapboard house had yielded the food for the family.
And the love of this family had eased the burden of being black. But
there were segregated schools and warnings to avoid white neigh-
borhoods after dark. I always had to sit in the peanut gallery (the
Negro section) at the movies. We weren't allowed to drink soda in
the drugstore in town. I was stoned and beaten and called "nigger,"
"black boy," "darky," "shine." These indignities came so often I began
to accept them as normal. Yet I always fought back. Now I considered
myself lucky to be alive; three of my close friends had already died
of senseless brutality, and I was lucky that I hadn't killed someone
myself. Until the very day that I left Fort Scott on that train for the

North, there had been a fair chance of being shot or perhaps beaten to death. I could easily have been murdered by some violent member of my own race. There had been a lot of killing in the border states of Kansas, Oklahoma and Missouri, more than I cared to remember.

I was nine years old when the Tulsa riots took place in 1921. Whites had invaded the Negro neighborhood, which turned out to be an armed camp. Many white Tulsans were killed, and rumors had it that the fight would spread into Kansas and beyond. About this time a grown cousin of mine decided to go south to work in a mill. My mother, knowing his hot temper, pleaded with him not to go, but he caught a freight going south. Months passed and we had no word of him. Then one day his name flashed across the nation as one of the most-wanted men in the country. He had killed a white millhand who spat in his face and called him "nigger." He killed another white man while fleeing the scene and shot another on the viaduct between Kansas City, Missouri, and Kansas City, Kansas.

I asked Momma questions she couldn't possibly answer. Would they catch him? Would he be lynched? Where did she think he was hiding? How long did she think he could hold out? She knew what all the rest of us knew, that he would come back to our house if it was possible.

He came one night. It was storming, and I lay in the dark of my room, listening to the rain pound the roof. Suddenly, the window next to my bed slid up, and my cousin, wet and cautious, scrambled through the opening. I started to yell as he landed on my bed, but he quickly covered my mouth with his hand, whispered his name, and cautioned me into silence. I got out of bed and followed him. He went straight to Momma's room, kneeled down and shook her awake. "Momma Parks," he whispered, "it's me, it's me. Wake up." And she awoke easily and put her hand on his head. "My Lord, son," she said, "you're in such bad trouble." Then she sat upon the side of the bed and began to pray over him. After she had finished, she tried to persuade him to give himself up. "They'll kill you, son. You can't run forever." But he refused. Then, going to our old icebox, he filled a sack with food and went back out my window into the cornfield.

None of us ever saw or heard of him again. And I would lie awake nights wondering if the whites had killed my cousin, praying that they hadn't. I remembered the huge sacks of peanut brittle he used to bring me and the rides he gave me on the back of his battered motorcycle. And my days were full of fantasies in which I helped him escape imaginary white mobs.

When I was eleven, I became possessed of an exaggerated fear of death. It started one quiet summer afternoon with an explosion in the alley behind our house. I jumped up from under a shade tree and tailed Poppa toward the scene. Black smoke billowed skyward, a large hole gaped in the wall of our barn and several maimed chickens and a headless turkey flopped about on the ground. Then Poppa stopped and muttered, "Good Lord." I clutched his overalls and looked. A man, or what was left of him, was strewn about in three parts. A gas main he had been repairing had somehow ignited and blown everything around it to bits.

Then once, with two friends, I had swum along the bottom of the muddy Marmaton River, trying to locate the body of a Negro man. We had been promised fifty cents apiece by the same white policeman who had shot him while he was in the water trying to escape arrest. The dead man had been in a crap game with several others who had managed to get away. My buddy, Johnny Young, was swimming beside me; we swam with ice hooks which we were to use for grappling. The two of us touched the corpse at the same instant. Fear streaked through me and the memory of his bloated body haunted my dreams for nights.

One night at the Empress Theater, I sat alone in the peanut gallery watching a motion picture, *The Phantom of the Opera*. When the curious heroine, against Lon Chaney's warning, snatched away his mask, and the skull of death filled the screen, I screamed out loud and ran out of the theater. I didn't stop until I reached home, crying to Momma, "I'm going to die! I'm going to die."

Momma, after several months of cajoling, had all but destroyed this fear when another cruel thing happened. A Negro gambler called Captain Tuck was mysteriously killed on the Frisco tracks. Elmer Kinard, a buddy, and I had gone to the Cheney Mortuary out of youthful, perhaps morbid, curiosity. Two white men, standing at the back door where bodies were received, smiled mischievously and beckoned to us. Elmer was wise and ran, but they caught me. "Come on in, boy. You want to see Captain Tuck, don't you?"

"No, no," I pleaded. "No, no, let me go."

The two men lifted me through the door and shoved me into a dark room. "Cap'n Tuck's in here, boy. You can say hello to him." The stench of embalming fluid mixed with fright. I started vomiting, screaming and pounding the door. Then a smeared light bulb flicked on and, there before me, his broken body covering the slab, was Captain Tuck. My body froze and I collapsed beside the door.

After they revived me and put me on the street, I ran home with the old fear again running the distance beside me. My brother Clem evened the score with his fists the next day, but from then on Poppa proclaimed that no Parks would ever be caught dead in Cheney's. "The Koonantz boys will do all our burying from now on," he told Orlando Cheney.

Another time, I saw a woman cut another woman to death. There were men around, but they didn't stop it. They all stood there as if they were watching a horror movie. Months later, I would shudder at the sight of Johnny Young, one of my closest buddies, lying, shot to death, at the feet of his father and the girl he loved. His murderer had been in love with the same girl. And not long after, Emphry Hawkins, who had helped us bear Johnny's coffin, was also shot to death.

As the train whistled through the evening, I realized that only hours before, during what seemed like a bottomless night, I had left my bed to sleep on the floor beside my mother's coffin. It was, I knew now, a final attempt to destroy this fear of death.

But in spite of the memories, I would miss this Kansas land that I was leaving. The great prairies filled with green and cornstalks; the flowering apple trees, the tall elms and oaks bordering the streams that gurgled and the rivers that rolled quiet. The summers of long, sleepy days for fishing, swimming and snatching crawdads from beneath the rocks. The endless tufts of high clouds billowing across the heavens. The butterflies to chase through grass high as the chin. The swallowtails, bobolinks and robins. Nights filled with soft laughter, with fireflies and restless stars, and the winding sound of the cricket rubbing dampness from its wing. The silver of September rain, the orange-red-brown Octobers and Novembers, and the white Decembers with the hungry smells of hams and pork butts curing in the smokehouses. Yet as the train sped along, the telegraph poles whizzing toward and past us, I had a feeling that I was escaping a doom which had already trapped the relatives and friends I was leaving behind. For, although I was departing from this beautiful land, it would be impossible ever to forget the fear, hatred and violence that Negroes had suffered upon it.

It was all behind me now. By the next day, there would be what my mother had called "another kind of world, one with more hope and promising things." She had said, "Make a man of yourself up there. Put something into it, and you'll get something out of it." It was her dream for me. When I stepped onto the chilly streets of St. Paul, Minnesota, two days later, I was determined to fulfill that dream.

I had never met my brother-in-law, and his handshake told me that I was to be tolerated rather than accepted. He was nearly white in color, big and fierce-looking. His whole person seemed formidable. His only words to me that first evening were about things I should not do in his house.

It was a nice house—two-storied, handsomely middle-class, with large, comfortable rooms. And that night, lying in bed, I marveled at the hundreds of deer leaping the bushes on the wallpaper around me, and my thoughts were charged with vague imaginings of the future. Yet I felt that whatever security lay ahead would be of my own making. There was no feeling of permanence in the softness of the ornate bed. I sensed that this was to be an uneasy stopover, and that it would be necessary to move on before long.

"Cut off your lamp! Electric light cost money, boy!" It was my brother-in-law outside the door. I didn't answer. I thought it better to remain silent, but I switched off the light and listened to him lumber down the hall. But, in spite of the long coach ride, I was restless and couldn't sleep. A few minutes later, my sister sneaked in the door with a handful of gingersnaps and a glass of milk and placed them on my night table. "Don't worry. Everything will work out all right," she whispered, then she slipped back into the hallway.

Even on this first night, I had bad feeling for this man. It was the kind of feeling I had for the whites whose indignities had pushed me to the edge of violence, whose injustices toward me had created one emotional crisis after another, all because my skin was black. My mind shifted back to those mornings when I stood before the cracked mirror in our house and wondered why God had made me black, and I remembered the dream I once had of being white, with skin so flabby and loose that I attempted to pull it into shape, to make it fit, only to awaken and find myself clutching at my underwear. But now I knew I was black and that I would always be black.

At fourteen, in the black-and-white world of Kansas, anyone whiter than I became my enemy. I had grown rebellious and once, while in a fit of temper, I knocked my crippled brother Leroy, who was a couple of shades lighter than I, to the floor. Immediately ashamed, I reached down to help him. He smiled and waved me aside, and I ran from the room crying. It hurt to learn several days later that he had known for months that he was incurably ill. Just before he died, the following winter, he called me to his bedside.

"Pedro," he said, using his favorite nickname for me, "for the life of me I don't know why you're so mad at the world. You can't whip it the way you're going. It's too big. If you're going to fight it, use your brain. It's got a lot more power than your fists." Before sleep came that night in St. Paul, it was clear to me that such reasoning was needed if I was to cope with my brother-in-law's hostility.

I awoke early the next day, dressed and went out of doors, eager for a look at the new surroundings. The morning was already brisk and alive, with sunshine full upon the big porch. The tree-lined avenue seemed clean and beautiful. The leaves, yielding to the first frosts, had taken on the golds and oranges of autumn. Stretching full length upon the steps, I was suddenly thankful to be in this bright new land.

People were now on the street, moving with the quickness that autumn mornings enforce. I thought that I too would have to move much faster here; otherwise I would be left behind....

MAYA ANGELOU

(1928–)

From *I Know Why the Caged Bird Sings*

As you might expect, bestselling author, poet, and playwright Maya Angelou had an extraordinary childhood. When she was only three, her parents divorced and sent Angelou and her older brother, Bailey, alone by train, to Stamps, Arkansas, to live with their paternal grandmother. Their grandmother owned a store in the black part of town, and for the most part, the children lived a sheltered life in a South where black men were still lynched and murdered.

Her uncle and grandmother encouraged learning, especially the works by black authors. Once when Angelou and her brother put on a play, they decided on a play by James Weldon Johnson because they knew their grandmother wouldn't stand for anything by a white playwright like William Shakespeare.

Little in their lives brought them in contact with whites in the segregated South, and the children learned to stay away from them. Grandmother Henderson, religious, stern, loving, and protective, was a strict guardian.

When Angelou was seven, she and her brother went to St. Louis to live with their mother and maternal grandmother, a quadroon or octoroon, who had been raised by a German family in Illinois and spoke English with a German accent. In addition, they were surrounded by strong, protective uncles. Their mother worked as a blues singer in city taverns and earned extra money cutting poker games in gambling parlors. The children had a flush toilet, wore store-bought clothes, and received an allowance. They even watched their glamorous mother perform. Soon after the children arrived, Angelou was raped by her mother's live-in boyfriend. The rapist was found guilty but allowed out on bail; he was soon *found dead near the stockyards. Angelou and her brother returned to Stamps.*

This excerpt describes her eighth grade graduation ceremony in 1940.

The children in Stamps trembled visibly with anticipation. Some adults were excited too, but to be certain the whole young population had come down with graduation epidemic. Large classes were graduating from both the grammar school and the high school. Even those who were years removed from their own day of glorious release were anxious to help with preparations as a kind of dry run. The junior students who were moving into the vacating classes' chairs were tradition-bound to show their talents for leadership and management. They strutted through the school and around the campus exerting pressure on the lower grades. Their authority was so new that occasionally if they pressed a little too hard it had to be overlooked. After all, next term was coming, and it never hurt a sixth grader to have a play sister in the eighth grade, or a tenth-year student to be able to call a twelfth grader Bubba. So all was endured in a spirit of shared understanding. But the graduating classes themselves were the nobility. Like travelers with exotic destinations on their minds, the graduates were remarkably forgetful. They came to school without their books, or tablets or even pencils. Volunteers fell over themselves to secure replacements for the missing equipment. When accepted, the willing workers might or might not be thanked, and it was of no importance to the pregraduation rites. Even teachers were respectful of the now quiet and aging seniors, and tended to speak to them, if not as equals, as beings only slightly lower than themselves. After tests were returned and grades given, the student body, which acted like an extended family, knew who did well, who excelled, and what piteous ones had failed.

Unlike the white high school, Lafayette County Training School distinguished itself by having neither lawn, nor hedges, nor tennis court, nor climbing ivy. Its two buildings (main classrooms, the grade school and home economics) were set on a dirt hill with no fence to limit either its boundaries or those of bordering farms. There was a large expanse to the left of the school which was used alternately as a baseball diamond or a basketball court. Rusty hoops on the swaying poles represented the permanent recreational equipment, although bats and balls could be borrowed from the P. E. teacher if the borrower was qualified and if the diamond wasn't occupied.

Over this rocky area relieved by a few shady tall persimmon trees the graduating class walked. The girls often held hands and no longer bothered to speak to the lower students. There was a sadness about them, as if this old world was not their home and they were bound for higher ground. The boys, on the other hand, had become more friendly, more outgoing. A decided change from the closed attitude they projected while studying for finals. Now they seemed not ready to give up the old school, the familiar paths and classrooms. Only a small percentage would be continuing on to college—one of the South's A & M (agricultural and mechanical) schools, which trained Negro youths to be carpenters, farmers, handymen, masons, maids, cooks and baby nurses. Their future rode heavily on their shoulders, and blinded them to the collective joy that had pervaded the lives of the boys and girls in the grammar school graduating class.

Parents who could afford it had ordered new shoes and ready-made clothes for themselves from Sears and Roebuck or Montgomery Ward. They also engaged the best seamstresses to make the floating graduating dresses and to cut down secondhand pants which would be pressed to a military slickness for the important event.

Oh, it was important, all right. Whitefolks would attend the ceremony, and two or three would speak of God and home, and the Southern way of life, and Mrs. Parsons, the principal's wife, would play the graduation march while the lower-grade graduates paraded down the aisles and took their seats below the platform. The high school seniors would wait in empty classrooms to make their dramatic entrance.

In the Store I was the person of the moment. The birthday girl. The center. Bailey had graduated the year before, although to do so he had had to forfeit all pleasures to make up for his time lost in Baton Rouge.

My class was wearing butter-yellow piqué dresses, and Momma launched out on mine. She smocked the yoke into tiny crisscrossing puckers, then shirred the rest of the bodice. Her dark fingers ducked in and out of the lemony cloth as she embroidered raised daisies around the hem. Before she considered herself finished she had added a crocheted cuff on the puff sleeves, and a pointy crocheted collar.

I was going to be lovely. A walking model of all the various styles of fine hand sewing and it didn't worry me that I was only twelve years old and merely graduating from the eighth grade. Besides, many teachers in Arkansas Negro schools had only that diploma and were licensed to impart wisdom.

The days had become longer and more noticeable. The faded beige of former times had been replaced with strong and sure colors. I began to see my classmates' clothes, their skin tones, and the dust that waved off pussy willows. Clouds that lazed across the sky were objects of great concern to me. Their shiftier shapes might have held a message that in my new happiness and with a little bit of time I'd soon decipher. During that period I looked at the arch of heaven so religiously my neck kept a steady ache. I had taken to smiling more often, and my jaws hurt from the unaccustomed activity. Between the two physical sore spots, I suppose I could have been uncomfortable, but that was not the case. As a member of the winning team (the graduating class of 1940) I had outdistanced unpleasant sensations by miles. I was headed for the freedom of open fields.

Youth and social approval allied themselves with me and we trammeled memories of slights and insults. The wind of our swift passage remodeled my features. Lost tears were pounded to mud and then to dust. Years of withdrawal were brushed aside and left behind, as hanging ropes of parasitic moss.

My work alone had awarded me a top place and I was going to be one of the first called in the graduating ceremonies. On the classroom blackboard, as well as on the bulletin board in the auditorium, there were blue stars and white stars and red stars. No absences, no tardinesses, and my academic work was among the best of the year. I could say the preamble to the Constitution even faster than Bailey. We timed ourselves often: "WethepeopleoftheUnitedStatesinorderto formamoreperfectunion..." I had memorized the Presidents of the United States from Washington to Roosevelt in chronological as well as alphabetical order.

My hair pleased me too. Gradually the black mass had lengthened and thickened, so that it kept at last to its braided pattern, and I didn't have to yank my scalp off when I tried to comb it.

Louise and I had rehearsed the exercises until we tired out ourselves. Henry Reed was class valedictorian. He was a small, very black boy with hooded eyes, a long, broad nose and an oddly shaped head. I had admired him for years because each term he and I vied for the best grades in our class. Most often he bested me, but instead of being disappointed I was pleased that we shared top places between us. Like many Southern Black children, he lived with his grandmother, who was as strict as Momma and as kind as she knew how to be. He was courteous, respectful and soft-spoken to elders, but on the playground he chose to play the roughest games. I admired him. Anyone, I reckoned, sufficiently afraid or sufficiently dull could be polite. But to be able to operate at a top level with both adults and children was admirable.

His valedictory speech was entitled "To Be or Not to Be." The rigid tenth-grade teacher had helped him write it. He'd been working on the dramatic stresses for months.

The weeks until graduation were filled with heady activities. A group of small children were to be presented in a play about buttercups and daisies and bunny rabbits. They could be heard throughout the building practicing their hops and their little songs that sounded like silver bells. The older girls (nongraduates, of course) were assigned the task of making refreshments for the night's festivities. A tangy scent of ginger, cinnamon, nutmeg and chocolate wafted around the home economics building as the budding cooks made samples for themselves and their teachers.

In every corner of the workshop, axes and saws split fresh timber as the woodshop boys made sets and stage scenery. Only the graduates were left out of the general bustle. We were free to sit in the library at the back of the building or look in quite detachedly, naturally, on the measures being taken for our event.

Even the minister preached on graduation the Sunday before. His subject was, "Let your light so shine that men will see your good works and praise your Father, Who is in Heaven." Although the sermon was purported to be addressed to us, he used the occasion to speak to backsliders, gamblers and general ne'er-do-wells. But since he had called our names at the beginning of the service we were mollified.

Among Negroes the tradition was to give presents to children going only from one grade to another. How much more important this was when the person was graduating at the top of the class. Uncle Willie and Momma had sent away for a Mickey Mouse watch like Bailey's. Louise gave me four embroidered handkerchiefs. (I gave her three crocheted doilies.) Mrs. Sneed, the minister's wife, made me an underskirt to wear for graduation, and nearly every customer gave me a nickel or maybe even a dime with the instruction "Keep on moving to higher ground," or some such encouragement.

Amazingly the great day finally dawned and I was out of bed before I knew it. I threw open the back door to see it more clearly, but Momma said, "Sister, come away from that door and put your robe on."

I hoped the memory of that morning would never leave me. Sunlight was itself still young, and the day had none of the insistence maturity would bring it in a few hours. In my robe and barefoot in the backyard, under cover of going to see about my new beans, I gave myself up to the gentle warmth and thanked God that no matter what evil I had done in my life He had allowed me to live to see this day. Somewhere in my fatalism I had expected to die, accidentally, and never have the chance to walk up the stairs in the auditorium and gracefully receive my hard-earned diploma. Out of God's merciful bosom I had won reprieve.

Bailey came out in his robe and gave me a box wrapped in Christmas paper. He said he had saved his money for months to pay for it. It felt like a box of chocolates, but I knew Bailey wouldn't save money to buy candy when we had all we could want under our noses.

He was as proud of the gift as I. It was a soft-leather-bound copy of a collection of poems by Edgar Allan Poe, or, as Bailey and I called him, "Eap." I turned to "Annabel Lee" and we walked up and down the garden rows, the cool dirt between our toes, reciting the beautifully sad lines.

Momma made a Sunday breakfast although it was only Friday. After we finished the blessing, I opened my eyes to find the watch on my plate. It was a dream of a day. Everything went smoothly and to my credit. I didn't have to be reminded or scolded for anything. Near evening I was too jittery to attend to chores, so Bailey volunteered to do all before his bath.

Days before, we had made a sign for the Store, and as we turned out the lights Momma hung the cardboard over the doorknob. It read clearly: CLOSED. GRADUATION.

My dress fitted perfectly and everyone said that I looked like a sunbeam in it. On the hill, going toward the school, Bailey walked behind with Uncle Willie, who muttered, "Go on, Ju." He wanted him to walk ahead with us because it embarrassed him to have to walk so slowly. Bailey said he'd let the ladies walk together, and the men would bring up the rear. We all laughed, nicely.

Little children dashed by out of the dark like fireflies. Their crepe-paper dresses and butterfly wings were not made for running and we heard more than one rip, dryly, and the regretful "uh uh" that followed.

The school blazed without gaiety. The windows seemed cold and unfriendly from the lower hill. A sense of ill-fated timing crept over me, and if Momma hadn't reached for my hand I would have drifted back to Bailey and Uncle Willie, and possibly beyond. She made a few slow jokes about my feet getting cold, and tugged me along to the now-strange building.

Around the front steps, assurance came back. There were my fellow "greats," the graduating class. Hair brushed back, legs oiled, new dresses and pressed pleats, fresh pocket handkerchiefs and little handbags, all homesewn. Oh, we were up to snuff, all right. I joined my comrades and didn't even see my family go in to find seats in the crowded auditorium.

The school band struck up a march and all classes filed in as had been rehearsed. We stood in front of our seats, as assigned, and on a signal from the choir director, we sat. No sooner had this been accomplished than the band started to play the national anthem. We rose again and sang the song, after which we recited the pledge of allegiance. We remained standing for a brief minute before the choir director and the principal signaled to us, rather desperately I thought, to take our seats. The command was so unusual that our carefully rehearsed and smooth-running machine was thrown off. For a full minute we fumbled for our chairs and bumped into each other awkwardly. Habits change or solidify under pressure, so in our state of nervous tension we had been ready to follow our usual assembly pattern: the American national anthem, then the pledge of allegiance, then the song every Black person I knew called the Negro National Anthem. All done in the same key, with the same passion and most often standing on the same foot.

Finding my seat at last, I was overcome with a presentiment of worse things to come. Something unrehearsed, unplanned, was going to happen, and we were going to be made to look bad. I distinctly remember being explicit in the choice of pronoun. It was "we," the graduating class, the unit, that concerned me then.

The principal welcomed "parents and friends" and asked the Baptist minister to lead us in prayer. His invocation was brief and punchy, and for a second I thought we were getting back on the high road to right action. When the principal came back to the dais, however, his voice had changed. Sounds always affected me profoundly and the principal's voice was one of my favorites. During assembly it melted and lowed weakly into the audience. It had not been in my plan to listen to him, but my curiosity was piqued and I straightened up to give him my attention.

He was talking about Booker T. Washington, our "late great leader," who said we can be as close as the fingers on the hand, etc.... Then he said a few vague things about friendship and the friendship of kindly people to those less fortunate than themselves. With that his voice nearly faded, thin, away. Like a river diminishing to a stream and then to a trickle. But he cleared his throat and said, "Our speaker tonight, who is also our friend, came from Texarkana to deliver the commencement address, but due to the irregularity of the train schedule, he's going to, as they say, 'speak and run.'" He said that we understood and wanted the man to know that we were most grateful for the time he was able to give us and then something about how we were willing always to adjust to another's program, and without more ado—"I give you Mr. Edward Donleavy."

Not one but two white men came through the door offstage. The shorter one walked to the speaker's platform, and the tall one moved over to the center seat and sat down. But that was our principal's seat, and already occupied. The dislodged gentleman bounced around for a long breath or two before the Baptist minister gave him his chair, then with more dignity than the situation deserved, the minister walked off the stage.

Donleavy looked at the audience once (on reflection, I'm sure that he wanted only to reassure himself that we were really there), adjusted his glasses and began to read from a sheaf of papers.

He was glad "to be here and to see the work going on just as it was in the other schools."

At the first "Amen" from the audience I willed the offender to immediate death by choking on the word. But Amens and Yes, sir's began to fall around the room like rain through a ragged umbrella.

He told us of the wonderful changes we children in Stamps had in store. The Central School (naturally, the white school was Central) had already been granted improvements that would be in use in the fall. A well-known artist was coming from Little Rock to teach art to them. They were going to have the newest microscopes and chemistry equipment for their laboratory. Mr. Donleavy didn't leave us long in the dark over who made these improvements available to Central High. Nor were we to be ignored in the general betterment scheme he had in mind.

He said that he had pointed out to people at a very high level that one of the first-line football tacklers at Arkansas Agricultural and Mechanical College had graduated from good old Lafayette County Training School. Here fewer Amens were heard. Those few that did break through lay dully in the air with the heaviness of habit.

He went on to praise us. He went on to say how he had bragged that "one of the best basketball players at Fisk sank his first ball right here at Lafayette County Training School."

The white kids were going to have a chance to become Galileos and Madame Curies and Edisons and Gauguins, and our boys (the girls weren't even in on it) would try to be Jesse Owenses and Joe Louises.

Owens and the Brown Bomber were great heroes in our world, but what school official in the white-goddom of Little Rock had the right to decide that those two men must be our only heroes? Who decided that for Henry Reed to become a scientist he had to work like George Washington Carver, as a bootblack, to buy a lousy microscope? Bailey was obviously always going to be too small to be an athlete, so which concrete angel glued to what country seat had decided that if my brother wanted to become a lawyer he had to first pay penance for his skin by picking cotton and hoeing corn and studying correspondence books at night for twenty years?

The man's dead words fell like bricks around the auditorium and too many settled in my belly. Constrained by hard-learned manners I couldn't look behind me, but to my left and right the proud graduating class of 1940 had dropped their heads. Every girl in my row had found something new to do with her handkerchief. Some folded the tiny squares into love knots, some into triangles, but most were wadding them, then pressing them flat on their yellow laps.

On the dais, the ancient tragedy was being replayed. Professor Parsons sat, a sculptor's reject, rigid. His large, heavy body seemed devoid of will or willingness, and his eyes said he was no longer with us. The other teachers examined the flag (which was draped stage right) or their notes, or the windows which opened on our now-famous playing diamond.

Graduation, the hush-hush magic time of frills and gifts and congratulations and diplomas, was finished for me before my name was called. The accomplishment was nothing. The meticulous maps, drawn in three colors of ink, learning and spelling decasyllabic words, memorizing the whole of *The Rape of Lucrece*—it was for nothing. Donleavy had exposed us.

We were maids and farmers, handymen and washerwomen, and

anything higher that we aspired to was farcical and presumptuous.

Then I wished that Gabriel Prosser and Nat Turner had killed all whitefolks in their beds and that Abraham Lincoln had been assassinated before the signing of the Emancipation Proclamation, and that Harriet Tubman had been killed by that blow on her head and Christopher Columbus had drowned in the *Santa María*.

It was awful to be Negro and have no control over my life. It was brutal to be young and already trained to sit quietly and listen to charges brought against my color with no chance of defense. We should all be dead. I thought I should like to see us all dead, one on top of the other. A pyramid of flesh with the whitefolks on the bottom, as the broad base, then the Indians with their silly tomahawks and teepees and wigwams and treaties, the Negroes with their mops and recipes and cotton sacks and spirituals sticking out of their mouths. The Dutch children should all stumble in their wooden shoes and break their necks. The French should choke to death on the Louisiana Purchase (1803) while silkworms ate all the Chinese with their stupid pigtails. As a species, we were an abomination. All of us.

Donleavy was running for election, and assured our parents that if he won we could count on having the only colored paved playing field in that part of Arkansas. Also—he never looked up to acknowledge the grunts of acceptance—also, we were bound to get some new equipment for the home economics building and the workshop.

He finished, and since there was no need to give any more than the most perfunctory thank-you's, he nodded to the men on the stage, and the tall white man who was never introduced joined him at the door. They left with the attitude that now they were off to something really important. (The graduation ceremonies at Lafayette County Training School had been a mere preliminary.)

The ugliness they left was palpable. An uninvited guest who wouldn't leave. The choir was summoned and sang a modern arrangement of "Onward, Christian Soldiers," with new words pertaining to graduates seeking their place in the world. But it didn't work. Elouise, the daughter of the Baptist minister, recited "Invictus," and I could have cried at the impertinence of "I am the master of my fate, I am the captain of my soul."

My name had lost its ring of familiarity and I had to be nudged to go and receive my diploma. All my preparations had fled. I neither marched up to the stage like a conquering Amazon, nor did I look in the audience for Bailey's nod of approval. Marguerite Johnson, I heard the name again, my honors were read, there were noises in the audience of appreciation, and I took my place on the stage as rehearsed.

I thought about colors I hated: ecru, puce, lavender, beige and black.

There was shuffling and rustling around me, then Henry Reed was giving his valedictory address, "To Be or Not to Be." Hadn't he heard the whitefolks? We couldn't *be*, so the question was a waste of time.

Henry's voice came out clear and strong. I feared to look at him. Hadn't he got the message? There was no "nobler in the mind" for Negroes because the world didn't think we had minds, and they let us know it. "Outrageous fortune"? Now, that was a joke. When the ceremony was over I had to tell Henry Reed some things. That is, if I still cared. Not "rub," Henry, "erase." "Ah, there's the erase." Us.

Henry had been a good student in elocution. His voice rose on tides of promise and fell on waves of warnings. The English teacher had helped him to create a sermon winging through Hamlet's soliloquy. To be a man, a doer, a builder, a leader, or to be a tool, an unfunny joke, a crusher of funky toadstools. I marveled that Henry could go through with the speech as if we had a choice.

I had been listening and silently rebutting each sentence with my eyes closed; then there was a hush, which in an audience warns that something unplanned is happening. I looked up and saw Henry Reed, the conservative, the proper, the A student, turn his back to the audience and turn to us (the proud graduating class of 1940) and sing, nearly speaking,

> *Lift ev'ry voice and sing*
> *Till earth and heaven ring*
> *Ring with the harmonies of Liberty...*

It was the poem written by James Weldon Johnson. It was the music composed by J. Rosamond Johnson. It was the Negro national anthem. Out of habit we were singing it.

Our mothers and fathers stood in the dark hall and joined the hymn of encouragement. A kindergarten teacher led the small children onto the stage and the buttercups and daisies and bunny rabbits marked time and tried to follow:

> *Stony the road we trod*
> *Bitter the chastening rod*
> *Felt in the days when hope, unborn, had died.*
> *Yet with a steady beat*
> *Have not our weary feet*
> *Come to the place for which our fathers sighed?*

Every child I knew had learned that song with his ABC's and along with "Jesus Loves Me This I Know." But I personally had never heard it before. Never heard the words, despite the thousands of times I had sung them. Never thought they had anything to do with me.

On the other hand, the words of Patrick Henry had made such an impression on me that I had been able to stretch myself tall and trembling and say, "I know not what course others may take, but as for me, give me liberty or give me death."

And now I heard, really for the first time:

*"We have come over a way that with tears
has been watered,
We have come, treading our path through
the blood of the slaughtered."*

While echoes of the song shivered in the air, Henry Reed bowed his head, said "Thank you," and returned to his place in the line. The tears that slipped down many faces were not wiped away in shame.

We were on top again. As always, again. We survived. The depths had been icy and dark, but now a bright sun spoke to our souls. I was no longer simply a member of the proud graduating class of 1940; I was a proud member of the wonderful, beautiful Negro race.

Oh, Black known and unknown poets, how often have your auctioned pains sustained us? Who will compute the lonely nights made less lonely by your songs, or by the empty pots made less tragic by your tales?

If we were a people much given to revealing secrets, we might raise monuments and sacrifice to the memories of our poets, but slavery cured us of that weakness. It may be enough, however, to have it said that we survive in exact relationship to the dedication of our poets (include preachers, musicians and blues singers).

M. CARL HOLMAN
(1919–1988)

From *Anger and Beyond:*
The Negro Writer in the U.S.
The Afternoon of a Young Poet

Perhaps best-known for his work as civil rights activist, M. Carl Holman was a skilled writer and poet. Before serving as president of the National Urban Coalition, he taught English at Clark College in Atlanta for fourteen years. Always a good student, he began writing short stories and poetry when he was a child.

Born in Minter City, Mississippi, he grew up in St. Louis, where his father worked in a steel mill. He graduated magna cum laude from Lincoln University in Missouri, received his master of arts degree in English from the University of Chicago, and went on to claim a master of fine arts from Yale in 1954. Holman taught at Clark from 1948 to 1962. During the height of the civil rights movement, he guided and counseled student demonstrators. He was a quiet activist, but effective. His newspaper, the Atlanta Inquirer, *refused to accept advertising from segregated businesses.*

In 1962 he was tapped to serve on the U.S. Commission on Civil Rights. He served both the Kennedy and Johnson administrations. He remained there for six years and was deputy director by the time he left to become vice president of programs at the new National Urban Coalition. Within a year, he was president of the coalition and remained there until his death. This excerpt concerns his youth in Mississippi.

* * *

43

In the late winter of my senior year in high school I entered a poem in an annual literary competition sponsored by the Arts Club of St. Louis. Because I was almost pathologically shy, and because I was not sure I actually intended to go through with it until I was picking my way back up the icy street from the corner mailbox, I told no one what I had done. Until that night I had submitted poems to Negro newspapers and magazines and had won one or two small prizes, but I had never before ventured to enter a "white" contest.

I had found the announcement of the Arts Club competition in the section of one of the white dailies where I read avidly about plays, concerts and ballets which might just as well have been taking place on the moon. During that period of my life I was strongly influenced by three or four university-trained teachers on our high school faculty who were still caught up in the afterglow of the Negro Renaissance. Mr. Watts, Miss Armstrong, Mr. Blanton and Miss Lewis taught us from the "lilywhite" textbooks prescribed by the St. Louis school system, but they also mounted on their bulletin boards the works and pictures of Langston Hughes, James Weldon Johnson, Claude McKay, Sterling Brown, Countee Cullen and Jean Toomer.

Entering the contest, however secretly, represented unusual daring for me, though it would have been as easy as breathing for Miss Armstrong, a vibrantly energetic mahogany-skinned woman whose voice flayed our budding manhood with contempt when she read McKay's poem "If We Must Die." (Her voice accused and disturbed me, conjuring up two confusing memories from my childhood down-town on Carroll Street—the first, that day in the depths of the Depression when half the fathers on the block straggled back from their protest march on City Hall, their heads broken and bleeding. Some of them weeping, but only one of them laughing. The potbellied little man next door who came stumbling up the alley apart from the others, tittering like a drunken woman, one eye puffed shut, his bloody rag of a shirt dragging in the dust. Giggling and whispering, *"Don't hit me no mo, Cap'n. You the boss. You sho God is the boss. . . ."* And less than five years later, Big Crew, standing in the middle of the yard, his lips drawn back from his blue gums in a wolfish grin, smashing his black fist like a hammer into the rent man's face, picking the man up like a sack of flour and knocking him down again. All the time talking to him as quietly as one friend to another: *"Git up and fight, you peckerwood sonuvabitch. Git up and fight for your country."*)

I yearned during those high school years to write something as defiantly bitter as McKay's "If We Must Die" or Sterling Brown's "Strong Men." My temper was capable of flaring up and consuming me so utterly that during a period of a few months I found myself in wildly hopeless fights with the older boys. Deep in hostile north St. Louis I had placed my life and those of two boys with me in jeopardy when, without thinking, I spat in the face of a young white boy seated on the stoop surrounded by at least seven members of his beefy family, because he called me a "skinny black nigger" as my friends and I were passing. My mother's long campaign to curb my temper had only taught me at last to swallow my feelings, hiding them so deep that I could not have dredged up my rages and despairs and found words for them even if I had wanted to. The long poem I finally mailed to the Arts Club was called "Nocturne on a Hill." Though it was probably honest enough in its way, it echoed more of the white writers I had been reading and told more about my reactions to the shapes and sounds of the city than it did about the people I loved and hated, or the things which delighted, hurt or confused me most.

We had moved from Carroll Street downtown three years earlier and we were living that year on Driscoll Avenue in midtown, halfway between the river on the east and that section of West End the whites had ceded to the Negro doctors, schoolteachers and postal workers. For a long time after the move to Driscoll Avenue I had continued to go back to the old neighborhood. In part this was because the customers to whom I sold Negro weekly newspapers lived there (ranging from an ancient self-ordained bishop, whose wife was never permitted to expose anything more than a slender wax-yellow hand and a black-clad sleeve as I handed the paper through the double-chained door, to the heavily powdered ladies in the big house on Seymour Street who had bought a dozen papers from me every Friday for a month before I learned how they made their living). But even on days when I had no papers to sell, Carroll Street for a long time continued to have the same love-fear magnetism for me it had exercised when I lived there; racked by sweaty nightmares on nights when the patrol wagons and ambulances pounded past our house, listening by the hour to the Italians singing from the backyards where they had strung light bulbs for the parties that left the alley littered with snail shells and the discarded bottles the winos fought over the next morning. On Carroll Street we had lived closely, though not intimately, with whites: the Italians on Bouie Avenue to the rear, the Jewish store-keepers, the Germans who worked in the bakery and the bank, the Irish truck drivers and policemen (and one saloon keeper who re-converted his storefront when Prohibition ended, returning to its old place in the window the faded, flyspecked sign whose legend we chanted up and down the street: "Coolidge Blew the Whistle, Mellon Rang the Bell, Hoover Pulled the Throttle and the Country Went to Hell").

Driscoll Avenue was a less impoverished and more self-contained world than Carroll Street. Except for the merchants and bill collectors, it was possible to walk through midtown for blocks without seeing a white face. We lived on the first floor of a three-story brick house set on a concrete terrace from which three stone steps led down to the street. My chores during that long winter included keeping the steps salted down and making sure the heavy hall door was kept tightly shut.

My mother was ill for a long time that winter, and the grown-ups came to visit her, stamped into the house wrapped like mummies with only their eyes showing, bringing pots of stew, pickled preserves and the latest tale of some drunk who had been found frozen stiff in an alley or a neighbor who had been taken to "Old Number Two" with double pneumonia. Number Two was the nearest city hospital, and the neighborhood saying was that they did more killing there than Mr. Swift did over at his packing house. Old people in the neighborhood sometimes clung stubbornly to their beds at home, hiding the seriousness of their ailments, for fear they would be sent to Number Two to die. My mother was not old, but I lay awake many nights that winter, listening to her rasping breathing and praying that she would not have to be taken to Number Two. Sometimes, after her breathing had smoothed out and she had fallen asleep, I would get out of bed and go over to the window, raising the shade enough to let in the white winter moonlight. Fumbling for a pencil and piece of paper, I would write lines and fragments which I could not see, then fold the paper and stuff it into my hiding place back of the piano which nobody in the house played.

My mother's conviction that both her children were going to finish high school and college and "amount to something" had persisted in the face of the bleakest realities her native Mississippi and a half-flat near the tracks in south St. Louis could marshal against her. Even in her illness, hollow-eyed and feverish, she wanted to know what we had done in school daily, what the teachers had said, whether our homework was done. A gifted seamstress and a careful manager of small change for most of her life, she never doubted she would one day find the proper use for the patterns, scraps of cloth, Eagle stamps, buttons and pins she scrupulously put aside, each in its proper place. She cooked huge pots of soup, with opulent aromas suggesting magnitudes of power and promise out of all proportion to the amount of meat in the pot. She felt she had ample reason to sing "He Leadeth Me," and when we had amazed ourselves and our teachers by prodigies of nerve-straining effort she only said mildly, "Didn't He promise He would make a way out of no way for those who believed in Him?"

Lacking her faith, I was so beset with premonitions and terrors during those months of her illness that I lost all recollection of the poem I had mailed to the Arts Club. The cousin I loved most had died in childbirth just two years before, at the age of nineteen, and I had been tormented ever since by the fragility of the web separating life and death. Though she met the slightest ache or pain visited on her children as if it were an outrider of the Devil's legions fully armed, my mother regarded her own illnesses as nuisances to be gotten through with as little fuss as possible. By the time the snow had melted in the gutters she was on her feet again, halfway through her spring cleaning and fretting to have the last frost gone so that she could start planting the narrow rectangle of earth out front she called her garden.

I came home from school one afternoon in early May to find a letter from the Arts Club in our mailbox. I was afraid to open it until I had first made sure it was not bulky enough to contain the rejected poem. There was only a single sheet inside, a note typed on the most elegant stationery I had ever seen, congratulating me on the selection of my poem as one of the five best works submitted in that year's contest and inviting me to meet the other winners at the club two weeks later.

The first surge of surprise and pleasure was followed almost at once by a seizure of blind panic. How could I go out there to Westmoreland Place, a street I had never seen, to meet a group of strangers, most if not all of them white—when I stammered or fell silent whenever I had to talk to one of my teachers without the supporting presence of the rest of the class? Reading the note again I saw that the meeting had been scheduled for midafternoon of a school day. For most of that next week I debated whether I should accept the club's invitation or prepare to be sick on that day. Finally, just forty-eight hours before the date set in the letter, I went down to the principal and secured permission to be excused from my afternoon classes to attend the Arts Club meeting.

That same afternoon I showed my mother the letter. She knew me well enough to play down the pride she felt, complaining instead about people who would miss Heaven one day because they always waited until the last minute. She consulted with a friend who worked in the section where the club was located and wrote down the directions for me, dryly reminding me to have the conductor give me a transfer when I boarded the trolley outside the school. I had once had to walk home a distance of some six miles away because I forgot to ask for a transfer. Actually, I was less concerned about the transfer than about the possibility that on the way out to the club I might develop motion sickness. This often happened when I rode the trolleys. Usually I got off the car as soon as the first queasy stirrings began in the pit of my stomach, and walked the rest of the way. But this time I would be in a part of town that I did not know at all. I resolved to ride standing up all the way, trusting that my mother's God would not let me be sick.

I left school on a hazily bright afternoon alive with the tarry tang of smoke and the green smell of growing things which I associate still with spring in St. Louis. It was good to be a privileged truant with the whole block in front of the school to myself, the typewriters clicking behind me in the principal's office and the unheeded voices of the teachers floating out of the classroom windows overhead. The first trolley was a long time coming. When I got on I remembered to ask for the transfer, and though over half the seats were empty on both trolleys, I stood up all the way. But when I got off the second car I found that I had managed to lose the directions my mother had given me. I could not remember whether I was to go north or south from the trolley stop. My palms promptly began sweating and I took out the letter from the Arts Club, reading the address again as if that would give me a clue. In my neighborhood most of the houses were row houses, or were separated from each other by nothing more than a narrow passageway. Even houses like the one we lived in, though not flush with the pavement, were close enough so that the addresses could be easily read from the sidewalk. But out here the houses were set back from wide lawns under shade trees and there was no way of making out the addresses without going up a long walk to the front door. No small children were playing outside, there were no stores into which a stranger might go and ask directions, and the whole neighborhood was wrapped in a fragrant but forbidding stillness. Remembering that my mother had said the club was only two blocks away from the trolley stop, I started walking south, deciding that if it turned out I was going the wrong way I could always come back and go two blocks in the other direction. I walked three blocks for good measure without finding Westmoreland Place, then turned and started back.

A red-faced old man with bushy military whiskers that reminded me of pictures I had seen of the Kaiser came down one of the walks with a bulldog on a leash. I braced myself to ask him where Westmoreland Place was, but before I could speak, his china blue eyes suddenly glared at me with such venomous hatred that I had the feeling he was about to set the dog on me. I averted my eyes and walked on, trembling suddenly with an answering hatred as senseless as his. Not noticing where I was going, I was about to cross into the next block when I looked up at the street sign and found that I was on Westmoreland Place. It was a street of thick hedges and houses which, if anything, were more inaccessible than those I had already passed. I walked up the street in one direction, then crossed and reversed my course. By now the letter was wilting in my hand. The trolley ride had taken longer than I had estimated and I was sure I was already late. One of the last things my mother had said to me that morning was, "Now try to be sure not to get out there on Colored People's Time." My mind groped for a plausible lie that would let me give up the whole business and go home. I thought of saying that the meeting had been called off, that the place was closed when I got there, that I had caught the wrong car and gone too far out of the way to get back in time. At one point, I almost convinced myself that I should go back to the trolley stop and catch a car that would take me downtown to my old refuge, the main public library. I could stay there reading for an hour or two, then claim I had actually attended the tea. But my spirit quailed at the prospect of inventing answers to all the questions that would follow. And what if in the meantime someone from the club had already called my home or the school? I hated myself for entering the competition and felt sick with envy when I thought of my schoolmates who by now were idling down the halls on free period or dreaming their way through the last classes before the liberating bell.

I was plodding down the same block for the second time when around the corner of a big stone house across the street came an unmistakably colored man in work clothes, uncoiling a garden hose. We might have been the only two living souls on a desert island. Almost faint with relief I angled across the street toward him. But the handyman, his high shiny forehead furrowed in elaborate concentration, adjusted the nozzle and began playing rainbow jets of spray across the grass. I halted at the edge of the lawn and waited for him to take note of my presence. In due time he worked himself close enough so that I was able to ask him if he knew where the Arts Club was. I held out the letter as I asked him, but he merely turned his rusty deepset eyes on me with a look that plainly said, *I hope to God you ain't come out here to make trouble for the rest of us.* In later years I have seen that look in the eyes of Negro businessmen, schoolteachers, college presidents, reverend ministers—and a trio of cooks and dishwashers peering through the swinging doors of a restaurant kitchen at the dark-skinned students sitting at counters where no one of their color ever presumed to sit before.

But I was of another generation, another temperament and state of mind from those students. So when the handyman flicked one hand in the direction from which I had just come and said, "There 'tis, over there," I thanked him—rather thanked his back, which was already turned to me.

I would never have taken the two-story brick building at the end of the flagstone walk to be anything other than the residence of a comfortably well-off family. Just before I pushed the button beside the broad door it occurred to me that the handyman might be playing his notion of a joke on me. Then I looked down at the thick mat on which I was standing and saw the letters "A-C." I pressed the button, waited and was about to press it again when the door swung open. The rake-thin white maid standing there had composed for her plain freckled face a smile of deferential welcome. The smile faded and her body stiffened in the neat gray uniform. For an instant I thought she would close the door in my face, but she braked it so that it was barely ajar and said, "Yes?" I mumbled something and held out the letter. She squinted at the envelope and said, "You wait here." The door closed and I stood there with my face burning, wanting to turn and go away but unwilling to confront the expression of sour satisfaction I expected to see on the face of the handyman across the street. After what seemed fifteen full minutes a gray-haired woman in a blue uniform with starched cuffs came to the door. "All right, what is it now?" she said, sounding like a very busy woman. I held out the letter and she took it, measured me up and down with her shrewd eyes and said to the younger woman hovering behind her, "I'll be right back." The freckle-faced thin one looked miles above my head toward the street but we shared the unspoken understanding that I was not to move from where I stood and that she was to watch me.

I stood rooted there, calling myself every kind of black fool for coming in the first place, my undershirt cleaving to my damp skin. It had become clear to me that I had received the invitation by mistake. And now that I had surrendered the letter, the only proof that I had been invited, my sole excuse for being there at all was gone. I pictured them huddled inside, talking in whispers, waiting for me to have the good sense to leave. Then I heard voices coming toward the door. My keeper faded back into the gloom of the hallway and an attractive woman in her forties held the door open and smiled at me. Everything about her, her fine-textured skin, the soft-colored dress and the necklace she was wearing, her candid gaze, defined an order of relationships which did away with any need for me to deal further with the other two women. "Hello," she said. "So you're the boy who came over to tell us Mr. Holman couldn't come?"

I stared dumbly at her, wondering how I could have been fooled into thinking she was one of those white women my mother would have described approvingly as "a real lady, as nice as they come."

"Please tell him we hope he'll be feeling better soon," the woman said. "We had so hoped to meet him."

"I'm—I got the letter saying to come out here," I blurted. We stood there for a minute staring at one another and then her pink skin flushed red. "Oh, you mean you—oh, I *am* so sorry," she said. "Please do come in. I didn't know." She glanced back at the maids. "I mean, we thought—"

It was finally clear to all of us what she had thought. That the white boy who wrote the poem had been unable to come so his family had thoughtfully sent their colored boy to tender his regrets.

"You come right on in," the woman said. "I'm your hostess. All the others are already here and we've been waiting for you." She drew me inside the cool, dim hallway and guided me up the stairs like an invalid. I could not remember ever walking on such thick carpets. I had a hazy impression of cut flowers in vases, and paintings hanging along the walls like those I had seen in the Art Museum in the park. As she went up she kept on talking, but I made very little of what she was saying because now I could hear the murmur of other voices and laughter coming from the floor above us. I had the feeling that an intimate and very pleasant family party was in progress which we were about to ruin and I wanted to ask my hostess if I might not be excused after all. Instead I let myself be piloted into a sunny high-ceilinged room which at one and the same time seemed as spacious as a playing field and so intimate that no one could move without touching the person beside him. A blur of white faces turned toward us, some of them young, some middle-aged, some older, but all of them clearly belonging to a different world from that of the uniformed women downstairs. A different world from mine. For a flickering moment there was a drop in energy like that sudden dimming of lights during a summer storm and then I was being introduced in a flurry of smiles, bobbing heads and a refrain seeming to consist of variations on "Delightful ... delighted ... so good you could come ... a pleasure."

Whenever I have tried to recollect that afternoon since, the faces in that upstairs room elude me like objects seen through sunlit water. I remember that one of the girls was blonde and turned eagerly from one speaker to another as if anxious not to miss one word, that there was a boy there from a school out in the country who talked and moved with the casual, almost insulting assurance which for a long time afterward I automatically associated with private schools. All of the other students there who had won prizes or honorable mentions in the area-wide competition were either from private schools or from white high schools whose very names were new to me. One of the girls was from a Catholic school and one of the sisters from the faculty had come along with her. I discovered that other winners were accompanied by their teacher and I mentally kicked myself for not realizing that I might have been buttressed by the presence of Miss Armstrong or Mr. Blanton. Certainly they would have been much more at home in this company than I was. Gradually, as cookies, tea and punch were passed and the talk again swirled back and forth, I began to relax somewhat, content to be on the periphery of that closed circle. I kept stealing glances around the room, taking in the wide fireplace and the portrait above the mantel of some famous man whose identity kept eluding me, the rows of books in the recessed shelves along the wall, and the magazines scattered tantalizingly just out of reach on the long oaken table in the center of the room.

In school, except to recite, I had rarely ever talked even to my English teachers about poems, books and writers. But this group, comfortably seated or standing about the pleasant room with the haze of spring sunlight sifting through the windows, shared a community of language and interests which enabled them largely to ignore differences of age and individual preference and to move from one idea or work to another as effortlessly as fish in a pond. They talked of Shakespeare and Keats, Milton and Shelley, but there were other writers whose lines I had spoken aloud, sometimes in puzzlement, when I was alone. Now they were being argued over, attacked, defended, ridiculed: Eliot, Frost, Sandburg, Millay, Vachel Lindsay, Amy

Lowell, Yeats. There were moments when someone touched on something I had read and I was tempted to speak out in agreement or disagreement. At other times I was overcome by the gloomy conviction that I could never in the years that were left to me read all the works some of them seemed to know by heart. I felt particularly lost as the talk shifted to novels only recently written, to concerts they had attended and plays seen at the American Theatre downtown or "on our last trip to New York." (I had been drunk for days on the free concert given for Negro high school students by the St. Louis Symphony the year before, shutting myself off in my room with an umbrella spoke for a baton, trying to be all the voices of the orchestra and graceful Mr. Golschmann conducting the *New World Symphony*. Later I was to go to the American as often as I could to see the road companies in performance and, during intermissions, to devour the posters advertising the plays I would not be able to see. Often my companion and I were among less than a dozen Negroes present. Years afterward, on a trip back to St. Louis I was triumphantly informed that Negroes were no longer segregated in the second-balcony seats at the American. Second-balcony seats being all we could afford, my friend and I had never asked for anything else, a neat dovetailing of covert discrimination and economic necessity.)

Toward the end of the long afternoon, it was proposed that the young writers read their poems. Once again I was plunged into sweaty-palmed agony. My torment only increased as the first two readers read their poems like seasoned professionals, or so it seemed to me. When my turn came I tried to beg off, but the additional attention this focused upon me only increased my discomfort and I plunged in, at first reading too fast and almost inaudibly but finally recollecting some of the admonitions my teachers had dinned into my head in preparation for "recitations" before Negro school and church audiences as far back as the second grade. I had not realized how long a poem it was when I was writing it and I was squirmingly conscious of certain flaws and failures which had never before loomed so large. The applause and praise that followed when I finished, if anything, exceeded that given the others; a situation which, even then, aroused the fleeting suspicion that the dancing bear was being given higher marks than a man might get for the same performance. One of the older women murmured something about Paul Laurence Dunbar. Someone else asked me if I liked Pushkin. I could only look blank, since at that time I knew almost nothing about the great Russian's poetry and even less about his Negro lineage. Inevitably, there was a flattering and irrelevant comparison to Langston Hughes. A wavy-haired gentleman took his pipe out of his mouth to ask if I didn't think "The Negro Speaks of Rivers" was a marvelous poem. I said I certainly did. (But stopped short of trying to explain why the Mississippi always made me think not of Lincoln at New Orleans but of the playmate on Carroll Street drowned during an Easter baptism, the cold, feral grin of the garfish skeleton which two of us stumbled on as we moped along the riverfront toward the pickle factory and the high platform beyond where the city garbage trucks dumped their loads into the frothing stream, and the dimly remembered "high waters" sucking at the edge of the roadbed as the train brought my father and me back to St. Louis from our grandfather's funeral.)

Gradually, as the light faded outside the window, people began looking at their watches and saying good-by. One of the club members thanked all of us for coming and said she could not remember when the Arts Club had had such a fine and talented group. The blonde girl clapped her hands for attention, her eyes shining with the enthusiasm of the born organizer. Why, she wanted to know, did this year's group really have to scatter? It seemed to her that we should not let our companionship, our new friendships die. Some of us were going away for the summer, but there were still several weeks left yet before school would be out. Some might be going off to college in the fall, but others would not, and probably some of those who would be entering college would be going no farther away than the University of Missouri at Columbia, or St. Louis, Washington, or one of the other schools in the St. Louis area. I was silent as the others chimed in, suggesting that we meet at the various high schools or rotate meetings from one home to another before and after summer vacations. Such a point was made of including me in and I felt already so much the witch at the wedding party that I was not inclined to remind them that I would have a much harder time getting into a meeting at the schools they attended or the colleges in the area than I had had getting into the Arts Club that afternoon. To say nothing of what their parents and friends and mine would make of those meetings in the homes. I tried to picture those well-dressed and half-assured young white poets strolling past the cleaning and pressing shop to a meeting at my house. Nevertheless, my Driscoll Avenue cynicism began crumbling under the effervescent pressures of their youth and mine. We made our way down the thick-carpeted stairs, true poets and comrades, a verbal skyscraper of plans and projects rising as we descended. We would exchange our favorite original poems by phone and by mail. We would do a volume of poems together and a famous novelist who was a good friend of our hostess would get the book published for us. The Arts Club would serve as secretariat and haven, keeping track of addresses and phone numbers and providing a place where we could meet, read and write.

Good will, mutual admiration, flowering ambition united us as we parted in the gathering spring dusk. The air was scented with the watermelony smell of freshly cut grass. The lights were on in the stone house across the street, but the handyman was gone.

* * *

I did not hear from the young men and women I met that afternoon at the Arts Club the next week, the next month, or ever. But I had a great many more serious disappointments than that, along with a decent amount of good fortune, in the two remaining years I spent in my home town. Like many other young men similarly situated I was involved during those prewar years in the quiet but no less desperate scramble simply to hold on to life and not go under. By the end of that period of twenty-odd months I had run an elevator, worked as a machine operator, delivered parcels, patrolled a lake stocked with fish nobody ever tried to steal, and stood in half a hundred job lines with white and black men who showed up every morning less out of hope than the need to put off as long as possible that time of day when they must once again face their families. For me and a good many others my age it was not a question really of having something to eat and a place to sleep. The battle was, rather, to find ways of withstanding the daily erosion, through tedium, through humiliation, through various short-term pleasures, of the sense of your own possibilities. Necessary, too, was some sensitivity to possibilities outside yourself. Here I do not exclude chance, the lucky break. For me it came with the opportunity to become a part-time student at a college I might have attended full time two years earlier.

On the night before I left for college my mother gave a party for me, inviting a dozen of my friends. Some of them brought gifts. As I was walking past the Catholic church on Garth Avenue, shortly after midnight, going home to the flat I shared with my father, a squad car pulled up and two officers jumped out. Night sticks at the ready, they flashed a light in my face and wanted to know where I was coming from and where I had picked up all that stuff. They pawed through the presents I was carrying until they came across an anthology of poetry autographed for me that night by my friends. The first officer grunted and snapped off his light. The second seemed tempted to take a swipe at me anyhow for wasting their time. They got back in the car and drove off, leaving me to walk the two blocks remaining between the church and home.

The next morning, on a cold, sooty, old-style St. Louis day, I left home. I got on a bus and headed for Jefferson City, Missouri. That trip away from home has been a much longer journey than I had anticipated and a very much different one. On certain occasions, as when my poetry was published or while lecturing at Atlanta University, I have remembered that afternoon. And I have thought that perhaps when I next visited St. Louis, I would try once again to find my way to the Arts Club. I never have and it is probably just as well. It may be that I got as much as could reasonably be expected on that first visit.

LORENE CARY
(1957-)

From *Black Ice*

*Fall 1971 found fourteen-year-old Lorene Cary attending a west
Philadelphia public high school and working weekends at the
Woolworth soda fountain. One year later, she had earned a full
scholarship to St. Paul's School, an exclusive boarding school in
New Hampshire. She was in the second class of girls to attend the
school that had been for more than one hundred twenty-five years
exclusively male, and almost exclusively white. In the first year
she attended, there were forty black and five hundred white students.*

*In 1972 Cary left her secure, middle-class family home for a
dormitory of strangers, her familiar school where she did well
for competitive classes where she always worked hard but didn't
always excel. In herself she confronted her racist attitudes about
non-blacks, but she often found herself the target of a subtle,
insidious racism. Were expectations lower for her? Could she
make it at St. Paul's? She knew she was at St. Paul's because of
the protests, the sit-ins, and the boycotts, but she was also there
because she deserved to be there, because she earned the privilege. Still she had doubts.*

*In the end, she had what it takes. Cary graduated from St.
Paul's, and in 1982 returned to the school to teach. This excerpt
describes a time during the fall of her first year at St. Paul's.*

Girls came and went in my room. I liked it that way. I wanted the
company—and the prosperous appearance of company. They taught
me about tollhouse cookies; Switzerland; the names of automobiles,
shampoos, rock groups, Connecticut cities; casual shoes and outdoor-

equipment catalogues. I learned that other girls, too, tired during sports, that their calf muscles, like mine, screamed out pain when they walked down the stairs. I learned about brands of tampons. I learned that these girls thought their hair dirty when they did not wash it daily.

"I hear what you're saying, but I just don't see it. I'm looking at your hair, but I just don't see grease."

"Oh, my God, it's, like, hanging down in clumps!" One girl pulled a few strands from her scalp to display the offending sheen. "Look."

I learned that their romanticized lusts sounded like mine felt, as did their ambivalent homesickness, and their guarded, girlish competitiveness.

As they came to sit and stay, however, differences emerged between us. Taken together, these girls seemed more certain than I that they deserved our good fortune. They were sorry for people who were poorer than they, but they did not feel guilty to think of the resources we were sucking up—forests, meadows and ponds, the erudition of well-educated teachers, water for roaring showers, heat that blew out of opened windows everywhere, food not eaten but mixed together for disgusting fun after lunch. They took it as their due. It was boot-camp preparation for America's leaders, which we were told we would one day be. They gave no indication that they worried that others, smarter or more worthy, might, at that very moment, be giving up hope of getting what we had.

I did not, however, tell the girls what I was thinking. We did not talk about how differently we saw the world. Indeed my black and their white heritage was not a starting point for our relationship, but rather was the outer boundary. I could not cross it, because there sprang up a hard wall of denial impervious to my inexperienced and insecure assault. "Well, as far as I'm concerned," one girl after another would say, "it doesn't matter to me if somebody's white or black or green or purple. I mean people are just people."

The motion, having been made, would invariably be seconded.

"Really. I mean, it's the person that counts."

Having castigated whites' widespread inability to see individuals for the skin in which they were wrapped, I could hardly argue with "it's the person that counts." I didn't know why they always chose green and purple to dramatize their indifference, but my ethnicity seemed diminished when the talk turned to Muppets. It was like they were taking something from me.

"I'm not purple." What else could you say?

"The truth is," somebody said, "I...this is *so* silly...I'm really embarrassed, but, it's like, there *are* some things you, God, you just feel ashamed to admit that you think about this stuff, but I always kind of wondered if, like, black guys and white guys were, like, different..."

They shrieked with laughter. Sitting on the afghan my mother had crocheted for me in the school colors of red and white, their rusty-dusty feet all over my good afghan, they laughed and had themselves a ball.

"Now, see, that's why people don't want to say anything," one girl said. "Look, you're getting all mad."

"I'm not mad."

"You look it."

"I'm not mad. I don't even know about any differences between white guys and black guys," I said deliberately avoiding the word boys. (Black manhood seemed at stake. Everything seemed at stake.) Then I added as archly as possible: "I don't mess around with white boys."

The party broke up soon after. I sat still, the better to control my righteous anger. It always came down to this, I thought, the old song of the South. I wanted something more meaningful. I wanted it to mean something that I had come four hundred miles from home, and sat day after day with them in Chapel, in class. I wanted it to mean something that after Martin Luther King's and Malcolm X's assassinations, we kids sweated together in sports, ate together at Seated Meal, studied and talked together at night. It couldn't be just that I was to become like them or hang onto what I'd been. It couldn't be that lonely and pointless.

I looked across the quad to Jimmy's window, and waved. He was not in his room, but the mere sight of his lighted window brought me back to my purpose. It was not to run my ass ragged trying to wrench some honesty out of this most disingenuous of God's people. I had come to St. Paul's to turn it out. How had I lost sight of the simple fact?

In a few days "inside" grades for the Fall Term caught me by surprise. I had barely settled in. During reports the Rector said that interim grades were merely to give us an idea of our progress. Students called them "warning" grades. Groupmasters handed them to each student in the evening.

I churned with anticipation all day. At one moment it seemed to me that I'd been doing brilliantly. I was understanding Sr. Fuster's musical Spanish, speaking glibly in religion about "systems of belief," hiding from Mr. Buxton the crush I was developing, trooping good-naturedly through the inanity of trigonometry, drawing and redrawing the folds of a draped cloth in art.

One wrong answer, however, would change my perspective completely. Sure, I was understanding Sr. Fuster better, but my essays were grammatical disasters. In religion, I skittered over the surface of the language, never quite knowing what I meant to say until the moment I opened my mouth. I only *thought* Mr. Buxton hadn't noticed my crush. I had fallen asleep during eighth-period trig. In art class, my colors were timid; my perspective was off.

Mr. Hawley handed me the thin piece of paper on which the computer in the Schoolhouse basement had recorded my warning grades. On my sheet were five grades, two Honors and three High Passes. What I saw when I looked at my warning grades were two Bs and three Cs. The school had made it quite clear in the catalog and elsewhere that St. Paul's grades were not letter-grade equivalents. They'd told us that High Honors were rare as A-pluses, and that Honors meant just that. No matter. I saw average. I saw failure. And what I saw on that paper, Mr. Hawley saw in my face.

"There are several things about these warning grades you should keep in mind," he said. "The first is that although they may look like real grades and feel like real grades, they are not real grades.

"OK. Now, how accurate an indicator are these? Well, I'm sure that in some of your courses, there hasn't been enough work assigned and graded for teachers to evaluate. And in that case, many teachers feel safer grading on the low side, just so that no one gets a false sense of security. So, it is possible that you might be doing better than these grades, and it is extremely unlikely that you'd be doing any worse."

He told me that High Passes were not the end of the world. "The other thing that I doubt you are giving yourself credit for," he said, "is that you've just come in, as a new Fifth Former—not many people come in the Fifth Form, as you've noticed, and there's a reason why, many reasons—and you've just come straight from your old hometown high. Some of these other students have had a different preparation. I am certain that you'll catch on fast. Look, you *have* caught on fast. I've got old girls in this house who'd kill for those grades. But the fact is, I don't see how you can expect much more of yourself right now."

Mr. Hawley told me that he'd seen students take a year or two to adjust to St. Paul's, not just public-school students, but kids from fancy day schools.

"I've only *got* two years," I said.

"You're doing great."

When girls on my hall asked about my grades, I joked: "It's like when the Ghost of Christmas Yet To Come points to the gravestone," I said. "All I want to know is: Is this what will be or what may be?"

"Oh, you'll do fine."

I wondered if anyone here had ever expected me to do better than this. White faces of the adults flashed in my head, smiling, encouraging, tilted to one side, asking if I'd like to talk, extending their welcome. "If you need anything..." Early on they'd told me that I'd do fine. I felt betrayed, first by them, then by my own naiveté. HPs were probably what they'd meant by fine—for black scholarship kids. Maybe that's what they'd been saying all along, only I hadn't heard it.

No sooner had the furor of warning grades subsided than the excitement of Parents' Day began. A few parents appeared on the last Friday afternoon in October, and by Saturday morning they were everywhere, cars clogging the roads, adult voices filling the Schoolhouse, where they waited in long lines for ten-minute talks with our teachers.

Parents who had no money or no time did not come, but mine did. And so did my grandparents. They surrounded me as we walked slowly along the paths. Seeing them made me know how much I'd missed them. I guided them through the days' activities as if marching through a dream.

In the evening, they came to the show we'd prepared for them. I sang in the chorus, and they saw me sing. I showed them my books and my papers. I walked them to each of my favorite places along the paths and pointed out where gardeners had been working all week to spruce up the grounds. My father remembered that dorm proctors at Lincoln University had handed out fresh new blankets on anniversary weekends, just before festivities, and then collected them again when parents went home. We laughed about that. But St. Paul's was no Lincoln, they kept saying, that tiny black college in rural Pennsylvania where milk from the nearby cows had tasted of onion grass in the spring.

I recalled the photographs of my father and his classmates, young black men with shiny hair, baring their legs and hamming it up for the camera; the photo of my father and mother, who had married the Saturday before my father graduated. They stood under a huge old tree, grinning broadly, my mother in her pedal-pusher pants, her body curving like an S against his, her arm waving in the air. Every time one of us mentioned Lincoln—and we did, again and again, because it was the only college we knew well—I thought of those photographs. As often as I saw the image in my mind, I heard snatches of what had been their old favorite song:

> *. . . Our day will come*
> *And we'll have ev'rything,*
> *We'll share the joy*
> *Falling in love can bring.*
> *No one can tell me that I'm too young to know*
> *I love you so,*
> *And you love me . . .*
> *Our day wi-ill come.*

I could not stop thinking of them like that, their arms entwined like the branches of a mulberry, certain that they would do together what their parents had been unable to do. "We decided we were *not* going to end up divorced. We just decided it," they always said. I'd wondered how they could have been so sure. "Our dreams have magic because we'll always stay/In love this way/Our day will come."

Lincoln looked green in the pictures, and, as if it were not full enough with their promise, and the promise of so many young men, black Greeks, black gods ready to march out into the world and grab it for their own, it was also home to the prepubescent Julian Bond "just running around the campus like any other little faculty kid," and, he, of course, was now in government.

My mother lit a cigarette in my room, and my father made a face. I could not take my eyes off the pack. My mother had changed brands. So absorbed had I been with my own changes, that I had not expected any from them, and my mother least of all. It was a small thing, the brand of cigarettes, but it occurred to me for the first time that in leaving home, I gave up the right to know the details of their daily life. Things might be the same when I got back for the next vacation, or they might not. I had no way of knowing, because I wasn't there.

Whatever I had planned to tell them—about how I did not feel like myself here, how I was worried that the recruiters expected little more than survival from us, how I was beginning to doubt that they could *see* excellence in us, because it might pop out through thick lips and eyes or walk on flat feet or sit on big, bodacious behinds— I kept to myself. I showed off my familiarity with my new school. Why, I was fitting in fine. My teachers said so. My new friends said so— Hey, girls, come meet my folks....

Soon they had to leave. Because it was more convenient, St. Paul's School did not switch to Standard Time until Sunday night when the parents were gone. My family was amused by the custom; I was not. "It's just like St. Paul's. It's practically a metaphor," I said ("metaphor" having become one of my favorite new words), "for the arrogance of this place. Isn't that the most arrogant thing you've ever seen, just changing *time!*"

"Well, honey," said my grandmother, "it's just for a little while. It's not as if they were going to keep it that way."

"When you think about it, it's an arbitrary change anyway," my father said. "And now that we need to save energy, who knows whether they might just change it some more to take better advantage of the daylight."

Everyone smiled mildly at me as if I were being unreasonable. I let the subject drop.

I fell asleep that night listening to the country sounds that replaced the parents' festive noise. In the branches, dead limbs creaked like old doors. Every hour until midnight the Chapel tower's metallic throat pealed out the wrong time, sharp and bright and sure.

November set in cold and damp. The work of the school chugged along: *I think I can, I think I can, I think I can.* The chipper refrain from childhood came chugging through my mind as I ran through the rain between classes. I did not have a raincoat that fall. *I think I can I think I can I think I can.* I slogged around the muddy field and hurled myself through wind sprints. Browner mud, grayer skies, blacker water. The wind penetrated the fiber of my clothing. The sun did not. But the engine of the school chugged on. Work and more work, with no way to get out. People and more people, with no way to get away from them, the same people day after day, becoming more familiar, their walks, their accents, their quirks and behavior. They said the same things, cracked the same jokes. So did I. I bored myself. We bored each other. Our teasing grew less witty and meaner.

It was in November that my soccer team played one of the boys' club teams. Our coach urged us to play aggressively. The ball flew up and down the field. I cursed its every reversal, knowing that I'd have to turn around and run back down the same field I'd just run up. Back and forth and back and forth, meaninglessly, mercilessly. The ball zinged, and I ran parallel to it, out on the edge of the field, in wing position, just like I didn't have any better sense. The drudgery was punctuated now and then by panic when a ball popped toward me. "Close up the hole! Close up the hole! Take it down. You're free, you're free!" and then I'd see the expanse of field between me and the goal, and I'd know that I could not tag along, but would have to run fast, faster than the mob coming at me. I wheezed and ran and wheezed. I opened my mouth wide, but I felt as if I were sucking air through a straw.

I think I can I think I can I think I can. Up jumped the good little girl inside, ever hopeful, she who believed that all she needed was one more win. Up she jumped as if this were a fifth-grade penmanship contest, the tie-breaker in a spelling bee, an audition for *Annie Get Your Gun:* "Anything you can do I can do better, I can do anything better than you." I knew this little girl. She looked like the freckled six-year-old in my mother's wallet. She felt like Pollyanna.

The ball came at me. The crazy little girl inside tore after it. Girls who had beaten me in wind sprints were unable to catch me. My arms pumped up and down as I ran. They helped push me forward. Maybe this was it, I thought, maybe. I almost cried with gratitude. Asthma came to clamp round my chest, but this time I was not afraid of suffocating. I huffed puffs of steam into the cold air.

I didn't see the little guy who came to steal the ball. I didn't see him at all until he was right in front of me like a sudden insult. I was stunned. The ball was mine. The goal was in sight. I could see the goal tender's fear, his awkward alarm. I loved how he called out to his fullbacks—as if they could stop me. But who was this little guy who would not be moved?

He put out his foot to snag the ball. He got it, and pulled it just to the side of me. I scooped the ball back with the inside of my foot, and knew I had to move it again, but could not, because he was there, the little guy again, his cleat coming, slender and tenacious. Then I charged. There was screaming around us, coming closer. I had to have the ball. I had to drive it in. I didn't realize I had fallen until the impact of the hard ground went up through my hip and reverberated inside my head. The ball rolled away. The whistle blew, and they stopped the game for us. His face contorted to hold back his tears. Clouds drifted overhead, wispy and beautiful.

I saw him a couple days later. He swung himself gingerly between his crutches as if his armpits were sore. He smiled bravely at me.

"I'm sorry," I said to him, trying to feel more intensely the throbbing in the purplish lump that had appeared on the side of my own leg.

"That's all right," he said, shrugging his shoulders above the crutches. "You couldn't help it. Are you all right?"

"Sure. Got a bruise or two." I felt like a brutish distortion of those big, black women I so admired, like Sojourner Truth as the actresses portrayed her: "Ah kin push a plow as far as a man—*And ain't I a woman?!*"

II

The Nineteenth Century—
A Time of Upheaval

IT IS EXTREMELY DIFFICULT, IF NOT IMPOSSIBLE, TO UNDERSTAND LIFE AS IT was in this country a little more than a century ago. If slavery, the "peculiar institution," did not exactly flourish, it most certainly existed, with all its unbelievable cruelty. By 1860 there were nearly 3,000,000 slaves in the South, but, contrary to belief, slave ownership was not widespread. Probably not more than 400,000 of the 8,000,000 Southern whites in that year were slaveholders. In addition, there was a class freed by their owners for one motive or another. They made up about 10 percent of the black population in the South.

Children of slaves had a most unnatural childhood. More often than not they did not know where or when they were born, or who their parents were since they were frequently separated from them at a very early age. It is interesting to reflect upon the fact that in many cases the father was the white plantation master. (It was, as a matter of fact, in his interest to have as many children as possible by his female slaves since the issue was regarded as additional property.) How did he feel to see his black child brutally whipped, perhaps by one of his legitimate white children? Did he feel any remorse? Or did he just regard the child as he would a piece of inanimate property?

Slave children were, of course, forbidden an education. Their function in that society was to serve. They were beaten if they deviated from their expected conduct in any way. Some were fortunate enough to escape to free states. Most did not.

Before the Civil War the number of blacks in the South climbed steadily. After the war, however, while many chose to remain on their former plantations on a sharecrop basis, others fled the South, and the decades following the 1860s show a gradual decline in the percentage of blacks in the total population of the South.

Children were still pressed into service, but this time by their families. Schools were opened for African-American children and the education of a race began. The twentieth century loomed ahead.

ISAAC JEFFERSON

(1775–1850?)

Memoirs of a Monticello Slave: The Life of Isaac Jefferson

As dictated to Charles Campbell in the 1840s by Isaac, one of Thomas Jefferson's slaves

Isaac Jefferson was born into slavery at Monticello in December, 1775. The country was in arms against England, and Isaac's earliest memories go back to the days when Thomas Jefferson was governor of Virginia, and the British captured Richmond in 1781. Isaac was taken to Yorktown as a prisoner of the British, but was released at the end of the war, at which time he returned to Monticello. When Jefferson went to Philadelphia in 1790 as Secretary of State (not as President, as Isaac mistakenly recalls) he took the fifteen-year-old slave with him. After Jefferson resigned in 1793, both Jefferson and Isaac returned to Monticello where Isaac remained for nine years. For the next quarter century he lived with Jefferson's son-in-law, Thomas Mann Randolph. He came back to nurse the ex-President in his old age, and after Jefferson died, spent the last years of his life in Petersburg where Charles Campbell, editor, scholar, and author, came to know him and record these reminiscences in the 1840s.

It is not often that we see a master from the viewpoint of a slave—particularly a master of such national and international prominence. Thomas Jefferson may have been a reluctant slaveholder, but he was a slaveholder, nevertheless. By 1774 he owned 50 slaves of his own, in addition to 135 whom he held on behalf of his wife. After the Revolution this number increased to over 200. He was a benevolent master. He tried to keep families together even when he bought or sold slaves, or when he accepted

65

or gave them in payment of debt. He maintained his landholdings by slave labor throughout his adult life.

Yet Thomas Jefferson, as paradoxical as it may seem, found slavery an abhorrent institution. As early as 1776 he favored and proposed abolition of the slave trade, and in his famous Notes on Virginia, *he admitted that slavery was a cruel institution that destroyed the morals of the masters while degrading the slaves. Freedom, he avowed, was a gift of God, and men had no right to take it away. (Nevertheless, at no time did he consider freeing his own slaves, partially because of the hostile attitude of Virginians toward freedmen at this time, and partially because it would have meant complete economic ruin for him personally.)*

The Notes *did provide for the gradual emancipation of slaves. Jefferson suggested that slaves born after a certain date should be freed, trained at public expense for useful employment, and then sent away to a colony either abroad, or further West on the American continent, at which time white settlers would be imported from Europe to replace them. Never did Jefferson contemplate a society where black and white would live side by side. He was nearing the end of his life when he summed up his thoughts by asserting, "Nothing is more certainly written in the book of fate than that these people are to be free. Nor is it less certain that the two races, equally free, cannot live in the same government." But even the idea of emancipation was radical enough in 1781 for Jefferson to withhold publication of his* Notes on Virginia. *As he himself put it, "The public mind would not bear the proposition."*

In the following selection, Isaac Jefferson recalls his life at Monticello in the late eighteenth century as a slave of the man who insisted that slavery was a "great political and moral evil."

LIFE OF ISAAC JEFFERSON OF PETERSBURG, VIRGINIA, BLACKSMITH, containing a full and faithful account of MONTICELLO & the FAMILY there, with notices of many of the distinguished CHARACTERS that visited there, with his REVOLUTIONARY experience & travels, adventures, observations & opinions, the whole taken down from his own words.

CHAPTER 1

Isaac Jefferson was born at Monticello: his mother was named Usler (Ursula) but nicknamed Queen, because her husband was named George & commonly called King George. She was pastry-cook &

washerwoman: Stayed in the laundry. Isaac toated wood for her: made fire & so on. Mrs. Jefferson would come out there with a cookery book in her hand & read out of it to Isaac's mother how to make cakes tarts & so on.

Mrs. Jefferson was named Patsy Wayles,[1] but when Mr. Jefferson married her she was the widow Skelton, widow of Batter (Bathurst) Skelton. Isaac was one year's child with Patsy Jefferson: she was suckled part of the time by Isaac's mother. Patsy married Thomas Mann Randolph.[2] Mr. Jefferson bought Isaac's mother from Col. Wm Fleming of Goochland. Isaac remembers John Nelson an Englishman at work at Monticello: he was an inside workers, a finisher. The blacksmith was Billy Ore; (Orr?) the carriage-maker Davy Watson: he worked also for Col. Carter of Blenheim, eight miles from Monticello. Monticello-house was pulled down in part & built up again some six or seven times. One time it was struck by lightning. It had a Franklin rod at one eend. Old master used to say, "If it hadn't been for that Franklin the whole house would have gone." They was forty years at work upon that house before Mr. Jefferson stopped building.

CHAPTER 2

Mr. Jefferson came down to Williamsburg in a phaeton made by Davy Watson. Billy Ore did the iron-work.[3] That phaeton was sent to London & the springs &c was gilded. This was when Mr. Jefferson was in Paris. Isaac remembers coming down to Williamsburg in a wagon at the time Mr. Jefferson was Governor. He came down in the phaeton: his family with him in a coach & four. Bob Hemings drove the phaeton: Jim Hemings was a body-servant: Martin Hemings—the butler. These three were brothers: Mary Hemings & Sally, their Sisters. Jim & Bob bright mulatoes, Martin, darker. Jim & Martin rode on horseback. Bob went afterwards to live with old Dr. Strauss in Richmond & unfortunately had his hand shot off with a blunderbuss. Mary Hemings rode in the wagon. Sally Hemings' mother Betty was a bright mulatto

[1]Martha, youngest daughter of John Wayles, a native of Lancaster, England, a lawyer, who lived at "the Forest" in Charles City county, Va. He was married three times & dying in May 1773 left three daughters one of whom married Francis Eppes, (Father of John W. Eppes who married Maria daughter of Thomas Jefferson) & the other Fulwar Skipwith. Mr. Jefferson inherited the Shadwell & Monticello estates. The portion that he acquired by marriage was encumbered with a (British) debt & resulted in a heavy loss. Martha Skelton was 23 years old in 1772 when She married Mr. Jefferson.

[2]Sometime Governor of Virginia.

[3]Capt. Bacon says: John Hemings made most of the wood-work & Joe Fosset made the iron-work.

woman & Sally mighty near white: She was the youngest child. Folks said that these Hemings'es was old Mr. Wayles' children. Sally was very handsome: long straight hair down her back. She was about eleven years old when Mr. Jefferson took her to France to wait on Miss Polly. She & Sally went out to France a year after Mr. Jefferson went. Patsy went with him at first, but she carried no maid with her. Harriet one of Sally's daughters was very handsome. Sally had a son named Madison, who learned to be a great fiddler. He has been in Petersburg twice: was here when the balloon went up—the balloon that Beverly sent off.

Mr. Jefferson drove faster in the phaeton than the wagon. When the wagon reached Williamsburg Mr. Jefferson was living in the College (of Wm. & Mary) Isaac & the rest of the servants stayed in the Assembly-house—a long wooden building. Lord Botetourt's picture (statue) was there. The Assembly-house had a gallery on top running round to the College. There was a well there then: none there now. Some white people was living in one end of the house: a man named Douglas was there: they called him Parson Douglas.[4] Mr. Jefferson's room in the College was down stairs. A tailor named Giovanni an Italian lived there too: made clothes for Mr. Jefferson & his servants. Mrs. Jefferson was there with Patsy & Polly (Maria). Mrs. Jefferson was small: She drawed from Old Madam Byrd[5] several hundred people & then married a rich man. (Bathurst Skelton). Old master had twelve quarters seated with black people: but mighty few come by him: he want rich himself—only his larnin. Patsy Jefferson was tall like her father; Polly low like her mother & longways the handsomest: pretty lady jist like her mother: pity she died—poor thing! She married John W. Eppes—a handsome man, but had a hare-lip.

Jupiter & John drove Mr. Jeffersons coach & four: one of em rode postilion: they rode postilion in them days. Travelling in the phaeton Mr. Jefferson used oftentimes to take the reins himself & drive. Whenever he wanted to travel fast he'd drive: would drive powerful hard himself. Jupiter & John wore caps & gilded bands. The names of the horses was Senegore, Gustavus, Otter, Remus, Romulus & Caractacus Mr. Jefferson's riding-horse.

---

[4]The Rev. Wm. Douglas in a school at Shadwell near Monticello, instructed Young Jefferson in the rudiments of Greek, Latin & French.

[5]Robert Beverley the historian married Ursula Byrd of Westover, from whom the Monticello Ursula may have derived her name.

CHAPTER 3

After one year the Government was moved from Williamsburg to Richmond. Mr. Jefferson moved there with his servants, among em Isaac. It was cold weather when they moved up. Mr. Jefferson lived in a wooden house near where the Palace (Governor's house) stands now. Richmond was a small place then: not more than two brick houses in the town: all wooden houses what there was. At that time from where the Powhatan house now stands clear down to the Old Market was pretty much in pines. It was a wooden house shedded round like a barn on the hill, where the Assemblymen used to meet, near where the Capitol stands now. Old Mr. Wiley had a saddler-shop in the same house. Isaac knew Billy Wiley mighty well—a saddler by trade: he was door-keeper at the Assembly. His wife was a baker & baked bread & ginger-cakes. Isaac would go into the bake-oven & make fire for; she had a great big bake oven. Isaac used to go way into the oven: when he came out Billy Wiley would chuck wood in. She sometimes gave Isaac a loaf of bread or a cake. One time she went up to Monticello to see Mr. Jefferson. She saw Isaac there & gave him a ninepence & said, "This is the boy that made fires for me." Mr. Jefferson's family-servants then at the palace were Bob. Hemings, Martin, Jim,—house-servants, Jupiter & John drivers, Mary Hemings & young Betty Hemings seamstress & house-woman, Sukey, Jupiter's wife the cook.

CHAPTER 4

The day before the British (under Arnold) came to Richmond Mr. Jefferson sent off his family in the carriage. Bob Hemings & Jim drove. When the British was expected (Jan. 6, 1781) Old master kept the spy-glass & git up by the sky-light window to the top of the palace looking towards Williamsburg. Some Other gentlemen went up with him, one of them old Mr. Marsdell: he owned where the basin is now & the basin-spring. Isaac used to fetch water from there up to the palace. The British reached Manchester about 1 o'clock.[6] Isaac larnt to beat drum about this time. Bob Anderson a white man was a blacksmith. Mat. Anderson was a black man & worked with Bob. Bob was a fifer Mat was a drummer. Mat bout that time was sort a-makin

---

[6]They didn't come by way of Manchester.

love to Mary Hemings. The soldiers at Richmond, in the camp at Bacon Quarter Branch would come every two or three days to salute the Governor at the Palace, marching about there drumming & fifing. Bob Anderson would go into the house to drink; Mat went into the kitchen to see Mary Hemings. He would take his drum with him into the kitchen & set it down there. Isaac would beat on it & Mat larnt him how to beat.

CHAPTER 5

As soon as the British formed a line three cannon was wheeled round all at once & fired three rounds. Till they fired the Richmond people thought they was a company come from Petersburg to join them: some of em even hurraed when they see them coming: but that moment they fired every body knew it was the British. One of the cannon-balls knocked off the top of a butcher's house: he was named Daly not far from the Governor's house. The butcher's wife screamed out & hollerd & her children too & all. In ten minutes not a white man was to be seen in Richmond: they ran as hard as they could stave to the camp at Bacon Quarter Branch. There was a monstrous hollering & screaming of women & children. Isaac was out in the yard: his mother ran out & cotch him up by the hand & carried him into the kitchen hollering. Mary Hemings, she jerked up her daughter the same way. Isaac run out again in a minute & his mother too: she was so skeered, she did'nt know whether to stay indoors or out. The British was dressed in red. Isaac saw them marching. The horsemen (Simcoe's cavalary) was with them: they come arter the artillerymen. They formed in line & marched up to the Palace with drums beating: it was an awful sight: seemed like the day of judgment was come. When they fired the cannon Old master called out to John to fetch his horse Caractacus from the stable & rode off.

CHAPTER 6

Isaac never see his old master arter dat for six months. When the British come in, an officer rode up & asked "Whar is the Governor?" Isaac's father (George) told him:—"He's gone to the mountains." The officer said, "Whar is the keys of the house?" Isaac's father gave him the keys: Mr. Jefferson had left them with him. The officer said: "Whar is the silver?" Isaac's father told him, "It was all sent up to the mountains." The old man had put all the silver about the house in a bedtick & hid it under a bed in the kitchen & saved it too & got his freedom by it. But he continued to sarve Mr. Jefferson & had forty pounds from old master & his wife. Isaac's mother had seven dollars a month for lifetime for washing, ironing, & making pastry. The British sarcht the house but didn't disturb none of the furniture: but they plundered the wine-cellar, rolled the pipes out & stove em in, knockin the heads out. The bottles they broke the necks off with their swords, drank some, threw the balance away. The wine-cellar was full: old master had plenty of wine & rum—the best: used to have Antigua rum—twelve years old. The British next went to the corn-crib & took all the corn out, st:ewed it in a line along the street towards where the Washington taverns[7] is now (1847) & brought their horses & fed them on it: took the bridles off. The British said they did'nt want anybody but the Governor: did'nt want to hurt him; only wanted to put a pair of silver handcuffs on him: had brought them along with them on purpose. While they was plunderin they took all of the meat out of the meat-house; cut it up, laid it out in parcels: every man took his ration & put it in his knapsack. When Isaac's mother found they was gwine to car him away she thought they was gwine to leave her: She was cryin & hollerin when one of the officers came on a horse & ordered us all to Hylton's. Then they marched off to Westham. Isaac heard the powder-magazine when it blew up—like an earthquake. Next morning between eight & nine they marched to Tuckahoe, fifteen miles: took a good many colored people from Old Tom. Mann Randolph. He was called "Tuckahoe Tom." Isaac has often been to Tuckahoe—a low-built house, but monstrous large. From Tuckahoe the British went to Daniel Hylton's. They carried off thirty people from Tuckahoe & some from Hylton's. When they come back to Richmond they took all old master's from his house: all of em had to walk except Daniel & Molly (children of Mary the pastry-cook) & Isaac. He was then big enough to beat the drum: but could'nt raise it off the ground: would hold it tilted over to one side & beat on it that way.

CHAPTER 7

There was about a dozen wagons along: they (the British) pressed the common wagons: four horses to a wagon: some black drivers, some white: every wagon guarded by ten men marching alongside.

One of the officers give Isaac name Sambo: all the time feedin him: put a cocked hat on his head & a red coat on him & all laughed. Coat

---

[7]At East end of Grace St.—now (1871) the Central Hotel.

a monstrous great big thing: when Isaac was in it could'nt see nothin of it but the sleeves dangling down. He remembers crossing the river somewhere in a periauger (piragua). And so the British carred them all down to Little York (Yorktown). They marched straight through town & camped jist below back of the battle-field. Mr. Jefferson's people there was Jupiter, Sukey the cook, Usley (Isaac's mother) George (Isaac's father) Mary the seamstress & children Molly, Daniel, Joe, Wormley, & Isaac. The British treated them mighty well, give em plenty of fresh meat & wheat bread. It was very sickly at York: great many colored people died there, but none of Mr. Jefferson's folks. Wallis (Cornwallis) had a cave dug & was hid in there. There was tremendous firing & smoke: seemed like heaven & earth was come together: every time the great guns fire Isaac jump up off the ground. Heard the wounded men hollerin: When the smoke blow off you see the dead men laying on the ground. General Washington brought all Mr. Jefferson's folks & about twenty of Tuckahoe Tom's (Tom Mann Randolph's) back to Richmond with him & sent word to Mr. Jefferson to send down to Richmond for his servants. Old master sent down two wagons right away & all of em that was carred away went up back to Monticello. At that time old master & his family was at Poplar Forest his place in Bedford. He stayed there after his arm was broke, when Caractacus threw him. Old master was mightly pleased to see his people come back safe & sound (Although "All men by nature are free & equal.") & to hear of the plate.

CHAPTER 8

Mr. Jefferson was a tall strait-bodied man as ever you see, right square-shouldered: nary man in this town walked so straight as my old master:neat a built man as ever was seen in Vaginny, I reckon or any place—a straight-up mans[8]: long face, high nose.

Jefferson Randolph (Mr. Jefferson's grandson) nothing like him, except in height—tall, like him: not built like him: old master was a Straight-up man. Jefferson Randolph pretty much like his mother. Old master wore Vaginny cloth & a Red Waistcoat, (all the gentlemen wore red waistcoats in dem days) & small clothes: arter dat he used to wear red breeches too.[9] Governor Page used to come up there to Monticello, wife & daughter wid him: drove four-in-hand: servants

---

[8]Capt Bacon describes him as "Six feet two & a half inches high, well proportioned & straight as a gun-barrel. He was like a fine horse: he had no surplus flesh."

[9]Capt. Bacon says: "He was always very neat in his dress: wore short breeches & bright shoe-buckles. When he rode on horseback he had a pair of overalls that he always put on."

John, Molly & a postilion. Patrick Henry visited old master: coach & two: his face for all the world like the images of Bonaparte: would stay a week or more. Mann Page used to beat Monticello—a plain mild-looking man: his wife & daughter along with him. Dr. Thomas Walker lived about ten miles from Monticello—a thin-faced man. John Walker[10] (of Belvoir), his brother, owned a great many black people.

CHAPTER 9

Old master was never seen to come out before breakfast—about 8 o'clock. If it was warm weather he would'nt ride out till evening: studied upstairs till bell ring for dinner. When writing he had a copyin machine: while he was a-writin he would'nt suffer nobody to come in his room: had a dumb-waiter: When he wanted anything he had nothin to do but turn a crank & the dumb-waiter would bring him water or fruit on a plate or anything he wanted. Old master had abundance of books: sometimes would have twenty of 'em down on the floor at once: read fust one, then tother. Isaac has often wondered how old master came to have such a mighty head: read so many of them books: & when they go to him to ax him anything, he go right straight to the book & tell you all about it. He talked French & Italian. Madzay[11] talked with him: his place was called Colle. General Redhazel (Riedesel) stayed there. He (Mazzei) lived at Monticello with old master some time: Didiot a Frenchman married his daughter Peggy: a heavy chunky looking woman—mighty handsome: She had a daughter Frances & a son Francis: called the daughter Franky. Mazzei brought to Monticello Antonine, Jovanini, Francis, Modena & Belligrini, all gardiners. My old master's garden was monstrous large: two rows of palings, all round ten feet high.

CHAPTER 10

Mr. Jefferson had a clock in his kitchen at Monticello; never went into the kitchen except to wind up the clock. He never would have less than eight covers at dinner—if nobody at table but himself; had from eight to thirty two covers for dinner; plenty of wine, best old Antigua rum & cider: very fond of wine & water, Isaac never heard of his

---

[10]John Walker member of Congress during the Revolution.

[11]Philip Mazzei—an Italian—author of "Recherches Sur Les Etats-Unis," 3 Vols. published at Paris, in 1788.

being disguised in drink. He kept three fiddles: played in the arternoons & sometimes arter supper. This was in his early time: When he begin to git so old he did'nt play: kept a spinnet made mostly in shape of a harpsichord: his daughter played on it. Mr. Fauble a Frenchman that lived at Mr. Walker's—a music-man used to come to Monticello & tune it. There was a forte piano & a guitar there: never seed anybody play on them but the French people. Isaac never could git acquainted with them: could hardly larn their names. Mr. Jefferson always singing when ridin or walkin: hardly see him anywhar out doors but what he was a-singin.[12] Had a fine clear voice, sung minnits (minuets) & sich: fiddled in the parlor. Old master very kind to servants.

CHAPTER 11

The fust year Mr. Jefferson was elected President, he took Isaac on to Philadelphia: he was then about fifteen years old: travelled on horseback in company with a Frenchman named Joseph Rattiff & Jim Hemings a body-servant. Fust day's journey they went from Monticello to old Nat. Gordon's on the Fredericksburg road next day to Fredericksburg, then to Georgetown, crossed the Potomac there, & so to Philadelphia: eight days a-goin. Had two ponies & Mr. Jefferson's tother riding-horse Odin. Mr. Jefferson went in the phaeton: Bob. Hemings drove: changed horses on the road. When they got to Philadelphia Isaac stayed three days at Mr. Jefferson's house: then he was bound prentice to one Bringhouse a tinner: he lived in the direction of the Water-works. Isaac remembers seeing the image of a woman thar holding a goose in her hand—the water spouting out of the goose's mouth. This was at the head of Market Street. Bringhouse was a short mighty small neat-made man: treated Isaac very well: went thar to larn the tinner's trade: fust week larnt to cut out & sodder, make little pepper-boxes & graters sich, out of scraps of tin, so as not to waste any till he had larnt. Then to making cups. Every Sunday Isaac would go to the President's House—large brick house, many windows: same house Ginral Washington lived in before when he was President. "Old master used to talk to me mighty free & ax me, how you come on Isaac, larnin de tin-business?" As soon as he could make cups pretty well he carred three or four to show him. Isaac made four dozen pint-cups a day & larnt to tin copper & sheets (sheet-iron)—make 'em tin. He lived four years with Old Bringhouse.

---

[12]Capt. Bacon says: "When he was not talking he was nearly always humming some tune; or singing in a low tone to himself."

One time Mr. Jefferson sent to Bringhouse to tin his copper-kittles & pans for kitchen use: Bringhouse sent Isaac & another prentice thar— a white boy named Charles: cant think of his other name. Isaac was the only black boy in Bringhouse's Shop. When Isaac carred the cups to his old master to show him he was mightily pleased: said, "Isaac you are larnin mighty fast: I bleeve I must send you back to Vaginny to car on the tin-business. You is growin too big: no use for you to stay here no longer." Arter dat Mr. Jefferson sent Isaac back to Monticello to car on the tin-business thar. Old master bought a sight of tin for the purpose. Mr. Jefferson had none of his family with him in Philadelphia. Polly his daughter stayed with her Aunt Patsy Carr: she lived seven or eight miles from old master's great house. Sam. Carr was Mr. Jefferson's sister's child. There were three brothers of the Carrs—Sam, Peter & Dabney. Patsy Jefferson while her father was President in Philadelphia stayed with Mrs. Eppes at Wintopoke: Mrs. Eppes was a sister of Mrs. Jefferson:—Mightily like her sister. Frank Eppes was a big heavy man.

Old master's servants at Philadelphia was Bob. & Jim Hemings, Joseph Ratiff a Frenchman—the hostler. Mr. Jefferson used to ride out on horseback in Philadelphia. Isaac went back to Monticello. When the tin came they fixed up a shop. Jim Bringhouse came on to Monticello all the way with old master to fix up the shop & start Isaac to work: Jim. Bringhouse stayed thar more than a month.

CHAPTER 12

Isaac knew old Colonel (Archibald) Cary mighty well: as dry a looking man as ever you see in your life. He has given Isaac more whippings than he has fingers & toes. Mr. Jefferson used to set Isaac to open gates for Col. Cary: there was three gates to open, the furst bout a mile from the house: tother one three quarters; then the yard-gate, at the stable three hundred yards from the house. Isaac had to open the gates. Col. Cary would write to old master what day he was coming. Whenever Isaac missed opening them gates in time, the Colonel soon as he git to the house, look about for him & whip him with his horsewhip. Old master used to keep dinner for Col. Cary. He was a tall thin-visaged man jist like Mr. Jefferson: he drove four-in-hand. The Colonel as soon as he git out of his carriage, walk right straight into the kitchen & ax de cooks what they hab for dinner? If they did'nt have what he wanted—bleeged to wait dinner till it was cooked. Col. Cary made freer at Monticello than he did at home: whip anybody: would stay several weeks: give servants money, sometimes five or six dollars among 'em. Tuckahoe Tom Randolph married Col. Cary's

daughter Nancy. The Colonel lived at Ampthill on the James river
where Col. Bob. Temple lived arterwards. Edgehill was the seat of
Tom. Mann Randolph father of Jefferson Randolph: it was three miles
from Monticello.

CHAPTER 13

Isaac carried on the tin-business two years:—it failed. He then carred
on the nail-business at Monticello seven years: made money at that.
Mr. Jefferson had the first (nail) cutting machine 'twas said, that ever
was in Vaginny,—sent over from England: made wrought nails & cut-
nails, to single & lathe: sold them out of the shop: got iron rods from
Philadelphia by water: boated them up from Richmond to Milton a
small town on the Rivanna: wagoned from thar.

CHAPTER 14

Thomas Mann Randolph had ten children.[13] Isaac lived with him fust
& last twenty six or seven years: treated him mighty well: one of the
finest masters in Virginia: his a wife mighty peacable woman: never
holler for servant: make no fuss nor racket: pity she ever died! Tom
Mann Randolph's eldest daughter Ann: a son named Jefferson, another
James & another Benjamin. Jefferson Randolph married Mr.
Nicholas'[14] daughter (Anne). Billy Giles[15] courted Miss Polly old master's daughter. Isaac one morning saw him talking to her in the garden,
right back of the nail-factory shop: she was lookin on de ground: all
at once she wheeled round & come off. That was the time she turned
him off. Isaac never so sorry for a man in all his life: sorry because
every body thought that she was going to marry him. Mr. Giles give
several dollars to the servants & when he went away dat time he
never come back no more. His servant Arthur was a big man. Isaac
wanted Mr. Giles to marry Miss Polly. Arthur always said that he was
a mighty fine man: he was very rich: used to come to Monticello in

---

[13]Thomas Mann Randolph's sons were Thomas Jefferson, James Madison, Benjamin
Franklin, Merriwether Lewis & George Wythe (Secy. of War. of C. S.) daughters Anne,
Ellen, Virginia, Cornelia & Septimia.

[14]Wilson Cary Nicholas, sometime Governor of Virginia.

[15]Wm. C. Giles. M. C. a celebrated debater. Sometime Governor of Virginia. He acquired
the sobriquet of "Farmer Giles."

a monstrous fine gig: mighty few gigs in dem days with plated moun-tins & harness.

CHAPTER 15

Elk Hill: old master had a small brick house there where he used to stay, about a mile from Elk Island on the North Side of the James river. The river forks there: one half runs one side of the island, tother the other side. When Mr. Jefferson was Governor he used to stay thar a month or sich a matter & when he was at the mountain he would come & stay a month or so & then go back again. Blenheim was a low large wooden house two storeys high, eight miles from Monticello. Old. Col. Carter lived thar: had a light red head like Mr. Jefferson. Isaac know'd him & every son he had:—did'nt know his daughters.

Mr. Jefferson used to hunt squirrels & partridges; kept five or six guns; oftentimes carred Isaac wid him: old master would'nt shoot partridges settin: said "he would'nt take advantage of em"—would give 'em a chance for thar life: would'nt shoot a hare settin, nuther; skeer him up fust. "My old master was as neat a hand as ever you see to make keys & locks & small chains, iron & brass:" he kept all kind of blacksmith and carpenter tools in a great case with shelves to it in his library—an upstairs room. Isaac went up thar constant: been up thar a thousand times; used to car coal up thar: old master had a couple of small bellowses up thar. The likeness of Mr. Jefferson (in Linn's Life of him) according to Isaac, is not much like him. "Old master never dat handsome in dis world: dat likeness right between old master & Ginral Washington: old master was squar-shouldered." For amusement he would work sometimes in the garden for half an hour at a time in right good earnest in the cool of the evening: never know'd him to go out anywhar before breakfast.

CHAPTER 16

The school at Monticello was in the out-chamber fifty yards off from the great house, on the same level. But the scholars went into the house to old master to git lessons—in the South end of the house called the South Octagon. Mrs. Skipper (Skipwith) had two daughters thar: Mrs. Eppes, one.

Mr. Jefferson's sister Polly married old Ned Bolling[16] of Chesterfield

---

[16]John Bolling of Cobbs in Chesterfield married a sister of Thomas Jefferson.

about ten miles from Petersburg. Isaac had been thar since his death: saw the old man's grave. Mr. John Bradley owns the place now. Isaac slept in the out-chamber where the scholars was: slept on the floor in a blanket: in the winter season git up in the morning & make fire for them. From Monticello you can see mountains all round as far as the eye can reach: sometimes see it rainin down this course & the sun shining over the tops of the clouds. Willis' mountain sometimes looked in the cloud like a great house with two chimneys to it: fifty miles from Monticello.

CHAPTER 17

Thar was a sight of pictures at Monticello: pictures of Ginral Washington & the Marcus Lafayette. Isaac saw him fust in the old war in the mountain with old master; saw him agin the last time he was in Vaginny. He gave Isaac a guinea: Isaac saw him in the Capitol at Richmond & talked with him & made him sensible when he fust saw him in the old war. Thar was a large marble at Monticello with twelve angels cut on it that came from Heaven: all cut in marble.

About the time when "my old master" begun to wear spectacles, he was took with a swellin in his legs: used to bathe 'em & bandage 'em: said it was setting too much: when he'd git up & walk it would'nt hurt him. Isaac & John Hemings nursed him two months: had to car him about on a han-barrow. John Hemings[17] went to the carpenter's trade same year Isaac went to the blacksmiths. Miss Lucy old master's daughter died quite a small child; died down the country at Mrs. Eppes' or Mrs. Bollings one of her young aunts. Old master was embassador to France at that time. He brought a great many clothes from France with him: a coat of blue cloth trimmed with gold lace; cloak trimmed so too: dar say it weighted fifty pounds: large buttons on the coat as big as half a dollar; cloth set in the button: edge shine like gold: in summer he war silk coat, pearl buttons.

Col. Jack Harvie[18] owned Belmont jinin Monticello. Four as big men as any in Petersburg could git in his waistcoat: he owned Belvidere near Richmond: the Colonel died thar: monstrous big man. The washerwoman once buttoned his waistcoat on Isaac & three others. Mrs. Harvie was a little woman.

---

[17]Capt. Bacon in his reminiscenses of Mr. Jefferson at Monticello says, "John Hemings was a carpenter. He was a first-rate workman, a very extra workman: he could make anything that was wanting in woodwork. He learned his trade with Dinsmore. John Hemings made most of the woodwork of Mr. Jefferson's fine carriage."

[18]He had command of the troops of Convention, for a time.

CHAPTER 18

Mr. Jefferson never had nothing to do with horse-racing or cock-fighting: bought two race horses once, but not in their racing day: bought em arter done runnin. One was Brimmer,[19] a pretty horse with two white feet: when he bought him he was in Philadelphia: kept him thar. One day Joseph Rattiff the Frenchman was ridin him in the Streets of Philadelphia: Brimmer got skeered: run agin shaft of a dray & got killed. Tother horse was Tarkill: (Tarquin?) in his race-day they called him the Roane colt: only rack-horse of a roane Isaac ever see: old master used him for a ridin-horse. Davy Watson & Billy were German soldiers: both workmen, both smoked pipes & both drinkers: drank whiskey: git drunk & sing: take a week at a time drinkin & singin. Col. Goode of Chesterfield was a great racer: used to visit Mr. Jefferson; had a trainer named Pompey.

Old master had a great many rabbits: made chains for the old buck-rabbits to keep them from killin the young ones: had a rabbit-house (a warren)—a long rock house: some of em white, some blue: they used to burrow under ground. Isaac expects thar is plenty of em bout dar yit: used to eat em at Monticello. Mr. Jefferson never danced nor played cards. He had dogs named Ceres, Bull, Armandy, & Claremont: most of em French dogs: he brought em over with him from France. Bull & Ceres were bull-dogs: he brought over Buzzy with him too: she pupped at Sea: Armandy & Claremont, Stump-tails—both black.

CHAPTER 19

John Brock the overseer that lived next to the great-house had gray hounds to hunt deer. Mr. Jefferson had a large park at Monticello: built in a sort of a flat on the side of the mountain. When the hunters ran the deer down thar, they'd jump into the park & could'nt git out. When old master heard hunters in the park he used to go down thar wid his gun & order em out. The park was two or three miles round & fenced in with a high fence, twelve rails double-staked & ridered:

---

[19]According to Capt. Bacon. "Brimmer was a son of imported Knowlsby. He was a bay, but a shade darker than any of the others. He was a horse of fair size, full, but not quite as tall as Eagle. He was a good riding-horse & excellent for the harness. Mr. Jefferson broke all his horses to both ride & work. I bought Brimmer of General John H. Cocke of Fluvanna County."

kept up four or five years arter old master was gone: Isaac & his father (George) fed the deer at sun-up & sun-down: called em up & fed em wid corn: had holes all along the fence at the feedin-place: gave em salt, got right gentle: come up & eat out of your hand.

No wild-cats at Monticello: some lower down at Buck Island: bears sometimes came on the plantation at Monticello: wolves so plenty that they had to build pens around black peoples' quarters & pen sheep in em to keep the wolves from catching them. But they killed five or six of a night in the winter season: come & steal in the pens in the night. When the snow was on the groun you could see the wolves in gangs runnin & howlin, same as a drove of hogs: made the deer run up to the feedin-place many a night. The feedin place was right by the house whar Isaac stayed. They raised many sheep & goats at Monticello.

The woods & mountains was often on fire: Isaac has gone out to help to put out the fire: everybody would turn out from Charlottesville & everywhere: git in the woods & sometimes work all night fightin the fire.

CHAPTER 20

Col. Cary of Chesterfield schooled old master: he went to school to old Mr. Wayles. Old master had six sisters: Polly married a Bolling; Patsy married old Dabney Carr in the low-grounds: one married Wm. Skipwith: Nancy married old Hastings Marks. Old master's brother, Mass Randall, (Randolph) was a mighty simple man: used to come out among black people, play the fiddle & dance half the night: had'nt much more sense than Isaac. Jack Eppes (John W. Eppes M. C.) that married Miss Polly (Jefferson) lived at Mount Black (Mt. Blanc?) on James river & then at Edge Hill, then in Cumberland at Millbrooks. Isaac left Monticello four years before Mr. Jefferson died. Tom Mann Randolph that married Mr. Jefferson's daughter, wanted Isaac to build a threshing machine at Varina. Old Henrico Court House was thar: pulled down now. Coxendale Island (Dutch Gap) jinin Varina was an Indian Situation: when fresh come, it washed up more Indian bones than ever you see. When Isaac was a boy there want more than ten houses at Jamestown. Charlottesville then not as big as Pocahontas (a village on the Appomattox, opposite Petersburg) is now. Mr. DeWitt kept tavern thar.

Isaac knowed Ginral Redhazel (Riedesel commander of the German troops of Convention.): he stayed at Colle, Mr. Mazzei's place, two miles & a quarter from Monticello—a long wood house built by Mazzei's servants. The servants' house built of little saplins of oak &

hickory instead of lathes: then plastered up: it seemed as if de folks in dem days had'nt sense enough to make lathes. The Italian people raised plenty of vegetables: cooked the most victuals of any people Isaac ever see.

Mr. Jefferson bowed to everybody he meet: talked wid his arms folded. Gave the boys in the nail-factory a pound of meat a week, a dozen herrings, a quart of molasses & peck of meal. Give them that wukked the best a suit of red or blue: encouraged them mightily. Isaac calls him a mighty good master. There would be a great many carriages at Monticello at a time, in particular when people was passing to the Springs.

Isaac is now (1847) at Petersburg, Va. seventy large odd years old: bears his years well: is a blacksmith by trade & has his shop not far from Pockahontas bridge. He is quite pleased at the idea of having his life written & protests that every word of it is true, that is of course according to the best of his knowledge & belief. Isaac is rather tall of strong frame, stoops a little, in color ebony:—sensible, intelligent pleasant: wears large circular iron-bound spectacles & a leather apron. A capital daguerrotype of him was taken by a Mr. Shew. Isaac was so much pleased with it that he had one taken of his wife, a large fat round-faced good-humoured looking black woman. My attention was first drawn to Isaac by Mr. Dandridge Spotswood who had often heard him talk about Mr. Jefferson & Monticello.

C. C.

P.S. Isaac died a few years after these his recollections were taken down. He bore a good character.

FREDERICK DOUGLASS

(1817?–1895)

From *Narrative of the Life of Frederick Douglass, An American Slave*

This selection is of interest for several reasons: it gives a vivid description of the cruelties of slavery on a Maryland plantation from the perspective of a young boy; it provides an account of the life of a slave in the city with comparisons to that of a rural slave; and it offers another example of the stirring determination with which some slaves pursued the golden dream of education. Finally, it gives a penetrating insight into the effects of slave-holding upon the owner, as we witness the rapid degradation of a decent family when confronted with the arbitrary power of human bondage.

Frederick Douglass never knew the exact year of his birth, but overheard his first owner say it was 1817 or 1818. When he was sent to Baltimore as a young boy it was to the house of people who had never before been slaveholders. There, in an unusual act of kindness, his mistress taught him to read.

He escaped to New York City in 1838 and married a free woman whom he had met in Baltimore. He agitated for abolition before the war, recruited black soldiers during it, and fought for the rights of the newly freed black population after it was over.

Later he was appointed Secretary of the Santo Domingo Commission, Marshal and Recorder of Deeds in the District of Columbia and United States Minister to Haiti.

* * *

I was born in Tuckahow, near Hillsborough, and about twelve miles from Easton, in Talbot county, Maryland. I have no accurate knowledge of my age, never having seen any authentic record containing it. By far the larger part of the slaves know as little of their ages as horses know of theirs, and it is the wish of most masters within my knowledge to keep their slaves thus ignorant. I do not remember to have ever met a slave who tells of his birthday. They seldom come nearer to it than planting-time. A want of information concerning my own was a source of unhappiness to me even during childhood. The white children could tell their ages. I could not tell why I ought to be deprived of the same privilege. I was not allowed to make any inquiries of my master concerning it. He deemed all such inquiries on the part of a slave improper and impertinent, and evidence of a restless spirit. The nearest estimate I can give makes me now between twenty-seven and twenty-eight years of age. I come to this, from hearing my master say, some time during 1835, I was about seventeen years old.

My mother was named Harriet Bailey. She was the daughter of Isaac and Betsey Bailey, both colored, and quite dark. My mother was of a darker complexion than either my grandmother or grandfather.

My father was a white man. He was admitted to be such by all I ever heard speak of my parentage. The opinion was also whispered that my master was my father; but of the correctness of this opinion, I know nothing; the means of knowing was withheld from me. My mother and I were separated when I was but an infant—before I knew her as my mother. It is a common custom, in the part of Maryland from which I ran away, to part children from their mothers at a very early age. Frequently, before the child has reached its twelfth month, its mother is taken from it, and hired on some farm a considerable distance off, and the child is placed under the care of an old woman, too old for field labor. For what this separation is done, I do not know, unless it be to hinder the development of the child's affection toward its mother, and to blunt and destroy the natural affection of the mother for the child. This is the inevitable result.

I never saw my mother, to know her as such, more than four or five times in my life; and each of these times was very short in duration, and at night. She was hired by Mr. Stewart, who lived about twelve miles from my home. She made her journeys to see me in the night, travelling the whole distance on foot, after the performance of her day's work. She was a field hand, and a whipping is the penalty of not being in the field at sunrise, unless a slave has special permission from his or her master to the contrary—a permission which they seldom get, and one that gives to him that gives it the proud name of being a kind master. I do not recollect of ever seeing my mother by the light of day. She was with me in the night. She would lie down with me, and get me to sleep, but long before I waked she was gone. Very little communication ever took place between us. Death soon ended what little we could have while she lived, and with it her hardships and suffering. She died when I was about seven years old, on one of my master's farms, near Lee's Mill. I was not allowed to be present during her illness, at her death, or burial. She was gone long before I knew anything about it. Never having enjoyed, to any considerable extent, her soothing presence, her tender and watchful care, I received the tidings of her death with much the same emotions I should have probably felt at the death of a stranger.

Called thus suddenly away, she left me without the slightest intimation of who my father was. The whisper that my master was my father, may or may not be true; and, true or false, it is of but little consequence to my purpose whilst the fact remains, in all its glaring odiousness, that slaveholders have ordained, and by law established, that the children of slave women shall in all cases follow the condition of their mothers; and this is done too obviously to administer to their own lusts, and make a gratification of their wicked desires profitable as well as pleasurable, for by this cunning arrangement, the slaveholder, in cases not a few, sustains to his slaves the double relation of master and father.

I know of such cases; and it is worthy of remark that such slaves invariably suffer greater hardships, and have more to contend with, than others. They are, in the first place, a constant offense to their mistress. She is ever disposed to find fault with them; they can seldom do any thing to please her; she is never better pleased than when she sees them under the lash, especially when she suspects her husband of showing to his mulatto children favors which he withholds from his black slaves. The master is frequently compelled to sell this class of his slaves, out of deference to the feelings of his white wife; and cruel as the deed may strike any one to be, for a man to sell his own children to human flesh-mongers, it is often the dictate of humanity for him to do so; for, unless he does this, he must not only whip them himself, but must stand by and see one white son tie up his brother, of but few shades darker complexion than himself, and ply the gory lash to his naked back; and if he lisp one word of disapproval, it is set down to his parental partiality, and only makes a bad matter worse, both for himself and the slave whom he would protect and defend.

Every year brings with it multitudes of this class of slaves. It was doubtless in consequence of a knowledge of this fact, that one great statesman of the south predicted the downfall of slavery by the inevitable laws of population. Whether this prophecy is ever fulfilled or not, it is nevertheless plain that a very different-looking class of people are springing up at the south, and are now held in slavery, from those originally brought to this country from Africa; and if their increase will do no other good, it will do away the force of the argument, that God cursed Ham, and therefore American slavery is right. If the lineal descendants of Ham are alone to be scripturally enslaved, it is certain that slavery at the south must soon become unscriptural; for thousands are ushered into the world, annually, who, like myself, owe their existence to white fathers, and those fathers most frequently their own masters.

I have had two masters. My first master's name was Anthony. I do not remember his first name. He was generally called Captain Anthony—a title which, I presume, he acquired by sailing a craft on the Chesapeake Bay. He was not considered a rich slaveholder. He owned two or three farms, and about thirty slaves. His farms and slaves were under the care of an overseer. The overseer's name was Plummer. Mr. Plummer was a miserable drunkard, a profane swearer, and a savage monster. He always went armed with a cowskin and a heavy cudgel. I have known him to cut and slash the women's heads so horribly, that even master would be enraged at his cruelty, and would threaten to whip him if he did not mind himself. Master, however, was not a humane slaveholder. It required extraordinary barbarity on the part of an overseer to affect him. He was a cruel man, hardened by a long life of slaveholding. He would at times seem to take great pleasure in whipping a slave. I have often been awakened at the dawn of day by the most heart-rending shrieks of an own aunt of mine, whom he used to tie up to a joist, and whip upon her naked back til she was literally covered with blood. No words, no tears, no prayers, from his gory victim, seemed to move his iron heart from its bloody purpose. The louder she screamed, the harder he whipped; and where the blood ran fastest, there he whipped longest. He would whip her to make her scream, and whip her to make her hush; and not until overcome by fatigue, would he cease to swing the blood-clotted cowskin. I remember the first time I ever witnessed this horrible exhibition. I was quite a child, but I will remember it. I never shall forget it whilst I remember anything. It was the first of a long series of such outrages, of which I was doomed to be a witness and a participant. It struck me with awful force. It was the blood-stained gate, the entrance to the hell of slavery, through which I was about to pass. It was a most terrible spectacle. I wish I could commit to paper the feelings with which I beheld it.

This occurrence took place very soon after I went to live with my old master, and under the following circumstances. Aunt Hester went out one night—where or for what I do not know,—and happened to be absent when my master desired her presence. He had ordered her not to go out evenings, and warned her that she must never let him catch her in company with a young man, who was paying attention to her belonging to Colonel Lloyd. The young man's name was Ned Roberts, generally called Lloyd's Ned. Why master was so careful of her, may be safely left to conjecture. She was a woman of noble form, and of graceful proportions, having very few equals, and fewer superiors, in personal appearance, among the colored or white women of our neighborhood.

Aunt Hester had not only disobeyed his orders in going out, but had been found in company with Lloyd's Ned; which circumstance, I found, from what he said while whipping her, was the chief offence. Had he been a man of pure morals himself, he might have been thought interested in protecting the innocence of my aunt; but those who knew him will not suspect him of any such virtue. Before he commenced whipping Aunt Hester, he took her into the kitchen, and stripped her from neck to waist, leaving her neck, shoulders, and back entirely naked. He then told her to cross her hands, calling her at the same time a d—d b—h. After crossing her hands, he tied them with a strong rope, and led her to a stool under a large hook in the joist, put in for the purpose. He made her get upon the stool, and tied her hands to the hook. She now stood fair for his infernal purpose. Her arms were stretched up at their full length, so that she stood upon the ends of her toes. He then said to her, "Now you d—d b—h, I'll learn you how to disobey my orders!" and after rolling up his sleeves, he commenced to lay on the heavy cowskin, and soon the warm, red blood (amid heart-rending shrieks from her, and horrid oaths from him) came dripping to the floor. I was so terrified and horror stricken at the sight, that I hid myself in a closet, and dared not venture out till long after the bloody transaction was over. I expected it would be my turn next. It was all new to me. I had never seen anything like it before. I had always lived with my grandmother on the outskirts of the plantation, where she was put to raise the children of the younger women. I had therefore been, until now, out of the way of the bloody scenes that often occurred on the plantation.

As to my own treatment while I lived on Colonel Lloyd's plantation, it was very similar to that of the other slave children. I was not old enough to work in the field, and there being little else than field work to do, I had a great deal of leisure time. The most I had to do was to drive up the cows at evening, keep the fowls out of the garden, keep the front yard clean, and run errands for my old master's daughter, Mrs. Lucretia Auld. The most of my leisure time I spent in helping Master Daniel Lloyd in finding his birds, after he had shot them. My connection with Master Daniel was of some advantage to me. He became quite attached to me, and was sort of a protector of me. He would not allow the older boys to impose upon me, and would divide his cakes with me.

I was seldom whipped by my old master, and suffered little from any thing else than hunger and cold. I suffered much from hunger, but much more from cold. In hottest summer and coldest winter, I was kept almost naked—no shoes, no stockings, no jacket, no trousers, nothing on but a coarse tow linen shirt, reaching only to my knees. I had no bed. I must have perished with cold, but that, the coldest nights, I used to steal a bag which was used for carrying corn to the mill. I would crawl into this bag, and there sleep on the cold, damp, clay floor, with my head in and feet out. My feet have been so cracked with the frost, that the pen with which I am writing might be laid in the gashes.

We were not regularly allowanced. Our food was coarse corn meal boiled. This was called *mush*. It was put into a large wooden tray or trough, and set down upon the ground. The children were then called, like so many pigs, and like so many pigs they would come and devour the mush; some with oyster-shells, others with pieces of shingle, some with naked hands, and none with spoons. He that ate fastest got most; he that was strongest secured the best place; and few left the trough satisfied.

I was probably between seven and eight years old when I left Colonel Lloyd's plantation. I left it with joy. I shall never forget the ecstasy with which I received the intelligence that my old master (Anthony) had determined to let me go to Baltimore, to live with Mr. Hugh Auld, brother to my old master's son-in-law, Captain Thomas Auld. I received this information about three days before my departure. They were three of the happiest days I ever enjoyed. I spent the most part of all these three days in the creek, washing off the plantation scurf, and preparing myself for my departure.

The pride of appearance which this would indicate was not my own. I spent the time in washing, not so much because I wished to, but because Mrs. Lucretia had told me I must get all the dead skin off my feet and knees before I could go to Baltimore; for the people in Baltimore were very cleanly, and would laugh at me if I looked dirty. Besides, she was going to give me a pair of trousers, which I should not put on unless I got all the dirt off me. The thought of owning a pair of trousers was great indeed! It was almost a sufficient motive, not only to make me take off what would be called by pig-drovers the mange, but the skin itself. I went at it in good earnest, working for the first time with the hope of reward.

The ties that ordinarily bind children to their homes were all suspended in my case. I found no severe trial in my departure. My home was charmless; it was not home to me; on parting from it, I could not feel that I was leaving any thing which I could have enjoyed by staying. My mother was dead, my grandmother lived far off, so that I seldom saw her. I had two sisters and one brother, that lived in the same house with me; but the early separation of us from our mother had well nigh blotted the fact of our relationship from our memories. I looked for home elsewhere, and was confident of finding none which I should relish less than the one which I was leaving. If, however, I found in my new home hardship, hunger, whipping, and nakedness,

I had the consolation that I should not have escaped any one of them by staying. Having already had more than a taste of them in the house of my old master, and having endured them there, I very naturally inferred my ability to endure them elsewhere, and especially in Baltimore; for I had something of the feeling about Baltimore, that is expressed in the proverb, that "being hanged in England is preferable to dying a natural death in Ireland." I had the strongest desire to see Baltimore. Cousin Tom, though not fluent in speech, had inspired me with that desire by his eloquent description of the place. I could never point out any thing at the Great House, no matter how beautiful or powerful, but that he had seen something at Baltimore far exceeding both in beauty and strength, the object which I pointed out to him. Even the Great House itself, with all its pictures, was far inferior to many buildings in Baltimore. So strong was my desire, that I thought a gratification of it would fully compensate for whatever loss of comforts I should sustain by the exchange. I left without regret, and with the highest hopes of future happiness.

We sailed out of Miles River for Baltimore on a Saturday morning. I remember only the day of the week, for at that time I had no knowledge of the days of the month, nor the months of the year. On setting sail, I walked aft, and gave to Colonel Lloyd's plantation what I hoped would be the last look. I then placed myself in the bows of the sloop, and there spent the remainder of the day in looking ahead, interesting myself in what was in the distance rather than in things near by or behind.

In the afternoon of that day, we reached Annapolis, the capital of the State. We stopped but a few moments, so that I had no time to go on shore. It was the first large town that I had ever seen, and though it would look small compared with some of our New England factory villages, I thought it a wonderful place for its size—more imposing even than the Great House Farm!

We arrived at Baltimore early on Sunday morning, landing at Smith's Wharf, not far from Bowley's Wharf. We had on board the sloop a large flock of sheep; and after aiding in driving them to the slaughterhouse of Mr. Curtis on Loudon Slater's Hill, I was conducted by Rich, one of the hands belonging on board of the sloop, to my new home in Alliciana Street, near Mr. Gardner's ship-yard, on Fells Point.

Mr. and Mrs. Auld were both at home, and met me at the door with their little son Thomas, to take care of whom I had been given. And here I saw what I had never seen before; it was a white face beaming with the most kindly emotions; it was the face of my new mistress, Sophia Auld. I wish I could describe the rapture that flashed through my soul as I beheld it. It was a new and strange sight to me, brightening up my pathway with the light of happiness. Little Thomas was told, there was his Freddy—and I was told to take care of little Thomas;

and thus I entered upon the duties of my new home with the most cheering prospect ahead.

I look upon my departure from Colonel Lloyd's plantation as one of the most interesting events of my life. It is possible, and even quite probably, that but for the mere circumstance of being removed from that plantation to Baltimore, I should have to-day, instead of being here seated by my own table, in the enjoyment of freedom and the happiness of home, writing this Narrative, been confined in the galling chains of slavery. Going to live at Baltimore laid the foundation, and opened the gateway, to all my subsequent prosperity. I have ever regarded it as the first plain manifestation of that kind providence which has ever since attended me, and marked my life with so many favors. I regarded the selection of myself as being somewhat re-markable. There were a number of slave children that might have been sent from the plantation to Baltimore. There were those younger, those older, and those of the same age. I was chosen from among them all, and was the first, last, and only choice.

I may be deemed superstitious, and even egotistical, in regarding this event as a special interposition of divine Providence in my favor. But I should be false to the earliest sentiments of my soul, if I sup-pressed the opinion. I prefer to be true to myself, even at the hazard of incurring the ridicule of others, rather than to be false, and incur my own abhorrence. From my earliest recollection, I date the enter-tainment of a deep conviction that slavery would not always be able to hold me within its foul embrace; and in the darkest hours of my career in slavery, this living word of faith and spirit of hope departed not from me, but remained like ministering angels to cheer me through the gloom. This good spirit was from God, and to him I offer thanksgiving and praise.

My new mistress proved to be all she appeared when I first met her at the door—a woman of the kindest heart and finest feelings. She had never had a slave under her control previously to myself, and prior to her marriage she had been dependent upon her own industry to get a living. She was by trade a weaver; and by constant application to her business, she had been in a good degree preserved from the blighting and dehumanizing effects of slavery. I was utterly astonished at her goodness. I scarcely knew how to behave towards her. She was entirely unlike any other white woman I had ever seen. I could not approach her as I was accustomed to approach other white ladies. My early instruction was all out of place. The crouching servility, usually so acceptable a quality in a slave, did not answer when manifested toward her. Her favor was not gained by it; she seemed to be disturbed by it. She did not deem it impudent or un-mannerly for a slave to look her in the face. The meanest slave was put fully at ease in her presence, and none left without feeling better for having seen her. Her face was made of heavenly smiles, and her voice of tranquil music.

But, alas! this kind heart had but a short time to remain such. The fatal poison of irresponsible power was already in her hands, and soon commenced its infernal work. That cheerful eye, under the influence of slavery, soon became red with rage; that voice, made all of sweet accord, changed to one of harsh and horrid discord; and that angelic face gave place to that of a demon.

Very soon after I went to live with Mr. and Mrs. Auld, she very kindly commenced to teach me the A, B, C. After I had learned this, she assisted me in learning to spell words of three or four letters. Just at this point of my progress, Mr. Auld found out what was going on, and at once forbade Mrs. Auld to instruct me further, telling her, among other things, that it was unlawful, as well as unsafe, to teach a slave to read. To use his own words, further, he said, "If you give a nigger an inch, he will take an ell. A nigger should know nothing but to obey his master—to do as he is told to do. Learning would *spoil* the best nigger in the world. Now," he said, "if you teach that nigger (speaking of myself) how to read, there would be no keeping him. It would be forever unfit for him to be a slave. He would at once become unmanageable, and of no value to his master. As to himself, it could do him no good, but a great deal of harm. It would make him discontented and unhappy." These words sank deep into my heart, stirring up sentiments within that lay slumbering, and called into existence an entirely new train of thought. It was a new and special revelation, explaining dark and mysterious things, with which my youthful understanding had struggled, but struggled in vain. I now understood what had been to me a most perplexing difficulty—to wit, the white man's power to enslave the black man. It was a grand achievement, and I prized it highly. From that moment, I understood the pathway from slavery to freedom. It was just what I wanted, and I got it at a time when I the least expected it. Whilst I was saddened by the thought of losing the aid of my kind mistress, I was gladdened by the invaluable instruction which, by the merest accident, I had gained from my master. Though conscious of the difficulty of learning without a teacher, I set out with high hope, and a fixed purpose, at whatever cost of trouble, to learn how to read. The very decided manner with which he spoke, and strove to impress his wife with the evil consequences of giving me instruction, served to convince me that he was deeply sensible of the truths he was uttering. It gave me the best assurance that I might rely with the utmost confidence on the results which, he said, would flow from teaching me to read. What he most dreaded, that I most desired. What he most loved, that I most hated. That which to him was a great evil, to be carefully shunned, was to me a great good, to be diligently sought; and the argument which he so warmly urged, against my learning to read, only served to inspire me with a desire and determination to learn. In learning to read, I owe almost as much to the bitter opposition of my master, as to the kindly aid of my mistress. I acknowledge the benefit of both.

I had resided but a short time in Baltimore before I observed a marked difference, in the treatment of slaves, from that which I had witnessed in the country. A city slave is almost a freeman, compared with a slave on the plantation. He is much better fed and clothed, and enjoys privileges altogether unknown to the slave on the plantation. There is a vestige of decency, a sense of shame, that does much to curb and check those outbreaks of atrocious cruelty so commonly enacted upon the plantation. He is a desperate slaveholder, who will shock the humanity of his non-slaveholding neighbors with the cries of his lacerated slave. Few are willing to incur the odium attaching to the reputation of being a cruel master; and above all things, they would not be known as not giving a slave enough to eat. Every city slaveholder is anxious to have it known of him, that he feeds his slaves well; and it is due to them to say, that most of them do give their slaves enough to eat. There are, however, some painful exceptions to this rule. Directly opposite to us, on Philpot Street, lived Mr. Thomas Hamilton. He owned two slaves. Their names were Henrietta and Mary. Henrietta was about twenty-two years of age, Mary was about fourteen; and of all the mangled and emaciated creatures I ever looked upon, these two were the most so. His heart must be harder than stone, that could look upon these unmoved. The head, neck, and shoulders of Mary were literally cut to pieces. I have frequently felt her head, and found it nearly covered with festering sores, caused by the lash of her cruel mistress. I do not know that her master ever whipped her, but I have been an eye-witness to the cruelty of Mrs. Hamilton. I used to be in Mr. Hamilton's house nearly every day. Mrs. Hamilton used to sit in a large chair in the middle of the room, with a heavy cowskin always by her side, and scarce an hour passed during the day but was marked by the blood of one of these slaves. The girls seldom passed her without her saying, "Move faster, you *black gip!*"—continuing, "If you don't move faster, I'll move you!" Added to the cruel lashings to which these slaves were subjected, they were kept nearly half starved. They seldom knew what it was to eat a full meal. I have seen Mary contending with the pigs for the offal thrown into the street. So much was Mary kicked and cut to pieces, that she was oftener called *"pecked"* than by her name.

I lived in Master Hugh's family about seven years. During this time, I succeeded in learning to read and write. In accomplishing this, I was compelled to resort to various stratagems. I had no regular teacher. My mistress, who had kindly commenced to instruct me, had, in compliance with the advice and direction of her husband, not only ceased to instruct, but had set her face against my being instructed by any one else. It is due, however, to my mistress to say of her, that she did not adopt this course of treatment immediately. She at first lacked the depravity indispensable to shutting me up in mental darkness. It was at least necessary for her to have some training in the exercise of irresponsible power, to make her equal to the task of treating me as though I were a brute.

My mistress was, as I have said, a kind and tenderhearted woman; and in the simplicity of her soul she commenced, when I first went to live with her, to treat me as she supposed one human being ought to treat another. In entering upon the duties of a slaveholder, she did not seem to perceive that I sustained to her the relation of a mere chattel, and that for her to treat me as a human being was not only wrong, but dangerously so. Slavery proved as injurious to her as it did to me. When I went there, she was a pious, warm, and tenderhearted woman. There was no sorrow or suffering for which she had not a tear. She had bread for the hungry, clothes for the naked, and comfort for every mourner that came within her reach. Slavery soon proved its ability to divest her of these heavenly qualities. Under its influence, the tender heart became stone, and the lamblike disposition gave way to one of tiger-like fierceness. The first step in her downward course, was in her ceasing to instruct me. She now commenced to practice her husband's precepts. She finally became even more violent in her opposition than her husband himself. She was not satisfied with simply doing as well as he had commanded; she seemed anxious to do better. Nothing seemed to make her more angry than to see me with a newspaper. She seemed to think that here lay the danger. I have had her rush at me with a face made all up of fury, and snatch from me a newspaper, in a manner that fully revealed her apprehension. She was an apt woman; and a little experience soon demonstrated, to her satisfaction, that education and slavery were incompatible with each other.

From this time I was most narrowly watched. If I was in a separate room any considerable length of time, I was sure to be suspected of having a book, and was at once called to give an account of myself. All this, however, was too late. The first step had been taken. Mistress, in teaching me the alphabet, had given me the *inch*, and no precaution could prevent me from taking the *ell*.

The plan which I adopted, and the one by which I was most successful, was that of making friends of all the little white boys whom I met in the street. As many of these as I could, I converted into teachers. With their kindly aid, obtained at different times and in different places, I finally succeeded in learning to read. When I was sent off on errands, I always took my book with me, and by going one part of my errand quickly, I found time to get a lesson before my return. I used also to carry bread with me, enough of which was always in the house, and to which I was always welcome; for I was much better off in this regard than many of the poor white children in our neighborhood. This bread I used to bestow upon the hungry little urchins, who, in return, would give me that more valuable bread of knowledge. I am strongly tempted to give the names of two or three of those little boys, as a testimonial of the gratitude and affection I bear them; but prudence forbids—not that it would injure me, but it might embarrass them; for it is almost an unpardonable offense to teach slaves to read in this Christian country. It is enough to say of the dear little fellows, that they lived on Philpot Street, very near Durgin and Bailey's ship-yard. I used to talk this matter of slavery over with them. I would sometimes say to them, I wished I could be as free as they would be when they got to be men. "You will be free as soon as you are twenty-one, *but I am a slave for life!* Have not I as good a right to be free as you have?" These words used to trouble them; they would express for me the liveliest sympathy, and console me with the hope that something would occur by which I might be free.

BOOKER T. WASHINGTON

(1858?–1915)

From *Up from Slavery*

Booker T. Washington was born in a Virginia slave cabin in 1858 or 1859. Although he was very young at the time of the Emancipation Proclamation, he vividly recalls his early days as a plantation slave.

Washington was an extraordinary individual by any standards, but that he achieved as much as he did with such truly humble beginnings is a remarkable feat. Washington's story is interesting on two counts: first, for its descriptions of the life of a slave boy on a Southern plantation, and second, for its exciting narration of his adventures in securing an education. Upon reading of the hardships that Washington willingly endured to obtain his education, we must reflect upon the almost unerring certainty with which an ambitious mind will seize upon education as the key to success and power.

Washington went on to international fame as the founder of Tuskegee Institute, a school for African-Americans which emphasized industrial training. By the turn of the century he was one of the most influential educators and racial advisors on the American scene.

This enlightening selection is a tribute not only to its author, but also to the inquiring nature of man himself.

I was born a slave on a plantation in Franklin County, Virginia. I am not quite sure of the exact place or exact date of my birth, but at any rate I suspect I must have been born somewhere and at some time. As nearly as I have been able to learn, I was born near a cross-roads post-office called Hale's Ford, and the year was 1858 or 1859. I do not know the month or the day. The earliest impressions I can now recall are of the plantation and the slave quarters—the latter being the part of the plantation where the slaves had their cabins.

My life had its beginning in the midst of the most miserable, desolate, and discouraging surroundings. This was so, however, not because my owners were especially cruel, for they were not, as compared with many others. I was born in a typical log cabin, about fourteen by sixteen feet square. In this cabin I lived with my mother and a brother and sister till after the Civil War, when we were all declared free.

Of my ancestry I know almost nothing. In the slave quarters, and even later, I heard whispered conversations among the coloured people of the tortures which the slaves, including, no doubt, my ancestors on my mother's side, suffered in the middle passage of the slave ship while being conveyed from Africa to America. I have been unsuccessful in securing any information that would throw any accurate light upon the history of my family beyond my mother. She, I remember, had a half-brother and a half-sister. In the days of slavery not very much attention was given to family history and family records—that is, black family records. My mother, I suppose, attracted the attention of a purchaser who was afterward my owner and hers. Her addition to the slave family attracted about as much attention as the purchase of a new horse or cow. Of my father I know even less than of my mother. I do not even know his name. I have heard reports to the effect that he was a white man who lived on one of the near-by plantations. Whoever he was, I never heard of his taking the least interest in me or providing in any way for my rearing. But I do not find especial fault with him. He was simply another unfortunate victim of the institution which the Nation unhappily had engrafted upon it at that time.

The cabin was not only our living place, but was also used as the kitchen for the plantation. My mother was the plantation cook. The cabin was without glass windows; it had only openings in the side which let in the light, and also the cold, chilly air of winter. There was a door to the cabin—that is, something that was called a door—but the uncertain hinges by which it was hung, and the large cracks in it, to say nothing of the fact that it was too small, made the room a very uncomfortable one. In addition to those openings there was, in the lower right-hand corner of the room, the "cat hole,"—a contrivance which almost every mansion or cabin in Virginia possessed during the ante-bellum period. The "cat hole" was a square opening, about seven by eight inches provided for the purpose of letting the cat pass in and out of the house at will during the night. In the case of our particular cabin I could never understand the necessity for this convenience, since there were at least a dozen or half dozen other places in the cabin that would have accommodated the cats.

There was no wooden floor in our cabin, the naked earth being used as a floor. In the center of the earthen floor there was a large, deep opening covered with boards, which was used as a place in which to store sweet potatoes, during the winter. An impression of this potato-hole is very distinctly engraved upon my memory, because I recall that during the process of putting the potatoes in or taking them out I would often come into possession of one or two, which I roasted and thoroughly enjoyed. There was no cooking-stove on our plantation, and all the cooking for the whites and slaves my mother had to do over an open fireplace, mostly in pots and "skillits." While the poorly built cabin caused us to suffer with cold in the winter, the heat from the open fireplace in summer was equally trying.

The early years of my life, which were spent in the little cabin, were not very different from those of thousands of other slaves. My mother, of course, had little time in which to give attention to the training of her children during the day. She snatched a few moments for our care in the early morning before her work began, and at night after the day's work was done. One of my earliest recollections is that of my mother cooking a chicken late at night, and awakening the children for the purpose of feeding them. How or where she got it I do not know. I presume, however, it was procured from our owner's farm. Some people may call this theft. If such a thing were to happen now, I should condemn it as theft myself. But taking place at the time it did, and for the reason that it did, no one could ever make me believe that my mother was guilty of thieving. She was simply a victim of the system of slavery. I cannot remember having slept in a bed until after our family was declared free by the Emancipation Proclamation. Three children—John, my older brother, Amanda, my sister, and myself—had a pallet on the dirt floor, or, to be more correct, we slept in and on a bundle of filthy rags laid upon the dirt floor.

I was asked not long ago to tell something about the sports and pastimes that I engaged in during my youth. Until that question was asked it had never occurred to me that there was no period of my life that was devoted to play. From the time that I can remember anything, almost every day of my life has been occupied in some kind of labour; though I think I would now be a more useful man if I had had time for sports. During the period that I spent in slavery I was not large enough to be of much service, still I was occupied most of the time in cleaning the yards, carrying water to men in the fields, or going to the mill to which I used to take the corn, once a week, to be ground. The mill was about three miles from the plantation. This work I always dreaded. The heavy bag of corn would be thrown across the back of the horse, and the corn divided about evenly on each side; but in some way, almost without exception, on these trips, the corn would shift as to become unbalanced and would fall off the horse, and often I would fall with it. As I was not strong enough to reload the corn upon the horse, I would have to wait, sometimes for many hours, till a chance passer-by came along who would help me out of my trouble. The hours while waiting for some one were usually spent in crying. The time consumed in this way made me late in reaching the mill, and by the time I got my corn ground and reached home it would be far into the night. The road was a lonely one, and often led through dense forests. I was always frightened. The woods were said to be full of soldiers who had deserted from the army, and I had been told that the first thing a deserter did to a Negro boy when he found him alone was to cut off his ears. Besides, when I was late in getting home I know I would always get a severe scolding or a flogging.

I had no schooling whatever while I was a slave, though I remember on several occasions I went as far as the schoolhouse door with one of my young mistresses to carry her books. The picture of several dozen boys and girls in a schoolroom engaged in study made a deep impression upon me, and I had the feeling that to get into a schoolhouse and study in this way would be about the same as getting into paradise.

So far as I can now recall, the first knowledge that I got of the fact that we were slaves, and that freedom of the slaves was being discussed, was early one morning before day, when I was awakened by my mother kneeling over her children and fervently praying that Lincoln and his armies might be successful, and that one day she and her children might be free. In this connection I have never been able to understand how the slaves throughout the South, completely ignorant as were the masses so far as books or newspapers were concerned, were able to keep themselves so accurately and completely informed about the great National questions that were agitating the country. From the time that Garrison, Lovejoy, and others began to agitate for freedom, the slaves throughout the South kept in close touch with the progress of the movement. Though I was a mere child during the preparation for the Civil War and during the war itself, I now recall the many late-at-night whispered discussions that I heard my mother and the other slaves on the plantation indulge in. These discussions showed that they understood the situation, and that they kept themselves informed of events by what was termed the "grapevine" telegraph.

During the campaign when Lincoln was first a candidate for the Presidency, the slaves on our far-off plantation, miles from any railroad or large city or daily newspaper, knew what the issues involved were. When war was begun between the North and the South, every slave on our plantation felt and knew that, though other issues were discussed, the primal one was that of slavery. Even the most ignorant members of my race on the remote plantations felt in their hearts, with a certainty that admitted of no doubt, that the freedom of the slaves would be the one great result of the war, if the Northern armies conquered. Every success of the Federal armies and every defeat of the Confederate forces was watched with the keenest and most intense interest. Often the slaves got knowledge of the results of great battles before the white people at the "big house," as the master's house was called.

I cannot remember a single instance during my childhood or early boyhood when our entire family sat down to the table together, and God's blessing was asked, and the family ate a meal in a civilized manner. On the plantation in Virginia, and even later, meals were gotten by the children very much as dumb animals get theirs. It was a piece of bread here and a scrap of meat there. It was a cup of milk at one time and some potatoes at another. Sometimes a portion of our family would eat out of the skillet or pot, while some one would eat from a tin plate held on the knees, and often using nothing but the hands with which to hold the food. When I had grown to sufficient size, I was required to go to the "big house" at meal-times to fan the flies from the table by means of a large set of paper fans operated by a pulley. Naturally much of the conversation of the white people turned upon the subject of freedom and the war, and I absorbed a good deal of it. I remember that at one time I saw two of my young mistresses and some lady visitors eating ginger-cakes in the yard. At that time those cakes seemed to me to be absolutely the most tempting and desirable things that I had ever seen; and I then and there resolved that, if I ever got free, the height of my ambition would be reached if I could get to the point where I could secure and eat ginger-cakes in the way that I saw those ladies doing.

Of course as the war was prolonged the white people, in many cases, often found it difficult to secure food for themselves. I think the slaves felt the deprivation less than the whites, because the usual diet for the slaves was corn bread and pork, and these could be raised on the plantation; but coffee, tea, sugar, and other articles which the whites had been accustomed to use could not be raised on the plantation, and the conditions brought about by the war frequently made it impossible to secure these things. The whites were often in great straits. Parched corn was used for coffee, and a kind of black molasses was used instead of sugar. Many times nothing was used to sweeten the so-called tea and coffee.

The first pair of shoes I recall wearing were wooden ones. They had rough leather on the top, but the bottoms, which were about an inch thick, were of wood. When I walked they made a fearful noise, and besides this they were very inconvenient, since there was no yielding to the natural pressure of the foot.

In wearing them one presented an exceedingly awkward appearance. The most trying ordeal that I was forced to endure as a slave boy, however, was the wearing of a flax shirt. In the portion of Virginia where I lived it was common to use flax as a part of the clothing for the slaves. That part of the flax from which our clothing was made was largely the refuse, which of course was the cheapest and roughest part. I can scarcely imagine any torture, except, perhaps, the pulling of a tooth, that is equal to that caused by putting on a new flax shirt for the first time. It is almost equal to the feeling that one would experience if he had a dozen or more chestnut burrs, or a hundred small pinpoints, in contact with his flesh. Even to this day I can recall accurately the tortures that I underwent when putting on one of these garments. The fact that my flesh was soft and tender added to the pain. But I had no choice. I had to wear the flax shirt or none; and had it been left to me to choose, I should have chosen to wear no covering. In connection with the flax shirt, my brother John, who is several years older than I am, performed one of the most generous acts that I ever heard of one slave relative doing for another. On several occasions when I was being forced to wear a new flax shirt, he generously agreed to put it on in my stead and wear it for several days, till it was "broken in." Until I had grown to be quite a youth this single garment was all that I wore.

My mother's husband, who was the stepfather of my brother John and myself, did not belong to the same owners as did my mother. In fact, he seldom came to our plantation. I remember seeing him there perhaps once a year, that being about Christmas time. In some way, during the war, by running away and following the Federal soldiers, it seems, he found his way into the new state of West Virginia. As soon as freedom was declared, he sent for my mother to come to the Kanawha Valley, in West Virginia. At that time a journey from Virginia over the mountains to West Virginia was rather a tedious and in some cases a painful undertaking. What little clothing and few household goods we had were placed in a cart, but the children walked the greater portion of the distance, which was several hundred miles.

I do not think any of us ever had been very far from the plantation, and the taking of a long journey into another state was quite an event. The parting from our former owners and the members of our own race on the plantation was a serious occasion. From the time of our parting till their death we kept up a correspondence with the older members of the family, and in later years we have kept in touch with those who were the younger members. We were several weeks making the trip, and most of the time we slept in the open air and did our cooking over a log fire out of doors. One night I recall that we camped near an abandoned log cabin, and my mother decided to build a fire in that for cooking, and afterward to make a "pallet" on the floor for our sleeping. Just as the fire had gotten well started a large black snake fully a yard and a half long dropped down the chimney and ran out on the floor. Of course we at once abandoned that cabin.

Finally we reached our destination—a little town called Malden, which is about five miles from Charleston, the present capital of the state.

At that time salt-mining was the great industry in that part of West Virginia, and the little town of Malden was right in the midst of the salt-furnaces. My stepfather had already secured a job at the salt-furnace and he had also secured a little cabin for us to live in. Our new house was no better than the one we had left on the old plantation in Virginia. In fact, in one respect it was worse. Notwithstanding the poor condition of our plantation cabin, we were at all times sure of pure air. Our new home was in the midst of a cluster of cabins crowded closely together, and as there were no sanitary regulations, the filth about the cabins was often intolerable. Some of our neighbors were coloured people, and some were the poorest and most ignorant and degraded white people. It was a motley mixture. Drinking, gambling, quarrels, fights, and shockingly immoral practices were frequent. All who lived in the little town were in one way or another connected with the salt business. Though I was a mere child, my stepfather put me and my brother at work in one of the furnaces. Often I began work as early as four o'clock in the morning.

The first thing I ever learned in the way of book knowledge was while working in the salt-furnace. Each salt-packer had his barrels marked with a certain number. The number allotted to my stepfather was "18." At the close of the day's work the boss of the packers would come around and put "18" on each of our barrels, and I soon learned to recognize that figure whenever I saw it, and after a while got to the point where I could make that figure, though I knew nothing about any other figures or letters.

From the time that I can remember having any thoughts about anything, I recall that I had an intense longing to learn to read. I determined, when quite a small child, that, if I accomplished nothing else in life, I would in some way get enough education to enable me to read common books and newspapers. Soon after we got settled in some manner in our new cabin in West Virginia, I induced my mother to get hold of a book for me. How or where she got it I do not know, but in some way she procured an old copy of Webster's "blue-back" spelling-book, which contained the alphabet, followed by such meaningless words as "ab," "ba," "ca," "da." I began at once to devour this book, and I think that it was the first one I have had in my hands. I had learned from somebody that the way to begin to read was to learn the alphabet, so I tried in all the ways I could think of to learn it—all of course without a teacher, for I could find no one to teach me. At that time there was not a single member of my race anywhere near us who could read, and I was too timid to approach any of the white people. In some way, within a few weeks, I mastered the greater portion of the alphabet. In all my efforts to learn to read my mother shared fully my ambition, and sympathized with me and aided me in every way that she could. Though she was totally ignorant, so far as mere book knowledge was concerned, she had high ambitions for her children, and a large fund of good, hard, common sense which seemed to enable her to meet and master every situation. If I have done anything in life worth attention, I feel sure that I inherited the disposition from my mother.

In the midst of my struggles and longing for an education, a young coloured boy who had learned to read in the state of Ohio came to Malden. As soon as the coloured people found out that he could read, a newspaper was secured, and at the close of nearly every day's work this young man would be surrounded by a group of men and women who were anxious to hear him read the news contained in the papers. How I used to envy this man! He seemed to me to be the one young man in all the world who ought to be satisfied with his attainments.

About this time the question of having some kind of a school opened for the coloured children in the village began to be discussed by members of the race. As it would be the first school for Negro children that had ever been opened in that part of Virginia, it was, of course, to be a great event, and the discussion excited the wildest interest. The most perplexing question was where to find a teacher. The young man from Ohio who had learned to read the papers was considered, but his age was against him. In the midst of the discussion about a teacher, another young coloured man from Ohio, who had been a soldier, in some way found his way into town. It was soon learned that he possessed considerable education, and he was engaged by the coloured people to teach their first school. As yet no free schools had been started for coloured people in that section, hence each family agreed to pay a certain amount per month, with the understanding that the teacher was to "board 'round"—that is, spend a day with each family. This was not bad for the teacher, for each family tried to provide the very best on the day the teacher was to be its guest. I recall that I looked forward with anxious appetite to the "teacher's day" at our little cabin.

This experience of a whole race beginning to go to school for the first time, presents one of the most interesting studies that has ever occurred in connection with the development of any race. Few people who were not right in the midst of the scenes can form any exact idea of the intense desire which the people of my race showed for an education. As I have stated, it was a whole race trying to go to school. Few were too young, and none too old, to make the attempt to learn. As fast as any kind of teachers could be secured, not only were day-schools filled, but night-schools as well. The great ambition of the older people was to try to learn to read the Bible before they died. With this end in view, men and women who were fifty or seventy-five years old would often be found in the night-school. Sunday-schools were formed soon after freedom, but the principal book studied in the Sunday-school was the spelling-book. Day-school, night-school, Sunday-school, were always crowded, and often many had to be turned away for want of room.

The opening of the school in the Kanawha Valley, however, brought to me one of the keenest disappointments that I ever experienced. I had been working in a salt-furnace for several months, and my stepfather had discovered that I had a financial value, and so, when the school opened, he decided that he would not spare me from my work. This decision seemed to cloud my every ambition. The disappointment was made all the more severe by reason of the fact that my place of work was where I could see the happy children passing to and from school, mornings and afternoons. Despite this disappointment, however, I determined that I would learn something, anyway. I applied myself with greater earnestness than ever to the mastering of what was in the "blue-back" speller.

My mother sympathized with me in my disappointment, and sought to comfort me in all the ways she could, and to help me find a way to learn. After a while I succeeded in making arrangements with the teacher to give me some lessons at night, after the day's work was done. These night lessons were so welcome that I think I learned more at night than the other children did during the day. My own experiences in the night-school gave me faith in the night-school idea, with which, in after years, I had to do both at Hampton and Tuskegee. But my boyish heart was still set upon going to day-school, and I let no opportunity slip to push my case. Finally, I won, and was permitted to go to the school in the day for a few months, with the understanding that I was to rise early in the morning and work in the furnace till nine o'clock, and return immediately after school closed in the afternoon for at least two more hours of work.

The schoolhouse was some distance from the furnace, and as I had to work till nine o'clock, and the school opened at nine, I found myself in a difficulty. School would always be begun before I reached it, and sometimes my class had recited. To get around this difficulty I yielded to a temptation for which most people, I suppose, will condemn me; but since it is a fact, I might as well state it. I have great faith in the power and influence of facts. It is seldom that anything is permanently gained by holding back a fact. There was a large clock in a little office in the furnace. This clock, of course, all the hundred or more workmen depended upon to regulate their hours of beginning and ending their day's work. I got the idea that the way for me to reach school on time was to move the clock hands from half-past eight up to the nine o'clock mark. This I found myself doing morning after morning, till the furnace "boss" discovered that something was wrong, and locked the clock in a case. I did not mean to inconvenience anybody. I simply meant to reach that schoolhouse in time.

When, however, I found myself at the school for the first time, I also found myself confronted with two other difficulties. In the first place, I found that all of the other children wore hats or caps on their heads, and I had neither hat nor cap. In fact, I do not remember that up to the time of going to school I had ever worn any kind of covering upon my head, nor do I recall that either I or anybody else had even thought anything about the need of covering for my head, But, of course, when I saw how all the other boys were dressed, I began to feel quite uncomfortable. As usual, I put the case before my mother, and she explained to me that she had no money with which to buy a "store hat," which was a rather new institution at that time among the members of my race and was considered quite the thing for young and old to own, but that she would find a way to help me out of the difficulty. She accordingly got two pieces of "homespun" (jeans) and sewed them together, and I was soon the proud possessor of my first cap.

The lesson that my mother taught me in this has always remained with me, and I have tried as best I could to teach it to others. I have always felt proud, whenever I think of the incident, that my mother had the strength of character enough not to be led into the temptation of seeming to be that which she was not—of trying to impress my schoolmates and others with the fact that she was able to buy me a "store hat" when she was not. I have always felt proud that she refused to go into debt for that which she did not have the money to pay for. Since that time I have owned many kinds of caps and hats, but never one of which I have felt so proud as of the cap made of the two pieces of cloth sewed together by my mother. I have noted the fact, but without satisfaction, I need not add, that several of the boys who began their careers with "store hats" and who were my schoolmates and used to join in the sport that was made of me because I had only a "homespun" cap, have ended their careers in the penitentiary, while others are not able now to buy any kind of hat.

My second difficulty was with regard to my name, or rather *a* name. From the time when I could remember anything, I had been called simply "Booker." Before going to school it had never occurred to me that it was needful or appropriate to have an additional name. When I heard the school-roll called, I noticed that all of the children had at least two names, and some of them indulged in what seemed to me the extravagance of having three. I was in deep perplexity, because I knew that the teacher would demand of me at least two names, and I had only one. By the time the occasion came for the enrolling of my name, an idea occurred to me which I thought would make me equal to the situation; and so, when the teacher asked me what my full name was, I calmly told him "Booker Washington," as if I had been called by that name all my life; and by that name I have since been known. Later in life I found that my mother had given me the name of "Booker Taliaferro" soon after I was born, but in some way that part of my name seemed to disappear, and for a long while was forgotten, but as soon as I found out about it I revived it and made my full name "Booker Taliaferro Washington." I think there are not many men in our country who have had the privilege of naming themselves in the way that I have.

More than once I have tried to picture myself in the position of a boy or man with an honoured and distinguished ancestry which I could trace back through a period of hundreds of years, and who had not only inherited a name, but fortune and a proud family homestead; and yet I have sometimes had the feeling that if I had inherited these, and had been a member of a more popular race, I should have been inclined to yield to the temptation of depending upon my ancestry and my colour to do that for me which I should do for myself. Years ago I resolved that because I had no ancestry myself I would leave a record of which my children would be proud, and which might encourage them to still higher effort.

The world should not pass judgement upon the Negro, and especially the Negro youth, too quickly or too harshly. The Negro boy has obstacles, discouragements, and temptations to battle with that are little known to those not situated as he is. When a white boy undertakes a task, it is taken for granted that he will succeed. On the other hand, people are usually surprised if the Negro boy does not fail. In a word, the Negro youth starts out with the presumption against him.

The influence of ancestry, however, is important in helping forward any individual or race, if too much reliance is not placed upon it. Those who constantly direct attention to the Negro youth's moral weaknesses, and compare his advancement with that of white youths, do not consider the influence of the memories which cling about the old family homesteads. I have no idea, as I have stated elsewhere, who my grandmother was. I have, or have had uncles and aunts and cousins, but I have no knowledge as to what most of them are. My case will illustrate that of hundreds of thousands of black people in every part of our country. The very fact that the white boy is conscious that, if he fails in life, he will disgrace the whole family record, extending back through many generations, is of tremendous value in helping him to resist temptations. The fact that the individual has behind and surrounding him proud family history and connection serves as a stimulus to help him to overcome obstacles when striving for success.

The time that I was permitted to attend school during the day was short, and my attendance was irregular. It was not long before I had to stop attending day-school altogether, and devote all of my time again to work. I resorted to the night-school again. In fact, the greater part of the education I secured in my boyhood was gathered through the night-school after my day's work was done. I had difficulty often in securing a satisfactory teacher. Sometimes, after I had secured some one to teach me at night, I would find, much to my disappointment, that the teacher knew little more than I did. Often I would have to walk several miles at night in order to recite my night-school lessons. There was never a time in my youth, no matter how dark and discouraging the days might be, when one resolve did not continually remain with me, and that was a determination to secure an education at any cost...

WILLIAM H. HOLTZCLAW

(1870?–1943)

From *The Black Man's Burden*

The emancipation of the slaves was the culmination of many years of hope and prayer for African-Americans, but they were soon to discover that the mere fact of freedom did not improve their lot to any significant degree. The only trade familiar to many slaves was farming, and the only way they could continue to farm after the Civil War was under some form of sharecropping system. The result was generally substitution of economic slavery for their former plight. It was a rugged struggle which many did not survive.

William Holtzclaw was born toward the end of the Reconstruction era in the Deep South, and later in life recalled quite clearly the hardships under the sharecrop system. After completing his own education with much difficulty, he tried to enlighten the Alabama community in which he lived by publishing a newspaper for the black community. Not satisfied with the results of this effort, he was determined to start a school for people of his own race, and did so in the early days of the new century. By 1915 Holtzclaw's school, the Utica Normal and Industrial Institute in Utica, Mississippi, could boast an enrollment of five hundred students.

I have some recollection of the house in which I was born, and of the great plantation which belonged, in the days of slavery, to one of those traditional Southern planters about whom we have read so much. I have seen the windowless house in which I first saw the light—the light that scantily streamed through the cracks in the wall. It was a little cabin, fourteen feet by sixteen feet, made of split pine poles, with only dirt for a floor.

It was in this cabin, near Roanoke, Randolf County, Alabama, that my mother was left alone one Saturday night. My father had gone away to secure food for her, and when he returned, Sunday morning, I was there to greet him. My mother and I were completely alone at the time of my birth.

I have always felt that I have an advantage over most men of my race in that I was born on a day of rest. It was the first piece of good fortune that came to me, and I want to be grateful for it.

This was in the closing days of Reconstruction, when there were stirring times in nearly every part of the country, but of course, I do not remember much about what happened then. I recall, however, some things that occurred four or five years later, when, although the South had been legally reconstructed, the law had not changed the sentiments of the people very much.

I distinctly remember that there were no colored school-teachers at that time and, in my own locality, there were no Northern white teachers. The few colored schools that existed at all were taught by Southern white men and women. Before I was old enough to attend school myself I used to go along now and then with the others, and I remember that one of these Southern white teachers took a great liking to me and, passing our house one day on his way home, predicted to my mother that I would some day be a lawyer. I did not know what that meant then, but I got the impression that it meant I was going to be something great, and I did not forget it.

Almost as soon as the Negro pupils got as far as "baker," and certainly when they got as far as "abasement," in the old blue-back speller, they were made assistant teachers, and in a short while, relieving the white teachers, they became the only teachers we had. When I was seven years old there was not a white teacher in our community. The colored teachers were doing pretty good work, but the best of them had advanced only about as far as the fourth grade. There is one thing, however, that they had learned to perfection, and that was the use of the rod, and of this kind of education I got my full share every day. My great trouble was that if I got a whipping at school, I was likely to get another one when I got home.

This was not always the case, however. One year it had been agreed that I should study nothing but arithmetic, and before I had been at school many days, I had undoubtedly reached the limit of my teacher's ability in that branch. For several days I had no lessons. At length, one day, without warning, he jumped at me like a fierce tiger, and with a hickory switch, which he had previously roasted in the fire, beat me to the floor and continued to flog me until some grown pupils interfered. When I started home that afternoon I became exhausted and sat down on a log on the roadside, from which I was not able to rise on account of the lacerated condition of my flesh. My father found me after dark and carried me home. That was the only time that I can now recall ever having seen my father very angry. He wanted to whip that school-teacher, but my mother's advice prevailed, and I was sent back to school as soon as I could walk. Those early experiences made me vow that if ever I got to be a school-teacher I would not whip the little ones and let the big ones go free.

My father—who, like my mother, had been a slave—was a young and inexperienced man when he married. My mother, however, had been married twice before, and she was the mother of three children. Her first marriage was performed in slavery time by the simple act of jumping back and forth over a broom in the presence of her master and mistress. In the course of time as more children, including myself, came along, until there were six of us, my father found it very difficult to keep the wolf from the door.

My mother helped him by cooking for the landlord's family, while my father worked on the plantation. Our landlord—one of those Southern planters, now commonly referred to as a "gentleman of the Old South"—like many others of his class, had had his fortune, consisting largely of slaves, swept away by the ravages of the Civil War. The result was that, although he had a large amount of land left, he was nevertheless a poor man. The agreement between him and Father, which was nothing more than a verbal contract between them, provided that he was to furnish land, mules, seed—in fact, everything but labor—and further provided that he was to help do the work and receive as his share three-fourths of all that the land produced, while we were to receive the other one-fourth.

Although he agreed to help, he seldom did any manual labor. He was in the fields every day, however, going from place to place among the various Negroes that were serving under contracts similar to ours. At one time my father ventured, in the most modest way, to call his attention to the fact that he was doing no work, but he very kindly, yet firmly, explained that he was doing more work in a day without a tool in his hand than my father was doing in a month. He tried to make my father understand this. I do not know whether my father understood it or not, but I could not.

We never prepared our land for cultivation, but simply planted the seeds on the hard ground in March and April and covered them with a turn plow; then we cultivated the crop for two months. Naturally, the returns were small. When the crop was divided in the fall of the year three loads of corn were thrown into the white man's crib and one into ours; but when it came to dividing the cotton, which was done up into bales weighing five hundred pounds each and which sold for seventeen cents a pound, every bale went to the white man. He was at great pains to explain to my father each year that we ate ours during the year.

I remember how puzzled I used to be trying to conceive how it was possible for people to eat a crop—especially cotton out of which cloth is made—before it was produced. In later years, however, and many times since then, I have seen whole crops eaten two or three years before they were planted.

Our landlord furnished us food from his smoke-house from March to July, and from September to December. This food consisted of corn meal, out of which we made corn-pone by mixing it with water and salt, and smoked sides of meat, from hogs that we raised. All the rest of the time we had to find something to do away from the plantation in order to keep supplied with bread and clothes, which were scanty enough to support all the people that lived on it, even if it had been under better cultivation.

Each year the landlord would "run" us, and he would charge from twenty-five to two hundred per cent for the advances, according to the time of the year. No wonder we ate our crops up.

The method of obtaining food and provisions on this plantation was interesting. The landlord owned the store—one large room about forty feet by sixty feet, which he kept well supplied with flour, meat, meal, and tobacco. This store was usually open only on Saturdays, when all the Negroes from the plantation would come up and pass the day in the store, which was a sort of "social center." Meantime their rations for the following week were being issued. For an un-married male laborer the usual ration was a pound of meat, a peck of meal, three pounds of flour, and a plug of tobacco.

I remember hearing the men complain very often that they were charged for rations that they did not get, and I remember that at one time a lawsuit arose between the landlord and a Negro on the plantation who could neither read nor write. When the trial came off at the store the landlord presented his books to show that the Negro had obtained certain rations during the year. The Negro denied having received such rations, and as proof he presented his "book," which consisted of a stick, one yard long, trimmed in hexagon fashion and filled with notches, each notch representing some purchase and in some ingenious way the time of the purchase. After the jury had examined the white man's books they began an examination of the Negro's stick, and the more he explained his way of keeping books, the more interested the jurors became. When the trial was over, the Negro won the case, the jurors having decided that he had kept his books properly and that a mistake had been made by the white bookkeeper.

My mother cooked for the "white folks," and, her work being very exacting, she could not always get home at night. At such times we children suffered an excruciating kind of pain—the pain of hunger. I can well remember how at night we would often cry for food until falling here and there on the floor we would sob ourselves to sleep. Late at night, sometimes after midnight, mother would reach home with a large pan of pot-liquor, or more often a variety of scraps from the "white folks'" table (she might have brought more, but she was not the kind of cook that slipped things out of the back door); waking us all, she would place the pan on the floor, or on her knees, and gathering around we would eat to our satisfaction. There was neither knife, fork nor spoon—nothing but the pan. We used our hands and sometimes in our haste dived head foremost into the pan, very much as pigs after swill. In the morning, when mother had to return to her work before we children awoke, she was accustomed to put the large pan on the dirt floor in the middle of the cabin where we could find it without difficulty. Sometimes, however, our pet pig would come in and find it first, and would be already helping himself before we could reach it. We never made any serious objection to dividing with him, and I do not recall that he showed any resentment about dividing with us.

One day my brother and I were given a meal of piecrust, which my mother had brought from the "white folks'" table. As we were eating it, Old Buck, the family dog, who resembled an emaciated panther, stole one of the crusts. We loved Old Buck, but we had to live, and so my brother "lit onto" him and a royal battle took place over that crust. As my brother was losing ground, I joined in the struggle. We saved the crust, but not until both of us had been scratched and bitten. I do not know who needed the crust most, we or the dog, for those were the days of hardships. Very often we would go two or three days at a time without prepared food, but we usually found our way into the potato patches, and the chickens were not always safe where we passed, for my brother occasionally, by accident, would step on a little one, and of course we would then have to cook it as a matter of economy. I recall that in that section of Alabama where I lived there is a kind of root called hog potato, which grows abundantly in the swamps and marshy places. I have never known it by any other name. I used to spend hours every day in the swamps about our house wading in the slush above my knees, turning up the mud in search of those potatoes. After they were roasted they had a taste like that of the white potato with which people in the Northern states are familiar. By means of these potatoes, together with berries and other wild fruits, we were able to keep body and soul together during those dark days.

As I now remember it, my father's continuous effort was to keep the wolf from the door. He presently quit the big plantation and spent a year working on the Western railway of Alabama, at Loachapoka in Lee county, about fifty miles from home. There were no railroads or stage coaches to carry him to and from his work, so it required two weeks to make the round trip, much of which lay through immense forests where a narrow footpath was the only passage. He would remain away from home three months at a time, working for the handsome sum of a dollar a day, out of which he boarded himself and furnished his working-clothes. I remember how mother and we children would sit in our dark little cabin many nights looking for him to come at any moment, and sometimes it would be nearly a week after we would begin to look for him before he would come. I don't think we ever had a letter from him; we only knew that the three months were up, and that it was time for him to come to us.

He usually brought from forty to fifty dollars home, but by the time we paid out of that amount what we owed the white gentleman, on whose place we still lived, for the advances obtained of him in my father's absence there would not be much left for us.

The lack of food was not the only hardship we had to endure. We found it very difficult to find clothes and even shoes, which was very trying when the winters were cold. I never wore a pair of shoes until I was fifteen, and when I did begin to wear shoes I never wore them until the weather was cold. In fact, I made it a rule never to put on my new shoes until Christmas morning, no matter how cold it was. Usually in the summertime the only garment that we children wore was a simple shirt. These shirts were not always made of shirting, but were often of homespun, and when this material could not be had a crocus sack, or something of the kind, was used instead.

I remember that the first suit of clothes I owned I paid for myself with the money I had made by splitting rails. It took me a good part of the fall season to split the two thousand rails that were required to get my little suit, but I succeeded in my undertaking, with occasional help from my father in finishing the job. The fact that I bought this suit with my own labor made me think all the more of it.

Although the census taker of 1880 classed my parents as illiterates, they had a very clear understanding of right and wrong; in their own way they were moral teachers, and they knew how to make their lessons impressive. By no stretch of the imagination could either of them have been classed with what was known at that time as an ignorant Negro, though neither of them could read or write.

One day while I was alone in the "white folks'" kitchen, where I had accompanied my mother to her daily work, I spied a little round box on the shelf. It was a box of matches such as I have not seen in twenty years. Curious to see what a match-head was like, I pinched one without removing it from the box. An explosion was heard, and the box was blown off the shelf, to my consternation. With a switch my mother began to administer to a rather tender part of my anatomy the treatment with which it was already familiar, explaining all the while that I must learn to mind my own business. The white lady, with whom I was a favorite, interceded for me, saying that I should not be whipped for a little thing like that; it was most natural; I had reached the age of investigation. My mother desisted, shaking her head as she left the scene, saying she would "investigate" me, and from time to time she did. So in matters of conduct, at least, whether large or small, I had the advantage of a loving but firm discipline.

In such matters of conduct, or of morality, if you please, my mother was always teaching me some little lesson. I remember that at one time, when I must have been five or six years old, I was sent up to the "big house" to borrow some meal from the "white folks" for supper. On my way back, while climbing over an old-fashioned rail fence, I discovered, while pausing for a few minutes on the top rail, a hen's nest full of eggs. The bait was tempting. I was hungry and wanted the eggs. I had never heard anybody say anything about taking that which did not belong to you, but somehow I felt that it was wrong to take those eggs. I knew they belonged to the white lady up at the "big house." After thinking the matter over for nearly a half hour, I decided to compromise by taking only a few of them, so I got as many as my little pocket would hold and carried them home. Sidling up to my mother in a rather sheepish fashion, I showed them to her and told her that I had found them, which was the truth. I remember that my mother was amused, but she kept her face turned from me and proceeded to teach me another one of those little lessons, which stayed by me and supported me in after years.

She told me it was wrong to steal from the "white folks," that "white folks" thought all Negroes would steal, and that we must show them that we would not. She said she knew I did not steal them, but that it would look that way, and that I must show that I did not by taking them right back to the white lady and giving them to her. That was a great task. After having spent an hour in going a distance of 300 yards, I reached the white lady with the eggs and told her that I had found them. I have always suspected that my mother had been there and had seen the white lady before my arrival. At least, that is the way it appears now, as I look back on it, for the good lady gave me an old-fashioned lecture about stealing and told me that, whenever I wanted anything she had, I should come up and ask for it. Then she gave me two of the eggs. I was quite young at that time, as I have said before, but was not too young to learn, and that lesson and others like it remained with me.

When I was four years old I was put to work on the farm—that is, at such work as I could do, such as riding a deaf and blind mule while my brother held the plow. When I was six years old my four-year-old brother and I had to go two miles through a lonely forest every morning in order to carry my father's breakfast and dinner to a saw-mill, where he was hauling logs for sixty cents a day. The white man, Frank Weathers, who employed a large number of hands, both Ne-groes and whites, was considered one of the best and most upright men in that section of the country.

In those days there were no public schools in that part of the country for the Negroes. Indeed, public schools for whites were just beginning to be established. This man set aside a little house in the neighborhood of the sawmill, employed a teacher, and urged all the Negroes to send their children to this school. Not a great many of them, however, took advantage of his generosity, for this was at the time when everybody seemed to think that the Negro's only hope was in politics.

But my father and mother had great faith in education, and they were determined that their children should have that blessing of which they themselves had been deprived.

Soon, however, Mr. Weathers had cut all the timber that he could get in that section, and he therefore moved his mills to another district. This left us without a school. But my father was not to be outdone. He called a meeting of the men in that community, and they agreed to build a schoolhouse themselves. They went to the forest and cut pine poles about eight inches in diameter, split them in halves, and carried them on their shoulders to a nice shady spot, and there erected a little schoolhouse. The benches were made of the same material, and there was no floor nor chimney. Some of the other boys' trousers suffered when they sat on the new pine benches, which exuded rosin, but I had an advantage of them in this respect, for I wore only a shirt. In fact, I never wore trousers until I got to be so large that the white neighbors complained of my insufficient clothes.

Those benches, I distinctly remember, were constructed for boys and girls larger than I was, and my feet were always about fourteen inches above the ground. In this manner I sat for hours at a time swinging my feet in an effort to balance myself on the pine bench. My feet often swelled, so that when I did get on the ground to recite I felt as if a thousand pins were sticking through them, and it was very difficult for me to stand. For this inability to stand I often got a good flogging, for I could not convince the teacher that I was not trying to "make believe."

School lasted two months in the year— through July and August. The house was three miles from our home, and we walked every day, my oldest sister carrying me astride her neck when my legs gave out. Sometimes we would have nothing more than an ear of roasted green corn in our baskets for dinner. Very often we had simply wild persimmons, or ripe fruit picked from our landlord's orchard, or nuts and muscadines from the forest. If we had meat, ten to one it was because "Old Buck" had caught a 'possum or a hare the night before. Many a night the dogs and I hunted all night in order to catch a 'possum for the next day's noon meal.

Although we were young, we were observant, and in this way we learned some things in that school—among them, that the teacher, who was a married man, had fallen in love with his assistant teacher. He was constantly "making eyes" at her. She evidently reciprocated his affection, for at the end of the school year they eloped, and there was a great stir in the community in consequence. The people met at the little schoolhouse and very nearly decided that they would have no more school, but my father was there and counselled them that we had all suffered enough already from the affair and that we ought not to punish ourselves further. I attended the meeting myself with my father and I remember that my sympathies were all with "Miss Deely." True, she had run away with the principal of the school and nobody knew where they were, but I could not see what right anybody had to interfere with her love affairs, and I ventured to tell my mother so. Mother did not argue the question, but sat down and took me across her lap and proceeded to correct my views on the subject. Then she put the matter to me in the form of a question. She asked me how would I like to have some nice little lady run away with my father and leave me there for her to take care of. That settled it with me. Miss Deely was forever afterward in the wrong.

At the end of the first school year there was a trying time in our family. On this occasion the teacher ordered all the pupils to appear dressed in white. We had no white clothes, nor many of any other sort, for that matter. Father and Mother discussed our predicament nearly all one night. Father said it was foolish to buy clothes which could be used only for that occasion. But my ever resourceful mother was still determined that her children should look as well on this important occasion as any of our neighbors. However, when we went to bed the night before the exhibition we still had no white clothes and no cloth from which to make them. Nevertheless, when we awoke the next morning, all three of us had beautiful white suits. It came about in this way: my mother had a beautiful white Sunday petticoat, which she had cut up and made into suits for us. As there is just so much cloth in a petticoat and no more, the stuff had to be cut close to cover all three of us children, and as the petticoat had been worn several times and was, therefore, likely to tear, we had to be very careful how we stooped in moving about the stage, lest there should be a general splitting and tearing, with consequences that we were afraid to imagine. At the exhibition the next night we said our little pieces, and I suppose we looked about as well as the others; at least, we thought so, and that was sufficient. One thing I am sure of—there was no mother there who was prouder of her children than ours. The thing that made her so pleased was the fact that my speech made such an impression that our white landlord lifted me off the stage when I had finished speaking and gave me a quarter of a dollar.

If there happened to be a school in the winter time, I had sometimes to go bare-footed and always with scant clothing. Our landlady was very kind in such cases. She would give me clothes that had already been worn by her sons, and in turn I would bring broom straw, from the sages, with which she made her brooms. In this way I usually got enough clothes to keep me warm.

So, with my mother's encouragement, I went to school in spite of my bare feet. Often the ground would be frozen, and often there would be snow. My feet would crack and bleed freely, but when I reached home Mother would have a tub full of hot water ready to plunge me into and thaw me out. Although this caused my feet and legs to swell, it usually got me into shape for school the next day.

I remember once, when I had helped "lay by" the crops at home and was ready to enter the little one-month school, it was decided that I could not go, because I had no hat. My mother told me that if I could catch a 'coon and cure the skin, she would make me a cap out of that material. That night I went far into the forest with my hounds, and finally located a 'coon. The 'coon was a mighty fighter, and when he had driven off all my dogs I saw that the only chance for me to get a cap was to whip the 'coon myself, so together with the dogs I went at him, and finally we conquered him. The next week I went to school wearing my new 'coon-skin cap.

Exertions of this kind, from time to time, strengthened my will and my body, and prepared me for more trying tests which were to come later.

As I grew older it became more and more difficult for me to go to school. When cotton first began to open—early in the fall—it brought a higher price than at any other time of the year. At this time the landlord wanted us all to stop school and pick cotton. But mother wanted me to remain in school, so, when the landlord came to the quarters early in the morning to stir up the cotton pickers, she used to outgeneral him by hiding me behind the skillets, ovens, and pots, throwing some old rags over me until he was gone. Then she would slip me off to school through the back way. I can see her now with her hands upon my shoulder, shoving me along through the woods and underbrush, in a roundabout way, keeping me all the time out of sight of the great plantation until we reached the point, a mile away from home, where we came to the public road. There my mother would bid me good-bye, whereupon she would return to the plantation and try to make up to the landlord for the work of us both in the field as cotton pickers.

But when I became too large to be conveniently hidden behind our few small pots I had to take my place on the farm. When I was nine years old I began to work as a regular field-hand. My mother now devised another plan to keep me in school: I took turns with my brother at the plow and in school; one day I plowed and he went to school, the next day he plowed and I went to school; what he learned on his school day he taught me at night and I did the same for him. In this way we each got a month of schooling during the year, and with that month of schooling we also acquired the habit of studying at home. That we learned little enough may be seen from the following incident: I was ordered to get a United States history, and my father went to the store to get one, but the storekeeper, not having one, sold him a "Biography of Martin Luther" instead, without telling him the difference, so I carried the book to school and studied it for a long time, thinking that I was learning something about the United States. My teacher had neglected to tell me the name of the land I lived in.

It was hard enough for me to find a way to go to school. When it was not one obstacle, it was another. More than once I worked hard for eleven months in the year without receiving a single penny. Then, in order to enter school, I split rails at fifty cents a hundred during the month of December to get money with which to buy clothes.

When I reached the age where my school days were for the time at an end I was hired out to a white man for wages, in order to help support the family. Seeing that there was no chance for further schooling, I became morose, disheartened, and pulled away from all social life, except the monthly religious meetings at the little cabin church. Nevertheless, I gathered all the books I could find or borrow and hid them in the white man's barn, where I spent every bit of my spare time in trying to satisfy my desire for knowledge of the world of books. In this manner I spent all my Sundays. It was during this time that I came across the "Life of Ignatius Sancho," who was an educated black West Indian. It was the first thing in the way of a biography of a colored man that I had found, and I cannot express the inspiration I received from learning for the first time that a colored man could really make history.

It was in 1880 that my father finally despaired of getting ahead by working on the share system—that is, by working crops for half the profit. Encouraged by the success of other Negroes around him and urged on by the determination of my mother and the persistence of us children, he determined to strike out for himself. His idea was, first, to rent land, furnish his own stock and farm implements, then after having paid for his stock, to buy land. I remember that when he announced this plan to us children we were so happy at the prospects of owning a wagon and a pair of mules and having only our father for boss that we shouted and leaped for joy.

Sure enough, he carried out his plans—in part, at least. He rented a farm of forty acres, for which he paid annually three bales of cotton, worth one hundred and fifty dollars. He bought a mule, a horse, and a yoke of oxen, and so we started out for ourselves. The effort brought about a transformation in the spirits of the whole family. We all became better workers and for the first time began to take an interest in our work. However, before the crops were laid by, many troubles arose: one of our oxen broke his neck, one mule was attacked with some peculiar disease (I think they called it the "hooks"), and the horse became so poor and thin that he could not plow.

I shall never forget that mule. His ailment was a peculiar one; he could plow all day with ease, seemingly in perfect health, but after he lay down for the night he could not get up again. If we would help him to his feet, he would eat a good meal and work faithfully all day long. Consequently, the first thing I heard in the morning was my father's voice arousing me from sleep, saying, "Son, son, get up, day is breaking; let's go and lift the old mule up." We also had to call in a neighbor each morning. Toward the end of the season old Jim began to get so weak that it was difficult for him to do any plowing, and before the crop was laid by he gave out entirely. At this juncture, not to be outdone, my brother and I took the mule's place at the plow, with my sister at the plow-handles, and in this way we helped to finish the crop after a fashion, so as to be ready to enter school the first day it opened in August.

The faithful ox that was left to us was always on hand, and it was my duty to plow and haul with him. In order to plow with an ox one has to put a half inch rope around his head, and let it extend to the plow-handles, for use as a line and bridle. That ox's head was so hard that a sore was cut into my hand, from jerking him for four years, and the scar is still there.

My father was without experience in self-direction and management, having always, up to that time, had a white man to direct him. As a consequence, our effort to do business for ourselves was not wholly successful. I have already spoken of our trials during that first year. Things went well during the early part of the second year, and the crop was laid by with little mishap, except that my father, who plowed without shoes, stepped on the stub of a cane, which entering his foot, made him useless as a field-hand for the greater part of the year. I recall that father carried a piece of cane two inches long in his foot for more than a month, until he finally drew it to the surface by the application of fat meat poultices. How much better it would have been if he could have had a modern surgeon who would have drawn the splinter in two minutes. The crops were laid by, however, by the first of August, and we entered the school, where we remained for one month. Our corn crop that year was splendid. We gathered it and piled it in heaps in the field one Friday and Saturday. On Sunday there was a cloudburst, and all the corn was washed away by the little creek that passed through the plantation. This was a severe blow to us, one from which we were never wholly able to recover.

However, we struggled on. The next year, just as we were ready to gather our crop, a disease called the "slow fever" broke out in our family. It was a great scourge and all the more serious because we were not able to employ a physician and because my father was compelled to be away from home during the day, working for food to keep us alive. My brother Lewis was born in the midst of this raging epidemic, and my mother was not able to leave her bed to wait on those who were sick. The only attention we got was that which neighbors could give, during the little time that they could spare from picking their own cotton. Although I never took to my bed during the two months that we suffered, I was almost as sick as any of the family. Mother had us put in little beds that hovered round her bed, and she waited on us the best she could until she was almost exhausted. But, in spite of her efforts, Lola, my oldest sister, and the most beloved member of the family, died. I distinctly remember that this so affected me that I did not care to live any longer. The fact is, I wanted to join her, for in my youthful mind I felt that she was better off than we were. It was after she had been buried and after we had returned from the little cemetery, all of us being still far from well, that I heard my father pray his first prayer before the family altar. The calamity was a great blow to him and brought about a change in his life that lasted as long as he lived.

The fourth and last year that we tried to get on by our own initiative we had several unique experiences. At the end of that year, we came out so far in debt that, after we had paid our creditors all the cotton we had made, they came and took our corn, and, finally, the vegetables from our little garden as well as the pig. I felt that we ought to fight and not to allow all our substance to be taken from us, and I told my father so, but he insisted that we must obey the law. My mother, however, was a woman with considerable fire in her make-up. When they came and entered the crib to take the corn we children commenced to cry; then my mother came out and with considerable warmth demanded that a certain amount of corn be left there. She said that was the law. I do not know how she knew anything about the law, but I do know that the white man who was getting the corn respected her knowledge of the law and left there the amount of corn that she demanded. Having succeeded thus far, she demanded that he leave the chickens and vegetables alone, and this he also did. However, we were so completely broken up at this time that we applied to a white man for a home on his place—a home under the old system. My father only lived a short while after that, and he was never able again to lift himself from the condition of a share tenant.

On the morning of Christmas Day, 1889, my father seated himself on the roots of a large oak tree in the yard just after breakfast, and, calling me to him, said: "Son, you are nearing manhood, and you have no education. Besides, if you remain with me till you are twenty-one, I will not be able to help you. For these reasons, your mother and I have decided to set you free, provided you will make us one promise— that you will educate yourself."

By that time Mother had come up, and there we all stood. My mother and I were crying, and I am not sure that my father was not. I accepted the proposition and hurried off across the forest, where about a mile away I secured work with a white man, at thirty cents a day and board. Although we usually took a week for Christmas, that day my Christmas ended. I was very much excited. It was difficult for me to restrain myself. I was free. I was now to enjoy that longed-for opportunity of being my own master. The white man for whom I worked could neither read nor write. For that reason I feared to let him see me with books lest he should resent it, but nothing ever came of my apprehensions.

At the end of six months, I ran across quite accidentally—I will say providentially—the *Tuskegee Student*, a little paper published by the Tuskegee Normal and Industrial Institute, at Tuskegee, Alabama. In it there was the following note:

"There is an opportunity for a few able-bodied young men to make their way through school, provided they are willing to work. Applications should be made to Booker T. Washington, Principal."

I scribbled up some sort of application and addressed it simply to "Booker T. Washington," with nothing else on the envelope. All the same, it reached him, and I was admitted....

III

The Twentieth Century:
The First 50 Years—

The Bitter Legacy

THE CIVIL WAR DESTROYED THE ECONOMIC BASIS OF THE SOUTH, AND, AS a result, both white and black groped for a way to earn a livelihood from the land. As previously described by William Holtzclaw, a system was developed whereby an African-American family was assigned to work a particular piece of property owned by a planter, and the family would receive a share of the crops for wages. Since the tenants were furnished by the planter with supplies on which to live during the year, and for which they mortgaged their share of the crops to come, the planter used this opportunity to charge exorbitant rates for these supplies. At the end of the farming season the tenants were lucky not to be in debt to the planter.

In the first two decades of the twentieth century two things happened to encourage African-Americans to leave the land in the South and try his luck in the cities to the North and West. The first event was a disastrous boll weevil attack which by 1921 had ruined cotton crops throughout the South and made the landlords turn, in great number, to livestock and dairying. The second incentive was World War I, which took a large percentage of white workers out of industry and into military service. Many African-Americans in the South saw this as their opportunity to get jobs in the North. The great migration began.

Since 1910 the African-American population has increased fivefold outside the Deep South. Fifty years ago about three-fourths of the Negro population lived in rural areas. Today it is just the opposite. Three out of four African-American families live in the city. But it has been a frightfully disillusioning experience. Housing discrimination resulted in crowded ghetto tenements. Unemployment was high and the jobs that were available offered low pay. Poverty became the norm. Educational facilities were poor and a serious dropout problem was created.

Children were hurt most by these conditions. Sibling rivalry mounted with material scarcity. Youngsters were farmed out to relatives because of broken homes. Their self-esteem was low and they found little desire to identify with their family. They took to the streets.

A vicious circle was created. Robert G. Goodwin, in *America Is for Everybody*, pointed out that job discrimination and lack of educational opportunity limit employment opportunities and result in low and unstable incomes. He wrote, "Low incomes, combined with discrimination, reduce attainable levels of health and skills, and thus limit occupational choice and income in the future. And limited job opportunities result in limited availability of education and apprenticeship training, thus completing the circle."*

This is the bitter legacy.

---

*Robert G. Goodwin, *America Is for Everybody* (U.S. Dept. of Labor, Government Printing Office, 1963).

CARL T. ROWAN

(1929-)

From *Breaking Barriers*

In 1952 Hodding Carter called Carl Rowan "a loyal and perhaps unquietly desperate American who will not find in his lifetime full acceptance as a first-class citizen anywhere in his country."

"Like hell I won't," swore the young Rowan.

The odds seemed against Rowan, born in the Jim Crow South of Tennessee. His father had a fifth-grade education and no steady work; his mother went through the eleventh grade and often cleaned houses for money. The family had five children, who were usually hungry and often cold. Rowan's mother wanted better things for her children, and she pushed him. She thought him college material and drilled him in spelling, reading, and math. Luck also was on his side. He was often in situations that could have landed him in jail—stealing peaches from trees because he was hungry, or coal from the trainyard because his family was cold—or six feet under—stealing booze from local bootleggers and selling it.

From his grandmother, who always told him, "Where there's a will, there's a way," to a high school English teacher who convinced him to strive for high standards and goals, Rowan had strong backers. At a time when others were going off to fight in World War II, he went to college—when less than 1 percent of black women and even fewer men attended. During his freshman year, he was one of a handful of blacks chosen to take the Navy's officer exam, when there had never been a black officer in the history of the Navy. He became a commissioned officer at nineteen.

After the war, Rowan went on to graduate from Oberlin College and to earn a master's degree in journalism from the University

123

of Minnesota. He was an award-winning young journalist and went on to work for the State Department, served as ambassador to Finland, and was chief of the U.S. Information Agency under President Johnson. Today he is a nationally syndicated columnist and a panelist on a political talk show—with full acceptance as a first-class citizen anywhere in his country. This excerpt covers the time from Rowan's high school years to the time he took the officer's exam for the Navy.

My Rescue—by Teachers and a Grisly War

It was so difficult in those depression years to focus on much other than getting enough to eat, and girls, and whupping Lynchburg or Gallatin on the gridiron. I shall be forever grateful that one marvelous teacher forced me to focus on some other things.

She was only an inch or so above five feet tall and probably never weighed more than 110 pounds in her eighty-five years, but she was the only woman tough enough to make me read *Beowulf* and think for a few foolish days that I liked it.

I refer to Miss Bessie—Mrs. Bessie Taylor Gwynn—the woman who taught me English, literature, history, civics, and a lot more than I realized when I attended Bernard High from 1938 to 1942.

I shall never forget the day she scolded me, insisting that I wasn't reading enough of the things she wanted me to read.

"But, Miss Bessie," I complained, "I ain't much interested in *Beowulf.*"

She fastened on me large brown eyes that became daggerish slits and said, "Boy, *I* am your *English* teacher, and I know I've taught you better than this. How dare you talk to me with 'I ain't' this and 'I ain't' that?"

"Miss Bessie," I said, "I'm trying to make first-string end on the football team. If I go around saying 'it isn't' and 'they aren't' the guys are gonna laugh me off the squad."

"Boy," she said, "you'll make first string only because you have guts and can play football. But do you know what *really* takes guts? Refusing to lower your standards to those of the dumb crowd. It takes guts to say to yourself that you've got to live and be somebody fifty years after these football games are over."

I started saying "we aren't" and "if I were," and I still made first-string left end and class valedictorian without losing the respect of my buddies. I remembered that with a special sense of tragedy when I read recently that many black kids were afraid to display knowledge or scholarship for fear that their peers would accuse them of acting white.

Miss Bessie died in 1980 after a remarkable forty-seven years in which she taught my mother, me, my brother and sisters, and hundreds of other black youngsters who were deprived economically, in terms of family backgrounds, and in almost every other measurement of disadvantage. She would be *unforgettable* to most of her pupils under any circumstance, but I remember her with special gratitude and affection in this era when Americans are so wrought up about a "rising tide of mediocrity" in public education and are worrying about finding competent, caring teachers to help their children to cope in an increasingly technological, sophisticated, and dangerous world.

Mrs. Gwynn was an example of an aphorism we must accept: An informed, dedicated teacher is a blessing to children and an asset to the nation—values not even remotely reflected in what most of our teachers are paid.

Miss Bessie had a bearing of dignity—an unpretentious pride that told anyone who met her she was educated in the best sense of that word. There was never a discipline problem in her classes. We knew instinctively that you didn't mess around with a woman who knew all about the Battle of Hastings, the Magna Charta and Runnymede, the Bill of Rights, the Kellogg-Briand Pact outlawing war, the Emancipation Proclamation—and could also play the piano.

This frail-looking woman, who could make sense of the writings of Shakespeare, Milton, Voltaire, and bring to life Booker T. Washington and W. E. B. Du Bois, was a towering presence in our classrooms. We students memorized the names of members of the Supreme Court and the president's cabinet, having learned early that it could be very embarrassing to be unprepared when Miss Bessie said, "Get up and tell the class who Frances Perkins is and what you know and think about her."

I wonder how many teachers today make their students learn the names of officials who spend the public's money and make policies that affect us all so profoundly.

Miss Bessie knew that my family, like so many in those hard days of the Great Depression, couldn't pay rent regularly, let alone maintain a subscription to a newspaper. She knew that my family didn't even own a radio. Still, she prodded me to "look out for your future and find some way to keep up with what's going on in the world." So I became a delivery boy for the *Chattanooga Times*, rarely making a dollar a week because most of my subscribers never paid. But I got to read a newspaper every day.

Miss Bessie noticed and heard things that had nothing to do with schoolwork but were so important to the well-being and development of a youngster. There was a time when a few of my classmates, especially her daughter, Ennys, made fun of my frayed, hand-me-down overcoat, calling it "strings." As I was leaving school one day Miss Bessie patted me on the back of that old overcoat and said, "Carl, never waste time fretting about what you *don't* have. Just make the most of what you *do* have—a brain."

Like millions of youngsters in today's ghettos and barrios, I needed the push and inspiration of a teacher who truly cared. Miss Bessie gave plenty of both as she immersed me in a wonderful world of similes, metaphors, alliteration, hyperbole, and even onomatopoeia. She acquainted me with dactylic verse, with the meter and scan of ballads, and set me to believing that I could write sonnets as good as any ever penned by Shakespeare, or iambic pentameter that would put Alexander Pope to shame.

You can't understand what a rare person Mrs. Gwynn was among black women, or even black men, in the 1930s and 1940s unless you know that in that era less than 1 percent of black women and even fewer black men went to college. Miss Bessie had gone to Fisk University in Nashville from 1909 to 1911, attending only the normal school; there she learned a lot about Shakespeare, but most of all about the profound importance of trained intelligence—especially for a people trying to move up from slavery.

"What you put in your head, boy," she said to me one day, "can never be pulled out by the Ku Klux Klan, the Congress, or anybody."

Poor black children in rigidly Jim Crow McMinnville didn't have much of an opportunity to put a lot in their heads in the 1930s and 1940s. Our little school was "no frills" to say the least.

Not only was our high school library outrageously inadequate, but blacks were not allowed to enter the town's Magness Memorial Library except to mop floors, dust tables, or do windows. But, through one of those Old South arrangements secretly arrived at by whites of good conscience and blacks of the stature of Miss Bessie, my teacher kept getting books smuggled out of the white library.

"If you don't read, you can't write, and if you can't write, you can stop dreaming," Miss Bessie told me.

So I read whatever she told me to read and tried to remember what she insisted that I store away.

The night of our graduation, May 25, 1942, three buddies and I walked near the persimmon tree, one guy toting a paper bag that turned out to contain a bottle of corncob wine that someone had gotten from my uncle McKinley Rowan. This product of fermented corncobs looked like horse liniment, tasted worse, and had the kick of a mule, so I grimaced at the prospect of my buddies proposing a toast. After each of us took a throat-burning swig from the bottle, Hogan announced that the three of them had decided to join the Navy the next day.

"You gonna join us and go help fight this war?" he asked me.

"Nope," I replied. "In the Navy a Negro can't be nothing but a cook or a mess attendant. I can't cook, and I don't want to tend mess. I'm going to college so that, when they draft me, I'll have a chance to become an officer."

There was a painful silence, then a soft, "OK, motherfucker." The bottle was passed around again, fists were rammed into shoulders as gestures of farewell, and we went home.

While my buddies went off to the Navy, I went back to the corner of the First National Bank building, waiting for someone to offer the jobs that would earn me enough money to go to college. The ranks of job seekers dwindled rapidly as the draft board swooped up able-bodied blacks, and others volunteered out of a belief that life in the military would have to be better.

So I had plenty of lawns to mow. When I came in from work around sundown I would notice how rapidly the war had become *the reality* in my town. Soldiers from Camp Forrest in Tullahoma seemed everywhere, and the girls of McMinnville were going GI crazy. I considered these guys to be poachers on my territory, so I would go to a movie and then the Slobbery Rock every night just to protect my turf. After playing the big spender one Saturday night, I went home and decided to take inventory of my cash before going to bed.

"My God," I said to myself, "I blew fifty-five cents on that chick tonight!"

But I didn't, or couldn't, change my lifestyle, so I woke up one July morning virtually broke. I had seventy-seven cents left of my go-to-college money. I felt sick just realizing that kids would be entering college in less than two months, and there I lay without even bus fare to Nashville. I told myself, scoldingly, that I'd have been better off joining the Navy with my buddies.

I washed up, made my hair look good with an application of Tuxedo-brand pomade, put on the best clothes I owned and put the rest into a cardboard box. I wrote a note to my parents, who were at work, saying "I've gone to Nashville for college" and went to the McBroom Lines trucking company. I asked a young woman which driver had the run to Nashville; she pointed to him without mumbling a word.

"I need a ride to Nashville real bad," I said to him.

"What's your problem?"

"I just woke up and realized I've been spending all my pay to take girls to movies and the honky-tonk, and I'm left with seventy-seven cents to get me to school."

"Hell, I'll give you a ride. But what school is going to let you in for seventy-seven cents?"

"I'm hoping to get a scholarship at Fisk. The rich boys there play lousy football. I play a helluva left end. Once I get the football scholarship, I'll work and save the money."

The driver looked me over with obvious skepticism. I wasn't sure whether he disbelieved that I played a helluva left end at my modest weight or doubted my vow not to blow my wages next time.

I already had met enough courageous, truly decent white people to know that I could never become an embittered racist. This truck driver reemphasized the rule of life that you judge and value people where and how you find them. He and I had a great conversation en route to Nashville, and not long after we passed Murfreesboro he said: "Hell, with just seventy-seven cents you don't need to hire any taxis or pay streetcar fare. If you can tell me how to get to Fisk, I'll drop you off there."

But that stop at Fisk was a quick and bitter disappointment. I only got to see some low-level guy who almost laughed when I told him I played a helluva left end. "You'd never make it here," he said and just waited for me to pick up my box of clothes and go.

I walked the mile or so to Grandmother Johnigan's house and was relieved somewhat by her warm embrace. My aunts Katie and Dixie, my mother's half sisters, expressed joy to see me again. I told them what a fool I had been all summer and how the guy at Fisk had almost spat in my face.

"You'll make it," my grandmother said in a tone that left no room for doubt. "Your grandfather has a job for you at the hospital—at one dollar a day."

The next morning I took the long journey out to the State Tuberculosis Hospital and got a job mopping floors, delivering food to patients, and getting my face mask incredibly dirty when I brushed down the screens around the porch wards where many patients were placed.

One day a young doctor said to me: "I've been talking with your grandfather, whom we admire very much. I'd like to give you a few things you might find helpful when you enter Tennessee State next month."

"What?"

We walked over to his Ford and he pulled out a couple of suits and a sport coat, all close to brand-new.

"You can't wear these?" I asked.

"Not with this expanding butt and belly. They're yours if you want them."

"God, do I want them! Thank you, sir!"

Later, I told my grandfather that this doctor didn't weigh a pound more than I did. "Do you think he just wanted to give me something decent to wear?"

"We don't know, and if I ever find out I won't tell *you*. Just wear them in ways that would make the doctor proud."

That doctor, whose name I wish I could remember, sure made me proud to be one of the best-dressed freshmen at Tennessee State, no small achievement considering the competition of studs from Pearl

High in Nashville. I would have been a bit ashamed to wear my "strings" onto campus, and this, added to the insecurities arising from my small-school background, would have put terrible pressures on me. But when I showed up in the light gray suit that the doctor had given me, a few coeds looked at me in ways that I interpreted to say, "*You* are *welcome*, Mister."

My new sense of security vanished fast when I learned of the high schools from which my classmates had graduated. But I had no doubts about my abilities regarding algebra and soon found classmates seeking me out for help on tough problems. This alone made me popular enough to get nominated for vice president of the freshman class, a post to which I was elected without opposition.

I was shocked to get A's in every course except algebra and to find that a couple of girls I tutored got A's while I got a B. But I took it philosophically, telling one of the girls, "I'm not coming back next quarter anyhow,'cause I'm broke, so what the hell difference does it make?"

A few days later I stood on the steps of the administration building, saying good-bye to my buddy Joe Bates, laughing with him about how we had struggled through the first quarter with one guy buying a bottle of milk and the other a day-old cake and making a lunch for two.

"I'm so sad to see you go," Joe said. "Before you go, walk with me to the Greasy Spoon so I can get a pack of cigarettes."

"The Greasy Spoon doesn't open till eleven."

"I gotta check,'cause I'm dying for a smoke."

We walked down to the little campus restaurant, and, as I predicted, it was padlocked. Bates and I walked away across the dirt circle where the Dinky Bus made its U-turn, discharging students who would throw their green bus transfers to the ground. The litterbugs seemed to have spread a zillion transfers around.

We had taken a few steps up the sidewalk when something said to me, "Carl Rowan, one of those wads you just passed in the weeds was not a bus transfer." I went back and reached into the weeds.

"Joe," I half shouted, "I just found a bill, and it doesn't look like a one!" I opened the wad to find that it was a twenty-dollar bill.

"Joe," I said, "I just pray to God that whoever lost this money doesn't need it as badly as I do."

I walked straight to the administration building, where I paid my tuition for the second quarter—for three months during which two teachers would give me blessed help.

I was stunned to learn that I was being put in Art 101, An Introduction to Art. Art was hardly heard of at Bernard High. I couldn't draw a box, let alone an apple.

"Jesus," I said to Bates, "if I had known they would sandbag me with this class I'd have gone home to tote bags at Brown's Hotel." I didn't mean it, of course, so I went to Art 101 to find that my teacher was a soft-spoken woman with a lovely brown face, Miss Frances Thompson.

I hated her when, as her first gesture, she asked the students to take a piece of paper and write the grade they expected to get in her class. This art illiterate summoned up a lot of courage and wrote a *C* on his paper. Miss Thompson collected the papers and studied each for a few seconds. "Would Carl Roe-ann from McMinnville please raise his hand?" she asked, mispronouncing my name.

I stuck up a trembling hand.

"Would you please stay after class for a few seconds to talk with me?"

"Ye...ye...yes, ma'am."

When the other students fled the classroom, she opened up an agonizing dialogue.

"Were you surprised that I knew you were from McMinnville?"

"No, ma'am."

"Will it surprise you if I tell you I know every grade you got in high school and at Tennessee State last quarter, and I know you never got a C? Why did you put a C on this piece of paper?"

"I don't know, ma'am."

I sat there paralyzed, like a bunny in a Ferrari's headlights, as she stared at me, finally saying to my relief, "I want to read you something."

Miss Thompson reached into her desk drawer and pulled out a piece of paper containing a quote from Daniel Burnham, a Chicago architect and city planner—words he spoke in 1925, the year of my birth. I listened intently as Miss Thompson quoted Burnham:

Make no little plans, they have no magic to stir men's blood and probably themselves will not be realized. Make big plans; aim high in hope and work, remembering that a noble, logical diagram once recorded will never die, but long after we are gone will be a living thing, asserting itself with evergrowing insistency. Remember that our sons and grandsons are going to do things that would stagger us. Let your watchword be order and your beacon beauty.

Miss Thompson handed me a clean piece of paper. I looked into her eyes once, then wrote a big *A* on it. I still doubt that any teacher in history ever worked harder to help a kid to earn an A in art. That woman had given me a gift far beyond the two suits and the suit coat from the doctor. She had made me believe in myself. She had given me a new measure of self-esteem.

More than thirty years later, I gave a speech in which I mentioned Frances Thompson had given me something that I needed desperately, something money could not have bought even if I had some money. A newspaper printed the story, and someone led a clipping to this beloved teacher. She wrote me a note that brings tears to my wife's eyes till this day:

You have no idea what that newspaper story meant to me, so long in retirement. For a lot of years I endured my brother's arguments that I had wasted my life. That I should have gotten married and had a family. When I read that newspaper article in which you gave me credit for helping to launch a marvelous career, I put the clipping in front of my brother. When he had read it I said, "You see, I didn't really waste my life, did I?"

Frances Thompson was sweet and quietly helpful, history professor Merle Eppse was just the opposite. During the first quarter I learned that his History of Civilization class was an exercise in handling insults. Eppse wanted achievement, scholarship, hard work, and study, and he brooked no excuses. In letting a student know what he expected, he probably went beyond the bounds of professorial behavior that any college should allow.

A McMinnville friend of mine, Vera Sims, and her family had moved to Nashville a couple of years earlier. She was in my class. One day, when she had no answer for an orally proffered Eppse question, he lit into her with a monologue: "I knew you would show up today, sleepy and ignorant, no sign of doing any homework, because I was driving down Jefferson Street last night and saw you out there leaning into some dummy's car. Now you can try to please some no-good jerk and get pregnant, or you can come to class ready to please me and go on to be somebody important....Mr. Roe-ann, tell her the answer to my question."

"My family pronounces it Rhau-wen, sir."

"Oh, goddammit, Roe-ann or Rhau-wen, the question is whether you're trying not to embarrass your old McMinnville buddy. No use you playing a dummy,'cause her favors will still go to that punk who was driving the car she was leaning in. Do you know the answer to my question?"

"I do, sir." I gave the answer to the man who had given me an A in the first quarter and would give me A's in the second and third quarters. Little did I know that this man, hated by so many and loved by a few, would also give me a chance to make history, to live a life I never thought possible.

One morning in the spring of '43 I sat in his class wondering why he was late. Suddenly, Eppse burst into the room, asked a favorite student to take over the class for a few minutes, and said: "Mr. Roe-en, come with me to the dean's office!"

Fear hit me with such force that my heart creased my scalp. In

1943, when a student went to the dean's office, the *student* was in trouble, not the *dean*. We walked to the office of Dean George W. Gore with Eppse saying nary a word.

When we entered, Eppse said to this man who would distinguish himself as an educator: "Here's the boy who's volunteering to join the Navy."

"Muh...muh...me?" I stammered. "I'm not volunteering to join the Navy."

"Yes, you are, boy," Eppse insisted.

Dean Gore raised his hand and said, "Just a minute, Professor Eppse." Then he turned to me and said calmly: "Are you aware that in the entire history of the United States there has never been a Negro officer in the Navy?"

"Yes, sir," I said proudly, "I read the *Pittsburgh Courier*." (This was the leading, nationally circulated black newspaper.)

"Are you also aware that here at all-Negro Tennessee State we often get messages from the government that are intended for the all-white University of Tennessee in Knoxville?"

"No, sir, I didn't know that."

"Well, let me show you a series of telegrams between the Navy Department and Tennessee State."

Gore read one from the Navy asking that Tennessee State have students take a national examination for admission to the Navy V–12 program to send officer candidates to reserve midshipman schools. Then he showed me his telegram asking the Navy, "Do you really mean *us*?" And he handed me the Navy's reply, "Yes, we mean *you*."

Gore gave me a solemn look and explained, "We don't want Tennessee State embarrassed. Someone here has got to pass this exam. So I've asked Professors Eppse and Boswell to pick out a half-dozen young men who might pass that exam, and Professor Eppse has chosen you. That is a wonderful endorsement from your professor. So I know that out of your loyalty to Professor Eppse, and to Tennessee State, and to your race, you are going to—"

"Yes, sir," I interrupted. "I volunteer to join the Navy!"

I went on to get all A's that third quarter at Tennessee State—and to pass the Navy exam. Meanwhile, part of my world was falling in around me.

My father had gambled himself into a hole and taken loans against the home he had bought with his World War I bonus. I understood why I had, in a year, received from my parents only three dollars to sustain me in college, but I had no idea that my mother was taking extra work as a domestic, sending my brother, Charles, down the railroad tracks to drum up extra laundry business, hoping to earn enough to save the home. She failed, and in desperation began to drink more and more.

Not that I could have stopped it, since I had no money, but the sheriff held an auction at which that little frame house was stripped away from my family without anyone telling me until years later, when my sister Jewel said, "You know, we're just renting this place now." Soon after Jewel spoke to me they were thrown out for failing to pay the rent.

My family had no telephone, so letters were the only way to stay in touch. I didn't write often, because I was so dedicated to succeeding. When I wrote, it might be a month before I got a reply, which invariably was full of bad news about which parent was getting drunk, who hurt whom in a marital brawl, how economically desperate the whole family was. I would become so depressed that for a day or two I could not concentrate on my studies. Subconsciously, I opted for an "out of sight, out of mind" existence. In pursuit of a dream, I was leaving my family behind.

Meanwhile, Grandmother Ella became sick from what the doctor told me was elephantiasis. He complained that "she hasn't always taken her medicine."

"I know," I said. "I now am convinced that she used her medicine money to keep me in college and in the running for a Navy commission."

Passing the written examination provided no sure entry into V–12 and midshipman's school. I had to get past two white Navy interviewers in Nashville, and then a physical exam.

"If one of 'em doesn't get you, the other will," said a skeptical professor.

"You will make it, son," my grandmother said the day I left for the interviews and the physical. She died a few days before I was notified that I had passed all exams and was to await assignment to a V–12 program.

At summer quarter's end, I went back to McMinnville, to the Edge-field Street house into which my family had moved after losing our Congo Street place. I had a card showing that I was in the Naval Reserve, awaiting assignment—a card that gave me protection from many local cops and military policemen who sometimes asked openly what "an able-bodied nigger is doing walking the streets."

That summer of '43 I ceased being a "black boy" and came to think of myself as a man.

By 1943, the local draft board had almost cleared the town of able-bodied Negroes (even though the Marines didn't want any blacks, the Navy wanted very few, and the Army wanted only so many as could fit into all-black units). The drafters of McMinnville figured they could not send white boys to war while black bucks were to be seen leaning against the bank building at Spring Street and Main.

But I was undraftable, with the Navy having a claim on me. So a lot of whites figured that I would handle a greater-than-normal share of their dirty work. They had no way of knowing that my status as a potential Navy officer, my year at college in an environment drastically different from McMinnville, had created revulsion in me for all the economic and social rules of my hometown. Even I did not realize that a year away from this little red-clay town had given me an air of haughtiness that would antagonize the white citizens for whom I had worked for years.

When a white person drove up to my little house on Edgefield Street and said he or she wanted someone to mow a lawn or serve food or wash dishes at a party, I did not take the easy way out, saying, "I have another job." I laced on the sarcasm of refusal by saying, "I'm giving a dinner tonight. You know anybody who might work for me?"

I was what the barber for whom I once worked called "a rebellious little sonofabitch." Rebellious I was. I flaunted my naval exemption every time a military policeman or local cop stopped me to inquire why I was strolling Main Street at midday in a suit and tie.

It was late October when I received orders to report to Washburn Municipal University of Topeka, Kansas. I had never heard of Washburn and thought how ironic it was that I could not go to the public library to learn something about it. I had only a general idea of the route to Topeka, since I still had never been out of Tennessee except for the time our football-team bus got lost and accidentally crossed into Alabama. But I had Navy travel orders that made it clear which trains I should take from where to where.

It has been said—correctly—that war is hell. This war turned out to be the great liberator, for it gave me a national mission of honor that would open up new horizons of opportunity and potential achievement.

IMAMU AMIRI BARAKA
(1934–)

From *The Autobiography of LeRoi Jones*

Things looked good for young LeRoi Jones. He came from a secure, lower-middle class black background in Newark, New Jersey—he had the childhood comfort that everything would be all right and nothing bad could happen. His mother had attended Fisk, and he also did well in school. When he dropped out of college and then was dishonorably discharged from the Air Force, it seemed he was going to fulfill his mother's nightmare that he would not amount to anything.

Today Amiri Baraka (LeRoi Jones) makes just about anyone's list of who's who. He's written plays, fiction, nonfiction, and poetry; he's been awarded a Whitney Fellowship and a Guggenheim Fellowship. He's taught at Columbia, Yale, and State University of New York at Stony Brook.

After leaving the Air Force, Baraka moved to Greenwich Village and began to write. He met and corresponded with the Beat artists of the era, published a literary magazine with his wife, and wrote his first book, Blues People. *Soon after his first play was produced, Baraka rejected white downtown society, moved to Harlem, and embraced political activism, putting together an incipient African cultural nationalism. Although his views have since changed, he hasn't stopped writing or fighting since.*

This excerpt, from Baraka's autobiography, captures the essence of his youth in Newark.

The games and sports of the playground and streets was one registration carried with us as long as we live. Our conduct, strategies and tactics, our ranking and comradeship. Our wins and losses. (Like I was a terrible terrible loser and still am.) I would fight, do anything to stop losing. I would play super-hard, attacking, with endless energy, to stop a loss. I would shout and drive my team on. Stick my hands in the opponents' faces, guard them chest to chest, or slash through the line from the backfield and catch them as they got the pass back from center. Or take the passes and cut around end and streak for the goal. Or double-step, skip, stop, leap, jump back, ram, twist, hop, back up, duck, get away, hustle, and rush into the end zone. I could leap and catch passes one-handed, backwards, on my back, on the run, over someone's shoulder, and take it in. And mostly I never got hurt. I had a fearlessness in games and sports. A feeling that I could win, that I could outrun or outhustle or outscramble or rassle or whatever to pull it out. I would slide head first into home, even first. On tar and cement. I would turn bunts into home runs, by just putting my head down and raging around the bases.

In ring-a-leerio, I was always with the little guys and I actually liked that. There was always more of us allowed on the team, cause we were little. But our secret was that we were fast and shifty. I had one move where just as the big boy would be about to snatch me after the run, I'd stop short very suddenly and duck down, and this would send this big dude literally flying over my shoulders. Me, Johnny Boy Holmes, Skippy, and a few others patented that move. So they had to be wary and not run so hard after you and instead try to hem you in and get a couple or three of them to run us down. So we were the dangerous ringy players. And sometimes we'd even break loose and slide into the box and free the others already caught. Streaking into the box, which was marked on the ground, and against the fence of one side of the playground, "Ring-a-leerio," we'd scream, whoever got that honor of charging through the ring of big boys to free the others. Sometimes we'd form a kind of flying wedge and come barreling in. But some other times them big dudes would smash us, block us, knock us down. Or if we didn't have our thing together, some of the really fast and shifty dudes wasn't playing for instance, they'd chop us off one by one and you had a hell of time if it was the big boys' time to run out to stop those dudes. But we could and did. If there was enough of us we'd roam in twos and threes and tackle them suckers and sit on them. But you also had to get them back to the box, and they'd be struggling and pulling and that could be worse than just catching them.

But ringy was the top game for my money. It involved all the senses and all the skills and might and main of little-boydom. We played everything, baseball, basketball, football, all day every day, according to what season it was (though we'd play basketball all the time, regardless of what the big leagues was doing). But Ringy was something else again. I'd like to see a big-league ringy game and league. It's just war pursuit and liberation without weapons. Imagine a ringy game in Yankee Stadium, with karate, boxing, wrestling, great speed, evasion tactics, plus the overall military strategy and tactics that would have to be used. That would really be something.

Ringy got you so you could get away from any assault and at the same time fear no one in terms of running directly against big odds trying to free your brothers in the box. And sometimes if you were the only one left, and could keep the bigs darting and running and twisting, and outspeeding them, with the whole playground watching, that was really something, really gratifying.

Another teaching experience I had was the game "Morning." It had its variations, "Afternoon," and perhaps there was also an "Evening," though I don't think so. "Morning" happened in the mornings. The first time we came in contact with each other the first one to see the other could hit him, saying, "Morning." And though the other varia- tions probably could be played, "Morning" was most happening I guess because at that time it was the first confrontation of the day and folks just getting up could be unawares and thus bashed.

And these suckers who most liked to play "Morning" were not kidding. When they hit they was trying to tear your shoulder off. The shoulder was the place most often hit. The real killers like this dude Big Shot would sneak up on you and hit you in the small of the back and that would take most people down and rolling on the ground in pain. Sometimes actual tears.

Close friends wouldn't actually play it or they wouldn't actually hit each other and if they did it wouldn't be a crushing blow. They'd just make believe they were playing it to keep you on your toes. But killers like Shot and some other dudes, little ugly Diddy and dudes like that, would actually try to take you off the planet.

If there was a slight tension, an outdoing or competitive thing, between dudes they would use "Morning" as an excuse to get off. But then the only thing that meant is that the other guy would come creeping around looking for an opening to bash the other one. I got hit a couple times, most times not hard—these were my main men who did it, cause I'd be watching, jim. I was not going to get "Morn- inged" too often. And I caught a couple of them terrible snake-ass niggers a couple times and tried to tear 'em up, though they were taller and huskier, so my mashing punch was more embarrassment and aggravation than physical wipeout. I got Shot one time and jumped off my feet punching this sucker in his back and he got mad (which was supposed to be against the "rules") and he started chasing me around the playground. But then he really got embarrassed, be- cause his ass was too heavy to catch me. I motored away from him, ducking and twisting, just like in ringy. And finally he got tired and

people was laid out on the fence of the playground laughing at his
sorry ass.

But then he runs over to my main man Love and catches him. You
see, you were supposed to say, "Morning," then the other dude
couldn't hit you. So Shot zooms over and catches Love right between
the shoulder blades and damn near killed him. Love and Shot were
always on the verge of going around anyway. Love had a close-cut
haircut and a funny, bony-looking head, according to us. And we
called him bonehead or saddlehead or some such. But it was the
usual joke time. With Shot it was some kind of bitter rebuke, cause
Love could play ball—any kind of ball—Shot couldn't do nothing but
terrorize people with his ugly-ass self.

Love was hurt but when he come up a fight almost started, and
then goddam Shot wanted to talk about the "rules." "Like how come
Love wanna fight . . . he just don't know how to play the goddam game.
If you a sissie you can't play."

"How come you can play then, Shot?" And people cracked up,
knowing he could not catch me. But from then on I had to watch Shot
very close.

The "rules." And he had just broke 'em himself. People like that I
knew about early. And also I learned how to terrorize the terrorizers.

The Dozens. You know the African Recrimination Songs! Yeh yeh,
see, I gotta anthropological tip for you as well. But Dozens always
floated around every whichaway, around my way, when you was small.
Or with close friends, half lit, when you got big. But that was either
fun, for fun-connected folks, or the sign that soon somebody's blood
would be spilt.

The lesson? The importance of language and invention. The place
of innovation. The heaviness of "high speech" and rhythm. And their
use. Not in abstract literary intaglios but on the sidewalk (or tar) in
the playground, with everything at stake, even your ass. How to rhyme.
How to reach in your head to its outermost reaches. How to invent
and create. Your mother's a man—Your father's a woman. Your
mother drink her own bath water—Your mother drink other people's.
Your mother wear combat boots—Your mother don't wear no shoes
at all with her country ass, she just come up here last week playin a
goddam harmonica. Or the rhymed variations. I fucked your mama
under a tree, she told everybody she wanted to marry me.—I fucked
your mama in the corner saloon, people want to know was I fucking
a baboon. Or: Your mother got a dick—Your mother got a dick bigger
than your fathers! Point and Counterpoint. Shot and Countershot. Up
and One Up.

(In the late 60's I was going through some usual state harassment—
to wit, I had supposedly cussed out a policeman in a bank. The truth
being that this dude had been harassing us every few evenings, riding
by the house, making remarks to the women, creep gestures at us,

&c. So he comes in this bank with a shotgun out on "bank patrol" and starts talking loudly about George Wallace, who was running for President. Hooking him up with some local creep, Imperiale, and saying he was voting for Wallace. I said, "You should, it's your brother!" Or something like that. There was an ensuing baiting, a scuffle, more cops summoned, and three of us who'd been in this bank talking bad to the cop, then cops, got taken away. But it was later thrown out because the prosecution said I'd baited the copy by talking about his father. My attorney and I pointed out that while that might be the mores of Irish Americans [the prosecutor] African Americans focused on de mama, so it was an obvious frame. The judge blinked, hmmm, case dismissed. Some street anthropology. And if you could've been there, Judge, in them playgrounds, and heard it, you'd see my point. But, miraculously, he did.)

I learned that you could keep people off you if you were mouth-dangerous as well as physically capable. But being Ebony Streak also helped just in case you had to express some physical adroitness. Cause your mouth might get your ass into a situation it could not handle! In which case it was the best thing to rapidly change your landscape.

Fighting, avoiding fights, observing fights, knowing when and when not to fight, were all part of our open-air playground-street side education. And fights were so constant, a kind of staged event of varying seriousness. Sometimes very serious. Sometimes just a diversion, for everyone. Like two dudes or girls woofing. Woof woof woof woof woof. They'd be standing somewhere, maybe the hands on the hips, the chicks especially, hands on hips. Maybe one hand gesturing. Or each with one hand on the hip and one hand gesturing. Or they'd get closer and closer. In the purely jive fights the audience would get drugged and push the would-be combatants into each other and that could either start a real fight or it would reveal the totally jive nature of the contest.

And these girls, the black ones, in Central would really get down. There were a couple, Edna, Charlene, plus Laverne and some others, who was so bad that dudes seriously didn't want to get into nothing with them. (Last time I saw Edna years later she was giving some white folks hell in Irvington about them trying to jack her kids up in that school near the Newark city line. When I saw her, shit, these motherfuckers just do not know what they are about to get into. I saw Edna kick so many little girls' asses when she was a not so little girl—she wasn't never really *little* when I was knowin her. She even jumped on some dudes and run 'em up Central Avenue with they eyes rollin.)

And they would fight. After school every day. The famous ones every other day. The corner of Newark Street and Central Avenue, a rumble. And when it was female, hey man, skirts rolling up, drawers in the wind. Dudes would press close up on that just to peep the flesh. But there were some terrible rumbles—clash and noise and conflict—eyes on fire. And the gathering of kids in motion to see, themselves a wild event. But we never got to the outer edge with the chicks' struggles. We thought they were serious, some even scary— as to the violence—but none we perceived as *deadly,* as when the dudes would get down. And then when a couple of famous knucklers and especially when they were representing some clear faction in the broader community, yeh, then that would seem deadly, deadly, like indeed death was easing close to our faces and our eyes would be propped open like at a horror movie with our favorites sounded loud, only if we were with one of the factions.

Yet, compared to today's constant communications of outright death in the streets every day, especially from the gangs, our clashes of yesterday seem tame. But then, death in those times was mostly unthinkable, though it happened. But when you fought you did not expect anybody to have a knife, let alone a piece. When today the pulling of shanks is normal, and guns, just about.

There were the gang clashes later that I knew about and almost got mashed up in several times. The story "The Screamers" talks about this, and in *The System of Dante's Hell.* I was caught between a small war inside a party between The Dukes and The North Newark Dudes. Hey, there was meat cleavers flying around in that one (during my teenage hip blue-light party roamings), the thing smacked my green Tyrolean lid off my head and sent me scrambling into the prone bodies. And there was a gang named The Geeks, uh uhm uhmp, the name itself could freeze you in your thirteen-year-old pimples. And those were titanic to us then, but the memory gets blunted by today's horrific reality, the projection of the dying monster trying to kill all life as it books.

But we had more experience day by day with individual confrontations. Gangs rose up in my experience more directly in my later teenage times.

Matthew Holden vs. Baxter Terrace's color bearer, Larry Thomas, was one standout of fixed tension and underlying terror. Matthew was known around Central Avenue as about the baddest of the big boys. He'd been kept back in school because he came up out of the South, so he was sixteen and in the eighth grade, just like the dead Haley. Matthew was big, lean, fast, and strong. He excelled at all sports and was a likable kind of guy but took absolutely no shit. We littler ones laughed with him sometimes and he might get upset if we said some off-the-wall stuff, like made mock of his Southern speech, and what's more, if you did you'd take two or three steps and he'd have your ass by the collar and punch you in your shoulder paralyzing you. But he didn't "take tech" as some of the monsters like Shot or

Diddy might. He was a straight-ahead dude, only you couldn't mess with him.

Thomas I knew only vaguely by rep. He was from Baxter Terrace, and about the same age as Matthew, only he had been born, I guess, up North, so he was already in high school. He was shorter than Matthew, stocky, built up, already playing high school football. And the Baxters relied on him as their baddest dude.

Baxter Terrace was actually in our neighborhood and most of the younger kids went to Central Avenue with us. But they had a Baxter Terrace playground in those projects where they played after school. And they had teams in another league, so there was some distance, though they played with us and around us often enough.

The fight was almost like some Passion play. It happened in the middle of the playground, a crowd had formed and the two moved around inside that thick crowd armed and slowed with tension. The crowd itself had ranged around like two halves of some giant organic creature, with much leering and balling of fists and the shouting somehow strained and shallow. Each half connected itself from the inside with its champion. For one thing, I didn't understand how this dude Larry expected he could seriously take on Matthew. That seemed dumb, but the fact that he did do that seemed to breach something important, it seemed a nasty corny affront and I thought he should be made to disappear.

Actually not much went on, there was much scrambling and twisting. Some blows got struck, none decisive. I think before it went too far both sides had somehow intervened. Perhaps neither the Baxter Terraces nor we Central Avenues wanted this conflict to go full up. It would have been too damaging. There was such fire in the preliminaries, and the feeling that this was it. That an Armageddon lurked in this conflict for us. Perhaps the world would blow up or split into pieces.

But for all that playground diplomacy, that tiff was deep. I know I kept some tension and distance with regards to Baxter Terrace after that, though I certainly had friends, even a couple girlfriends over there. But the feeling that the place and the people were *other* remained. And when we played their teams baseball or basketball that tension and resentment always partially surfaced.

So despite our various lives somehow there was a collective passion, a collective life, generated by our presence together on those streets, in that playground, and in that school. A collective description of us (whatever it was) that we had internalized. There were no real gangs at my age group (turning thirteen) but under that generalized dome of our youth there were indeed factions that could be mobilized more tightly by some threatened hostility.

* * *

I did belong to a basketball team, actually it was an ASC (Athletic Social Club)—most of the clubs and teams were termed such. Ours was the Cavaliers. This was junior high and early high school, when we were tightest. Really from late grammar school to middle high school, I guess. We won trophies in the junior league inside Central Avenue (which was an elementary school). Some of us had been in school together for some time. There was Love, Hines, Johnny Boy, Snooky, Skippy, Barry, J. D., and me at one time. Later, Johnny Boy, Skippy, and J. D. dropped out and Bob and Earl Early came in, then Leon and Dick plus Sess and Ray and toward the end even big Sleepy, who could have been a pro. We gave a couple dances through the years. When we got into high school we gave a few sets at Club Harold and made a little money. (Also most of us were on a baseball team called the Newark Cubs and with our country manager with big ideas we thought we were semipro and still in high school.)

But we could play ball and we had a good reputation, as ball players. We never came on like fighters. We were ball players and a couple dudes thought they was lovers.

We got our name from a group of older boys, also athletes, that we admired, called the Caballeros. And we picked out Cavaliers because it sounded like Caballeros, and now I know it's the same word. And that was our sense of ourselves, Knights, gentlemen of a certain kind. Later we even got some way-out jackets—red, white, and blue—reversible jackets with a white satin side and a blue wool side, both with the head of a Cavalier, slightly cross-eyed and staring off into space. I wanted hoods on the jacket, but that was voted down in some strange manner I have never been able to fathom. I thought we had decided to get hoods but when we got to the store that Saturday afternoon after we had paid all our money and the guy brought out the jackets, there were no hoods. I said, "Where's the hoods?" And everybody laughed. I was embarrassed and dropped the subject, but I never understood what happened to the hoods. But probably somebody undermined that idea behind my back.

I treasured that jacket, and would probably wear it today if it didn't get lost or stolen. I spilt ink on the satin side (which I am still doing today). But otherwise, until I got deep into high school and got a letter jacket, my Cavalier jacket was me in my high street style.

Basketball was our maximum game. In elementary school I was number 6 man, in junior high I got moved down, by high school I was about 8, definitely not a starter. But I almost never minded because we had a great team within our limitations (which we occasionally were well exposed to) and a great street rep that made you strut just to be a Cavalier, jim. I was a playmaker, a guard, me and Barry would bring the ball down and set up the plays. I was never a great shooter, but I could move the ball and connect with those passes. I got big off assists. But if I got matched with a small man I would go into my scoring act—such as it was.

Sometimes, in those games, in those various leagues we played in, even in some neighboring towns, as we got older, there was some element of violence, like we thought we might have to fight. And we would if pressed, but we was, like gentlemen, athletes, and lovers, not no head beaters.

We'd even tease each other after such encounters about how we knew we was going to fade. Especially we'd get on Love, everybody always teased him, because he was such a great player but so totally unsophisticated and country-like off the court. We'd say, "Love's ass was already down the street when this other dude was looking to fight. He'd have to be Rocket Man to catch Love's ass." But, in reality, we would do whatever the moment called for but we never fancied ourselves pugs.

I had the most mouth on the court. Constantly talking to the other team, harassing them, face-guarding them, stealing the ball. I guess to make up for my light shot. And that could stir up the other team where they wanted to "kick that little nigger's ass" but that never happened. Once we did get run out of this "country" town just west of Newark called Vaux Hall. We played baseball up there in what looked like a cow pasture. And we always had stories about the Negroes in Vaux Hall. But one night we played basketball up there and at the end of the game, because of some kind of encounter, we had to motor on down Springfield Avenue for several blocks until we got out of harm's way. We blamed that on Love too.

The focus of that club changed as we got older. Love and Hines, who were best friends, both went on to Central High School, and they were the emotional and spiritual center of our group, especially as an athletic team. And they began to gather dudes from Central High onto the squad. There was a heavy social underpinning to the club/team and when we were all in Central Avenue that was the focus. I went off to McKinley Junior High and later Barringer, which was almost all Italian, so I couldn't bring too many onto the squad or into the social circle that formed the basis for our team. So my influence, such as it was, lessened. Though Sess, who was a high school star, did come in from Barringer and he brought Ray, who went to South Side (now Malcolm X Shabazz), because they lived in the same project on Waverly Avenue cross town. Later I moved back cross town, onto The Hill again, around my junior year in high school, so Sess and Ray and I got tight. But Leon, Bobby, Earl, Dick, Barry (plus Love, Hines, and Snooky) were all Central High dudes, so that was the social and athletic center of the team when we were in our early high school days.

From time to time I see some of the old Cavaliers, and there is still that bond of fondness held high by memory. I know now that the club/team was a mixture of the lower middle class and the workers (and a couple of peasants turned workers just a couple minutes ago). But by high school the winnowing process had seriously begun. Central was a technical and commercial high school, Barringer supposedly college prep. And we had a couple dudes from West Side and South Side (a mixture of both, plus business) and so we got sprayed out into auto plants, utilities, electronic tube factories, mechanics, white-collar paper shuffling, teachers, small businessmen, security guards, commercial artists, and even a goddam poet.

For us, athletics was art, a high expression of culture. And as athletes the only expression of that, within the other framework of society, was as cool, dignified, profilin' dudes, self-sustaining and collective, but individually distinctive. That was at our best. At our worst, wow, we would mess with people. Especially egged on by one dude Love and Hines hooked up with later. Although we was all mischievous and even at times, from the narrow perch of that limited collectivity, somewhat arbitrary and cruel. I mean sometimes we would tap old dudes on the shoulder walking down the street, or say out-of-the-way things to women minding their business, or flip somebody's hat off they head, and shoot up the street laughing. We were great agitators. And mostly we agitated among ourselves. We would throw each other's hats and bags, nip each other's sneakers and run off with them. Talk about each other like dogs and about each other's mamas even worse. But we were comrades most of us—as it went on, some gaps grew in that fabric, because of the different social situations we got into—but at its strongest it was something to be treasured and now looked back at with great feeling.

By high school I'd gotten into several different sectors of community or social life that complicated my life somewhat, even more than I knew. But that was a constant in my life I recognized, change. And though sometimes it saddened me and I regretted it, I saw after a while that that was what was happening.

So there was a mist-life while very young on Barclay Street in the Douglas-Harrison apartments (and I always, for a long time, dug those small red buildings and park in the back with green slat benches. And even the people that seemed to live there. Sometimes I longed for those people, in some not totally explained way), but we had to cut out. And then Boston Street, two sites, one near South Orange Avenue and then for a minute in my grandparents' house up the street, near West Market. (I had a late-night knee operation in the last house, under oil lamps my knee formed a silhouette against the greenish wall and a baldhead doctor with a red wig—a blood with red freckles—meticulously picked the glass out of my messed-up knee while the family stood in one corner and watched.) That was right down the street from my grandfather's store which had closed in the Depression, though the tale persisted in our family that it was because my grandfather gave out too much credit—it was implied—to ungrateful niggers. Which meant simply that that is the myth they wanted to invest their lives with, not understanding the actual political economy of this United Snakes. And how depression always kills off the petty and small bourgeoisie rat away!

But the bias of that description is to put down both Tom Russ and black people, but not the ugly thang that actual did de damage! And so the twist you inherit of seeing from who teaches you to see. But the whole I came only much later to see and only now to sum up.

From there we went to Dey Street and the orange-red casa of my coming to little-boy consciousness. That was the center of my little-boy life. Central Avenue School, the playground, the evening recreation program we called "The Court" for some reason, The Secret Seven, wild fights, my athletic training, the Cavaliers, some of the remembered paths and lessons and teachers of whatever style, and even my first full-up meeting with white folks, though on my turf.

There was some other heavy stuff I found out and got into in them Dey Street days, a little romance, the church, and the Newark Eagles, and they need to be talked about. Why? Because they had something to do with it—the shaping, the answering—of the question how did you get to be you?

For one thing, the whites, almost all Italians and a few Irish and a German or two around somewhere, were definitely at the fringe, as I said before, of most of the Dey Street world. Not that they were sealed off by us in any way. It was just how we related, the deep cultural connects and the invisible and not so invisible antecedents of social organization. It seems obvious now that the blacks were expanding in all directions even then. And our westward thrust was some kind of frontier. We were aware that a few blocks away the world changed and Italians lived in growing numbers.

And though they were on the fringe of the Dey Street life there were some distinct and concrete effects of their existence among us, and out beyond us. A couple of them could play ball, like Augie D., for instance, but we thought in the main their game was baseball. As little boys we played mixed teams, but at another point the teams were mostly black, and then you could get a black vs. white game, which was still not much until we got older and it began to reflect and take on the tension of the whole society.

By the time we were teenagers we were playing all-white baseball teams and those games were for something other than little-boy note. The baseball team we put together always talked about playing the white teams for cases of beer, but most of us were teetotalers and that didn't mean much to us.

Then there was the weird situation in which we actually by time of seventh grade or so began to take certain liberties with the white girls that we did not would not had better not take with the black ones. Like a couple big ol' (for seventh grade) white girls I knew, we would "feel up" in the cloakroom. It never dawned on me to delve into why or maybe it did and I couldn't. But we certainly liked quite a few of the little black girls we went to school with but we would no more think of feeling any of them...except certain rogues I'm told did feel on certain of the wilder-repped sisters and that would cause a small shooting war in most cases. Maybe the other cases where that meant something else were kept from me young gourd by the benevolent moralists of me age. But some dudes later as we got into junior high would brag about women. What they did. But none of that was too clear to me anyway. That was real mystery. And there were a couple of these white girls who'd giggle and push you away, like they dug it. My God, what would they Italian fathers and brothers have said at seeing that. Wow, it makes me shudder even now.

And Augie was the first in the neighborhood I knew about to get a TV. (I remember clear as a bell when we got our first telephone—on Dey Street. MI 2–5921. Our first electric refrigerator—a Kelvinator, and we called it that, exchanging the brand name for the genre. We had to put quarters in it to keep it going. We didn't get our first TV until I was about thirteen or fourteen, one year I came back from summer Boy Scout camp and walked into the house and there was a 14-inch Motorola, later we got a 17-inch, we never had a really big screen when it was hip to brag about that.) But we would, some of us, pile up in Augie's house to watch the TV. Augie's father was some kind of worker, a medium-sized guy with black hair gray at the edges. He never said much, just nodded to us. I wonder what he thought about the crowd of colored kids that would push in there to watch that early tube.

But later I could tell that something was happening in the whole of that Dey Street/Newark Street/Lock Street world, bounded by Central and Sussex Avenues, when Augie began to say certain things. Like one time we were sitting on the auditorium steps in the playground bullshitting about something and he was combing his hair. Augie loved to comb his goddam hair, and I think his little brother was with him and fat (white) Norman and maybe staring Johnny, who had the weird disease that made him go into trances at odd times. So I says to Augie to lemme use the comb. My hair was always cut very close, we called them "Germans" the way our hair was cut. And later a little longer on the top and front was called a "German bush." But Augie nixes me and says, "Don't mix the breeds."

I didn't know what the fuck he was talking about, "Don't mix the breeds." Huh? I said. Huh? Whatta you talking about, ol' bean, don't mix the breeds? (Not exactly in those words, ya know.) But he says it again. And I did get the meaning. I got it the first fucking time, not literally but generally and emotionally and psychologically I understood exactly what he meant. And hey, I didn't even get mad. It didn't even faze me. Actually it confirmed some upside-down shit I had in my head. That we were white and black. And I knew the abstract social history of that. I also knew what I saw every day in various ways that manifested some meaning and connection with what Augie was saying.

Shit, I saw Mantan Moreland and Amos and Andy and Beulah and Stepin Fetchit. I knew what "Feets, don't fail me now" meant. And who Birmingham really was. And why Ellic in the Bob Hope picture *Ghost Breakers* had got so scared in the clock that when it opened he stood there shivering and turned completely white. I had seen Butterfly McQueen and Hattie McDaniel and Louise Beavers. I had seen the wild-eyed woogies in *Tarzan* and how knowledgeable Tarzan was. I had seen Al Jolson do his bullshit—hey and most of that *was* funny. HaHaHaHaHaHaHaHaHaHaHaHaHaHaHaHaHaHaHaHaHa (except Al Jolson, he wasn't shit). But still, anyway, down beneath that actual laughter there was something else. Besides the embarrassment and even shame for the feebleminded, beneath all that, boys and girls, there was something else that it took me a long time to fully dig. (I'll tell you about it later!)

Sure, I knew exactly what my best white friend Augie was saying, and I knew instinctively that his mother had probably put that shit in his head. What could have been the expression on my little round brown face with the big comical eyes? But what does it mean then, on the actual sidewalks and playgrounds of our lives? Whatever I said, it could only have been an acknowledgement of the time the place the condition. Like a fucking flag salute.

Another time, I'm hiking Augie, like his mother had all this gray hair and I'm calling her the Gray Terror, like we did. But Augie, then, pauses and asks me what color my mother's hair is. And I, like a sap, say black, which it was. And Augie looks half-eyed at I donno who, Normie or somebody, and says, "The Black Terror." It was a good hike, I guess. I ain't gonna be an objectivity freak—its my funking memoirs—but more than the hike *qua* hike was the thing it really raised, that Augie really was putting into the game that which could not have been kept out in any real take on the world. But it let you know that all that was abstract to you, about black and white and all that, was not really abstract, that it all could not be waved away, or laughed away, or forgot or not known about. It meant to me that there was real shit over which I did not have total control, that I did not even properly understand. And I could be, on such occasions, quietly stunned. Turned inward and set adrift in a world of my feelings I couldn't yet deal with.

Those were some of the steps, the paths, of our divergence. And I told you how in high school (at least for me) the old relationships completely fell apart. For one thing, it was an Italian high school and junior high I went to. (Heading for college prep in my jumbled-up but crystal-clear head.) And so all things were openly reversed. The Italians now sat in center stage and controlled the social life of those two institutions. And year after year (only four, really), I went through various kinds of bullshit and humiliations that actually made me feel at one point that I hated Italians straight out.

(Earlier, in the seventh grade, we'd gone to the Bronx Zoo, and I'm lagging behind in the elephant house, holding my nose but wanting to check close up on the elephants. So I see this guy, he's cleaning up or something in there, and I ask him, "Wow, how do you stand it in here?" Meaning the terrible odor of elephant shit. So he says to me, "I don't mind it. I live in Harlem." Yeh, a white guy said this, and it went through me like a frozen knife. And I knew exactly what he meant. Except I also wondered, even right then at that ugly moment, why he wanted to drop that kind of shit on me. I knew he was attacking me, saying a bad thing to me, my big eyes must have wheeled and caught his face for a second, then dropped down into the zoo dirt, and carried the rest of me out of there. But what did that do, I wonder, for Mr. Elephant Shit Shoveler to say that? Did it make him feel good or heroic or like he wasn't really shoveling elephant shit? And all that was nestled tightly in me gourd by time I got out of grammar school. And Augie's words and news of "race riots" and even a couple run-ins my mother had with cut-rate racists, one in a candy store down-town—the lady wanted to sell her some "nigger toes"—my mother says, "Those are Brazil nuts, lady," grabs my hand and stalks out. Later she had a near-rumble with a bus driver who wanted to talk to her funny. I took all that in, and carried it, carried it with me—who knows when you need such experiences? I felt subconsciously.)

But I was totally unprepared for the McKinley and Barringer experiences in which the whites ran the social and academic part of that institutional life. And I put up with many nigger callings and off-the-wall comments and intimidations, even getting cussed out regularly in Italian. I even learned Italian curse words (though not many precise meanings) and would fling them back sometimes. But I tried to hold my own. For instance, when a big schizophrenic white boy— a blond dude named Joe S.—threw a ball at me in the McKinley playground not long after I got there, I flung the bat at his head. The other white dudes kept him off me.

And later in school I developed an interior life that was split obviously like the exterior life. One half tied to Dey Street while we still lived there and the black life of the playground and streets. And the other tied to the school experiences of McKinley and Barringer. It must be true, maybe obvious, that the schizophrenic tenor of some of my life gets fueled from these initial sources (and farther back with words whispered into the little boy's ear, from mouths and radios). But the white thing was only periphery in me young days, a fringe thing I didn't even recognize. And then to go into McKinley and then

Barringer and be in a white world ruled by white Italians whose most consistent emotion regarding me was unconcern, that took me up by the ankles and dangled me in *no* space and put *not*'s in my head and *not me*'s.

The life of emotion, which is historical, like anything else, gets warped in high school I'm certain now. And to understand I must go back now several years to give a picture of one side of my life, feelings, mind, head, and then come back to this threshold of pain, then we can draw conclusions together!

RALPH DAVID ABERNATHY

(1926–1989)

From *And the Walls Came Tumbling Down*

When Ralph David Abernathy was born, the attending midwife predicted he would grow up into a man known throughout the world. The tenth of the twelve Abernathy children fulfilled that prophecy. During the heat of the civil rights movement, he fought the system that threatened the rights of the midwife's children and grandchildren.

All in all, Abernathy had a comparatively good childhood in rural Alabama. His father farmed over five hundred acres, and the family never wanted for much. His father was stern, hard-working, and respected in the local community. His mother was tender, supportive, and nurturing. Both were dedicated Baptists, and from an early age, Abernathy wanted to be a preacher.

When he was eighteen, he was drafted to fight in World War II but was sent home with rheumatic fever before he had a chance to confront his opposition to killing, even in war. After the war, he studied at Alabama State University in Montgomery and led his first nonviolent demonstration there—a hunger strike against truly terrible cafeteria food. Later he earned his master's degree at Atlanta University and met Martin Luther King, Jr. Abernathy returned to Alabama and soon became pastor of a large Baptist church in Montgomery.

When King moved to Montgomery, the two discovered a common vision of an active Gospel for social change. They discussed theory and tactics for the times to come and were well placed on that December day when Rosa Parks refused to give her bus seat to a white man. And so from Montgomery to Memphis, Abernathy *and King were at the heart of the civil rights movement. And after King's assassination, Abernathy continued the fight as head of the Southern Christian Leadership Conference.*

What in Abernathy's background gave him the fortitude to practice nonviolent protest in the face of snarling dogs and deadly bombs? This excerpt from his autobiography gives a sense of the stability, dignity, and love that made up his childhood.

In those days childhood was not all play, at least not in the country. On a family farm everybody worked; and while young people today look on such a life as tedious and hard, it had its advantages. For one thing, none of the children in our family had to worry about a job, the way black teenagers today do. We all had a job from the time we could walk—and it was not an unimportant job, one that was trivial in the eyes of the world. Children can't plant and plow and hoe and weed and pick as well as experienced adults, but we worked together and did things as well as we could.

At least my brothers and sisters did. As for me, I was given a slightly different role. Perhaps because I was the tenth child and there were already enough field workers in the family, perhaps because my hands were smaller than the hands of the others, for whatever reason, my father assigned me to my mother—to help her in the kitchen, around the house, and wherever else she might need me.

On August days, when everyone else came in sweating from laboring in the heat, I would smile, hold out my hands, and tell my brothers and sisters that the Good Lord had not made my hands to hold a plow or, for that matter, anything heavier than a pencil. Sometimes they would laugh and take it well; but I learned not to push the joke too far, because one of my outside duties was that of "waterboy," and if all of them timed their thirst just right, they could keep me running back and forth for the rest of the afternoon.

Not that my life was soft, as my brothers and sisters like to tell me these days. They forget that my father woke me around 4 every morning, while he and everyone else still lay in bed. He would call my name just once—"David!"—and I was expected to answer "Yes, sir!" and roll out of bed. During all those years it never occurred to me to go back to sleep, because I knew if I ever did, he would come into the room after me, maybe with a belt or a razor strop. One advantage of being the tenth child is the wisdom you gain from noting the mistakes of your older brothers and sisters. I had seen my father deal out punishment to them, and I wanted no part of such treatment. So I was a good boy in the early mornings.

In cold weather I would make the fires before the others got up to dress—and there were fireplaces all over the house, since in those days few people had furnaces. In addition, I had to make the fire in the wood stove, on which my mother cooked breakfast. I also milked the cows before dawn, fed the mules, and the chickens, and gathered the eggs. Then I would wash my hands and churn butter, all before we sat down to breakfast, just as the sun's rays began to cast shadows on the kitchen floor.

Later in the day I would do other tasks, like picking vegetables in the garden, peeling potatoes, snapping beans, slicing onions, and shucking corn. I didn't know who did these chores before I came along and didn't really care. I just knew that I had to get them done before there was any time to slip off and read a book or take a short nap.

There were also errands to run. If my mother needed anything from the store that my father hadn't picked up on his Saturday trip to town, I would be dispatched to get it. And every Saturday I would ride a mile to the mill, hauling heavy bags of corn for the miller to grind so that we could have meal and grits and "chops" (feed) for the chickens.

The chickens were entirely my responsibility. I not only fed them and watered them, but I was also the chief chicken killer in the family. Though at first the job made me queasy, very soon I learned to grab a chicken by the neck, twist it around three or four times the way you used to crank a car, and then pop the head off and watch the body flap around on the ground, quite unaware for a few seconds that it no longer had a head.

Back then, chicken was the best of all meals to serve—better than ham, better than pork chops, better even than roast beef or steak. We did not get to eat chicken every day. In fact, there were only three occasions when we were sure to get chicken. First, of course, we always had it for Sunday dinner, which was served in the early afternoon. Come Sunday, the Lord's Day, we would have a feast. On Monday, Tuesday, Wednesday, Thursday, and Friday, we would have ordinary meals—one meat, three or four vegetables, cornbread, butter, maybe some preserves, plenty of milk. And Saturday—well, that was a day when everyone was busy with special tasks. My father was in town, laying in the week's supplies. My mother was cleaning the house as diligently as most people today do their spring cleaning. Lula Mae and I swept the yard while Susie and James Earl, the babies, looked on and jeered. William was off courting. Louvenia was receiving company. So on Saturdays we were lucky to get leftovers.

But, come Sunday, things were different. Come Sunday, we would have a feast—we would always eat chicken. So we lived for Sunday.

We would also have chicken when the preacher came, because that too was a grand occasion, and one in which I played a special part. Our church—the Hopewell Baptist Church—was small, its congregation consisting of no more than our family and its connections, so we could not afford to have a full-time minister. As a consequence, the preacher came only on the second and fourth weekends of the month. The rest of the time he lived in another town, but when he did come he stayed with us, remaining for several days.

Because my father was the head deacon (what Baptists now call the chairman of the Board of Deacons), it was his responsibility to provide for the preacher when he came to the Hopewell community. The first preacher I remember was the Reverend G. H. Connor, who was associated with my family for over forty years, having married my parents and preached at my father's funeral. I also remember the Reverend J. W. Wilson, the Reverend J. R. Davis (our first educated preacher), the Reverend Columbus Young, and another man named Twilly. These men all stayed at our house, took their meals with us, and were entertained from the time they arrived on Friday afternoon till the time they left on Monday morning. And, like taking care of the children, the current preacher was also my responsibility.

When he was due on Friday, I would walk down the dirt road to the highway and stand there till the Greyhound bus lumbered into sight and squealed to a halt at precisely the same spot every time. The preacher would get off, wearing a black suit, a black tie, and carrying a dark leather suitcase. I would take the grip, which for me was a little heavy, and carry it back to the house, where I would set it in the front room, which was reserved for him because it had fine furniture and lace curtains.

While he was with us I was often excused from my usual chores so that I could wait on him, talk to him, and—if the occasion demanded it—even entertain him. I was always glad to see him come because it meant a lighter work load, despite the long haul from the highway; and it also meant chicken for dinner at least one additional night.

The third occasion on which we had chicken was when my father would hear one of the hens attempting to crow. A devout Christian who knew the Old Testament, chapter and verse, as well as the New Testament, he believed that men should behave like men and women should behave like women. And he extended that law to include chickens. If he heard a hen trying to behave like a rooster on our farm, she would be in a pot before the sun went down. But her wicked pride was our good fortune, and we were always happy when one of the hens got out of line.

As I look back on these times, I realize that even if we didn't have much money, we had the essential things: we had plenty to eat, a place to live, and many things to do—most of them useful and a few of them fun. There were sports to play—in open fields rather than in Little League parks—and several of my brothers were excellent athletes. In fact, one of them, K. T., was a prodigious baseball player who could do it all—pitch, field, and hit the ball a mile. People around our part of the country said he was as good as Babe Ruth, and in a later time I'm certain he would have been a major league star, though of course no such career was open to a black in the 1930s.

My brother William also played baseball as well as basketball; and he too might well have been a famous professional athlete, but I'm afraid I was a different matter. I had little aptitude for sports and therefore little interest. When I found a few free moments to amuse myself, I would usually go to a quiet corner in the house and read a book or a newspaper. More often than not the book was the Bible, which for me was more fascinating than any popular novel.

As was the case in most country homes, the Bible was the central book in our family, the single source of wisdom that bound us all together, and we spent a good deal of time learning about it. As children we had to memorize a verse every week and recite it at the family prayer meeting we held every Sunday morning before breakfast. No matter how busy the week had been, no one was excused from reciting, and my father's memory was too keen to repeat last week's verse, so we never tried.

After recitations, my father would teach from the Good Book and we would listen. Then, at some point, my mother would slip away to prepare breakfast, which was always a very special occasion. We would usually have biscuits, sausage, eggs, and at the end of the meal—the greatest treat of all—the residue from my parents' coffee cups!

Of course, coffee was a stimulant, so the only people who drank it in our family were my father and mother. But the younger children would get a taste of it on occasion, when my parents would pour sugar into the cup, drink the coffee almost to the dregs, and then leave a dark, sweet crystallized mixture at the bottom. After they left the table, we would fight over the remaining treat more that we would have fought over a candy bar.

Such moments come back to me now as more important than the troubles that plagued society, yet somehow never seemed to intrude on our sheltered world. Just as I had no experience of a Great Depression, so was I relatively unaware of racism or segregation, matters that would occupy much of my time and energy in later years. Of course, all the children in our family recognized that racial distinctions existed and that from time to time they could cause trouble. In fact, my father told us never to play with white children. "If you do," he said, "every joke will be at your expense. If you wrestle or box with a white child, you will always have to let him win, otherwise he may become aggravated, and that could lead to trouble."

But such a warning was merely hypothetical to us. We lived on five hundred acres, which gave us plenty of breathing space, and most of the farms around us were owned or run by our uncles and cousins. Our nearest white neighbors—Mr. and Mrs. Robert Jones—had children who were off at college. So we didn't sit around and brood about whether or not to play with whites our age. We'd never met any and had no desire to.

We were also perfectly content to drink out of our own water fountains and to enter and exit by doors marked "COLORED." We were so secure in the honor accorded our family that we didn't consider such practices demeaning or even important. If white people wanted their own fountains and doors, that was just fine with us.

Ironically, my first experience of racial animosity came out of my firm resolve to maintain my private vision of Jim Crow. I remember the occasion well—the words spoken, the hostile gestures, the man's name—though not with any bitterness. What happened was at worst annoying, at best highly amusing (at least in retrospect) then—though the society it was symptomatic of was no laughing matter.

One of my responsibilities as a child was to run errands at the country store, which was operated by our neighbor Mr. Jones. This store fronted on U.S. Highway 43, which ran from Mobile to Linden and then to points north (to places as strange and foreign as Tennessee). It was like most country stores of that day—a white, wooden building filled with anything that any reasonable human being could want, from flour and baking powder to hammers and shoes and bolts of cloth. You went about gathering up your own items, except for a few things on the shelves behind the massive counter where Mr. Jones stood and totaled your purchases on a fancy brass cash register. If you charged the goods instead of paying cash, he would pull out a huge, dog-eared ledger and record the items you had bought and their prices. We always paid cash or else brought eggs for barter.

That morning I had brought in a sack of three dozen eggs to trade for things my mother needed in the kitchen, and when I came through the door I knew from the sudden silence that something was different. Then I saw Mr. Fitzhugh, a white man who lived down the road. He was leaning up against the counter, drinking a Nehi soda, and from the expression on his face, I could tell he was drunk.

I moved down to the other end of the counter and told Mr. Jones my business, handing him the sack of eggs. In addition to being our neighbors, the Joneses were our friends. They came to call on us from time to time, visiting in our living room the way other friends did; and despite the fact that they were white, I was even allowed to go over to their house and help Mrs. Jones shake pecans out of the big trees in her backyard. But Mr. Fitzhugh was another kind of neighbor, another kind of white man.

After watching me deal with Mr. Jones, he took a gulp from his Nehi and held out the half-empty bottle.

"Here, boy," he said. "You finish this." It was more a command than an invitation.

Now, my mother had taught us never to drink behind anybody. Not behind members of the family. Particularly not behind a stranger. And *certainly* not behind a white man. So I shook my head and told him, "No, thank you."

His eyes narrowed immediately and he shoved the bottle in my direction.

"Drink this, nigger!"

I shook my head and said firmly, "I'm sorry, but I don't care for it."

He couldn't believe his ears.

"What in hell do you mean? Are you saying you won't drink after *me*?"

I stared at him for a moment, then nodded my head.

With a cry of rage he drew back his hand to hit me. At that moment Mr. Jones, who had been watching to see how far things would go, came halfway across the counter.

"Don't you touch that boy!" he cried. Then he added, "That's the son of W. L. Abernathy."

The change in Mr. Fitzhugh was remarkable. I can't think of a more dramatic testimony to the standing of my father in the community. From a towering bully he was transformed into a bundle of quivering nerves by the sound of a black man's name.

"Oh," he said quietly. "I didn't know that."

Mr. Jones relaxed a little and then turned to me and said, "Now, David, you run along home," and handed me my sack of groceries.

Of course, I did what he said, because he was our friend; but as I left the store, I glanced over my shoulder to see the two white men glaring at one another. To this day I don't know what happened after I left. If Mr. Jones said anything to my father about the confrontation, I never heard about it. I do know that it was the only such incident in my childhood, or at least the only one that stands out vividly in my memory, so strong a figure was my father, and so protective was his shadow.

CLAUDE BROWN
(1937–)

From *Manchild in the Promised Land*

*"By the time I was nine years old," recalls the author of this
selection, "I had been hit by a bus, thrown into the Harlem River
(intentionally), hit by a car, severely beaten with a chain, and I
had set the house afire." If any reader is dismayed by this statement, let him prepare himself for a far greater shock in the revelations that follow. And let it be remembered that boyhoods such
as Claude Brown's are not remarkable in Harlem or in any of
the big-city ghettos; on the contrary, they are only too common-
place. That such things as murder, theft, rioting, drug addiction,
prostitution, and the like could have become so common in the
life of a Harlem youth as to receive mention only in passing is
the real horror of this story.*

Claude Brown wrote Manchild in the Promised Land *in 1965
when he was twenty-eight years old, and it is remarkable that
the Claude Brown who went from one reform school to another,
who organized gang wars, who smoked pot and who was an
accomplished thief, is the same Claude Brown who became a law
student at one of America's leading universities.*

"Run!"

Where?

Oh, hell! Let's get out of here!

"Turk! Turk! I'm shot!"

I could hear Turk's voice calling from a far distance, telling me not
to go into the fish-and-chips joint. I heard, but I didn't understand.
The only thing I knew was that I was going to die.

I ran. There was a bullet in me trying to take my life, all thirteen years of it.

I climbed up on the bar yelling, "Walsh, I'm shot. I'm shot." I could feel the blood running down my leg. Walsh, the fellow who operated the fish-and-chips joint, pushed me off the bar and onto the floor. I couldn't move now, but I was still completely conscious.

Walsh was saying, "Git outta here, kid. I ain't got no time to play."

A woman was screaming, mumbling something about the Lord, and saying, "Somebody done shot that poor child."

Mama ran in. She jumped up and down, screaming like a crazy woman. I began to think about dying. The worst part of dying was thinking about the things and the people that I'd never see again. As I lay there trying to imagine what being dead was like, the policeman who had been trying to control Mama gave up and bent over me. He asked who had shot me. Before I could answer, he was asking me if I could hear him. I told him that I didn't know who had shot me and would he please tell Mama to stop jumping up and down. Every time Mama came down on that shabby floor, the bullet lodged in my stomach felt like a hot poker.

Another policeman had come in and was struggling to keep the crowd outside. I could see Turk in the front of the crowd. Before the cops came, he asked me if I was going to tell them that he was with me. I never answered. I looked at him and wondered if he saw who shot me. Then his question began to ring in my head: "Sonny, you gonna tell 'em I was with you?" I was bleeding on a dirty floor in a fish-and-chips joint, and Turk was standing there in the doorway hoping that I would die before I could tell the cops that he was with me. Not once did Turk ask me how I felt.

Hell, yeah, I thought, I'm gonna tell 'em.

It seemed like hours had passed before the ambulance finally arrived. Mama wanted to go to the hospital with me, but the ambulance attendant said she was too excited. On the way to Harlem Hospital, the cop who was riding with us asked Dad what he had to say. His answer was typical: "I told him about hanging out with those bad-ass boys." The cop was a little surprised. This must be a rookie, I thought.

The next day, Mama was at my bedside telling me that she had prayed and the Lord had told her that I was going to live. Mama said that many of my friends wanted to donate some blood for me, but the hospital would not accept it from narcotics users.

This was one of the worst situations I had ever been in. There was a tube in my nose that went all the way to the pit of my stomach. I was being fed intravenously, and there was a drain in my side. Everybody came to visit me, mainly out of curiosity. The girls were all anxious to know where I had gotten shot. They had heard all kinds of tales about where the bullet struck. The bolder ones wouldn't even bother to ask: they just snatched the cover off me and looked for themselves. In a few days, the word got around that I was in one piece.

On my fourth day in the hospital, I was awakened by a male nurse at about 3 A. M. When he said hello in a very ladyish voice, I thought that he had come to the wrong bed by mistake. After identifying himself, he told me that he had helped Dr. Freeman save my life. The next thing he said, which I didn't understand, had something to do with the hours he had put in working that day. He went on mumbling something about how tired he was and ended up asking me to rub his back. I had already told him that I was grateful to him for helping the doctor save my life. While I rubbed his back above the beltline, he kept pushing my hand down and saying, "Lower, like you are really grateful to me." I told him that I was sleepy from the needle a nurse had given me. He asked me to pat his behind. After I had done this, he left.

The next day when the fellows came to visit me, I told them about my early-morning visitor. Danny said he would like to meet him. Tito joked about being able to get a dose of clap in the hospital. The guy with the tired back never showed up again, so the fellows never got a chance to meet him. Some of them were disappointed.

After I had been in the hospital for about a week, I was visited by another character. I had noticed a woman visiting one of the patients on the far side of the ward. She was around fifty-five years old, short and fat, and she was wearing old-lady shoes. While I wondered who this woman was, she started across the room in my direction. After she had introduced herself, she told me that she was visiting her son. Her son had been stabbed in the chest with an ice pick by his wife. She said that his left lung had been punctured, but he was doing fine now, and that Jesus was so-o-o good.

Her name was Mrs. Ganey, and she lived on 145th Street. She said my getting shot when I did "was the work of the Lord." My gang had been stealing sheets and bedspreads off clotheslines for months before I had gotten shot. I asked this godly woman why she thought it was the work of the Lord or Jesus or whoever. She began in a sermonlike tone, saying, "Son, people was getting tired-a y'all stealing all dey sheets and spreads." She said that on the night that I had gotten shot, she baited her clothesline with two brand-new bedspreads, turned out all the lights in the apartment, and sat at the kitchen window waiting for us to show.

She waited with a double-barreled shotgun.

The godly woman said that most of our victims thought that we were winos or dope fiends and that most of them had vowed to kill us. At the end of the sermon, the godly woman said, "Thank the Lord I didn't shoot nobody's child." When the godly woman had finally departed, I thought, Thank the Lord for taking her away from my bed.

Later on that night, I was feeling a lot of pain and couldn't get to sleep. A nurse who had heard me moaning and groaning came over and gave me a shot of morphine. Less than twenty minutes later I was deep into a nightmare.

I was back in the fish-and-chips joint, lying on the floor dying. Only, now I was in more pain than before, and there were dozens of Mamas around me jumping up and screaming. I could feel myself dying in the rising pool of blood. The higher the blood rose the more I died.

I dreamt about the boy who Rock and big Stoop had thrown off that roof on 149th Street. None of us had stayed around to see him hit the ground, but I just knew that he died in a pool of blood too. I wished that he would stop screaming, and I wished that Mama would stop screaming. I wished they would let me die quietly.

As the screams began to die out—Mama's and the boy's—I began to think about the dilapidated old tenement building that I lived in, the one that still had the words "pussy" and "fuck you" on the walls where I had scribbled them years ago. The one where the super, Mr. Lawson, caught my little brother writing some more. Dad said he was going to kill Pimp for writing on that wall, and the way he was beating Pimp with that ironing cord, I thought he would. Mama was crying, I was crying, and Pimp had been crying for a long time. She ran out of the house and came back with a cop, who stopped Dad from beating Pimp.

I told Pimp not to cry anymore, just to wait until I got big: I was going to kill Dad, and he could help me if he wanted to.

This was the building where Mr. Lawson had killed a man for peeing in the hall. I remembered being afraid to go downstairs the morning after Mr. Lawson had busted that man's head open with a baseball bat. I could still see blood all over the hall. This was the building where somebody was always shooting out the windows in the hall. They were usually shooting at Johnny D., and they usually missed. This was the building I loved more than any place else in the world. The thought that I would never see this building again scared the hell out of me.

I dreamt about waking up in the middle of the night seven years before and thinking that the Germans or the Japs had come and that the loud noises I heard were bombs falling. Running into Mama's room, I squeezed in between her and Dad at the front window. Thinking that we were watching an air raid, I asked Dad where the sirens were and why the street lights were on. He said, "This ain't no air raid—just a whole lotta niggers gone fool. And git the hell back in that bed!" I went back to bed, but I couldn't go to sleep. The loud screams in the street and the crashing sound of falling plate-glass windows kept me awake for hours. While I listened to the noise, I imagined bombs falling and people running through the streets screaming. I could see mothers running with babies in their arms, grown men running over women and children to save their own lives, and the Japs stabbing babies with bayonets, just like in the movies. I thought, Boy, I sure wish I was out there. I bet the Stinky brothers are out there. Danny and Butch are probably out there having all the fun in the world.

The next day, as I was running out of the house without underwear or socks on, I could hear Mama yelling, "Boy, come back here and put a hat or something on your head!" When I reached the stoop, I was knocked back into the hall by a big man carrying a ham under his coat. While I looked up at him, wondering what was going on, he reached down with one hand and snatched me up, still holding the ham under his coat with his other hand. He stood me up against a wall and ran into the hall with his ham. Before I had a chance to move, other men came running through the hall carrying cases of whiskey, sacks of flour, and cartons of cigarettes. Just as I unglued myself from the wall and started out the door for the second time, I was bowled over again. This time by a copy with a gun in his hand. He never stopped, but after he had gone a couple of yards into the hall, I heard him say, "Look out, kid." On the third try, I got out of the building. But I wasn't sure that this was my street. None of the stores had any windows left, and glass was everywhere. It seemed that all the cops in the world were on 145th Street and Eighth Avenue that day. The cops were telling everybody to move on, and everybody was talking about the riot. I went over to a cop and asked him what a riot was. He told me to go on home. The next cop I asked told me that a riot was what had happened the night before. Putting two and two together I decided that a riot was "a whole lotta niggers gone fool!"

I went around the corner to Butch's house. After I convinced him that I was alone, he opened the door. He said that Kid and Danny were in the kitchen. I saw Kid sitting on the floor with his hand stuck way down in a gallon jar of pickled pigs' ears. Danny was cooking some bacon at the stove, and Butch was busy hiding stuff. It looked as though these guys had stolen a whole grocery store. While I joined the feast, they took turns telling me about the riot. Danny and Kid hadn't gone home the night before; they were out following the crowds and looting.

My only regret was that I had missed the excitement. I said, "Why don't we have another riot tonight? Then Butch and me can get in it."

Danny said that there were too many cops around to have a riot now. Butch said that they had eaten up all the bread and that he was going to steal some more. I asked if I could come along with him, and he said that I could if I promised to do nothing but watch. I promised, but we both knew that I was lying.

When we got to the street, Butch said he wanted to go across the street and look at the pawnshop. I tagged along. Like many of the stores where the rioters had been, the pawnshop had been set afire. The firemen had torn down a sidewall getting at the fire. So Butch and I just walked in where the wall used to be. Everything I picked up was broken or burned or both. My feet kept sinking into wet furs that had been burned and drenched. The whole place smelled of smoke and was as dirty as a Harlem gutter on a rainy day. The cop out front yelled to us to get out of there. He only had to say it once.

After stopping by the seafood joint and stealing some shrimp and oysters, we went to what was left of Mr. Gordon's grocery store. Butch just walked in, picked up a loaf of bread, and walked out. He told me to come on, but I ignored him and went into the grocery store instead. I picked up two loaves of bread and walked out. When I got outside, a copy looked at me, and I ran into a building and through the backyard to Butch's house. Running through the backyard, I lost all the oysters that I had; when I reached Butch's house, I had only two loaves of bread and two shrimp in my pocket.

Danny, who was doing most of the cooking, went into the street to steal something to drink. Danny, Butch and Kid were ten years old, four years older than I. Butch was busy making sandwiches on the floor, and Kid was trying to slice up a loaf of bologna. I had never eaten shrimp, but nobody seemed to care because they refused to cook it for me. I told Butch that I was going to cook it myself. He said that there was no more lard in the house and that I would need some grease.

I looked around the house until I came up with some Vaseline hair pomade. I put the shrimp in the frying pan with the hair grease, waited until they had gotten black and were smoking, then took them out and made a sandwich. A few years later I found out that shrimp were supposed to be shelled before cooking. I ate half of the sandwich and hated shrimp for years afterward.

The soft hand tapping on my face to wake me up was Jackie's. She and Della had been to a New Year's Eve party. Jackie wanted to come by the hospital and kiss me at midnight. This was the only time in my life that I ever admitted being glad to see Jackie. I asked them about the party, hoping that they would stay and talk to me for a while. I was afraid that if I went back to sleep, I would have another bad dream.

The next thing I knew, a nurse was waking me up for breakfast. I didn't recall saying goodnight to Jackie and Della, so I must have fallen asleep while they were talking to me. I thought about Sugar, how nice she was, and how she was a real friend. I knew she wanted to be my girl friend, and I liked her a lot. But what would everybody say if I had a buck-toothed girl friend. I remembered Knoxie asking me how I kissed her. That question led to the first fight I'd had with Knoxie in years. No, I couldn't let Sugar be my girl. It was hard enough having her for a friend.

The next day I asked the nurse why she hadn't changed my bed linen, and she said because they were evicting me. I had been in the hospital for eleven days, but I wasn't ready to go home. I left the hospital on January 2, and went to a convalescent home in Valhalla, New York. After I had been there for three weeks, the activity director took me aside and told me that I was going to New York City to see a judge and that I might be coming back. The following morning, I left to see that judge, but I never got back to Valhalla.

I stood there before Judge Pankin looking solemn and lying like a professional. I thought that he looked too nice to be a judge. A half hour after I had walked into the courtroom, Judge Pankin was telling me that he was sending me to the New York State Training School for Boys. The judge said that he thought I was a chronic liar and that he hoped I would be a better boy when I came out. I asked him if he wanted me to thank him. Mama stopped crying just long enough to say, "Hush your mouth, boy."

Mama tried to change the judge's mind by telling him that I had already been to Wiltwyck School for Boys for two and a half years. And before that, I had been ordered out of the state for at least one year. She said that I had been away from my family too much; that was why I was always getting into trouble.

The judge told Mama that he knew what he was doing and that one day she would be grateful to him for doing it.

I had been sent away before, but this was the first time I was ever afraid to go. When Mama came up to the detention room in Children's Court, I tried to act as though I wasn't afraid. After I told her that Warwick and where I was going were one and the same, Mama began to cry, and so did I.

Most of the guys I knew had been to Warwick and were too old to go back. I knew that there were many guys up there I had mistreated. The Stinky brothers were up there. They thought that I was one of the guys who had pulled a train on their sister in the park the summer before. Bumpy from 144th Street was up there. I had shot him in the leg with a zip gun in a rumble only a few months earlier. There were many guys up there I used to bully on the streets and at Wiltwyck, guys I had sold tea leaves as pot. There were rival gang members up there who just hated my name. All of these guys were waiting for me to show. The word was out that I couldn't fight any more—that I had slowed down since I was shot and that a good punch to the stomach would put my name in the undertaker's book.

When I got to the Youth House, I tried to find out who was up at

Warwick that I might know. Nobody knew any of the names I asked about. I knew that if I went up to Warwick in my condition, I'd never live to get out. I had a reputation for being a rugged little guy. This meant that I would have at least a half-dozen fights in the first week of my stay up there.

It seemed the best thing for me to do was to cop out on the nut. For the next two nights, I woke up screaming and banging on the walls. On the third day, I was sent to Bellevue for observation. This meant that I wouldn't be going to Warwick for at least twenty-eight days.

While I was in Bellevue, the fellows would come down and pass notes to me through the doors. Tito and Turk said they would get bagged and sent to Warwick by the time I got there. They were both bagged a week later for smoking pot in front of the police station. They were both sent to Bellevue. Two weeks after they showed, I went home. The judge still wanted to send me to Warwick, but Warwick had a full house, so he sent me home after two weeks.

The day before I went back to court, I ran into Turk, who had just gotten out of Bellevue. Tito had been sent to Warwick, but Turk had gotten a walk because his sheet wasn't too bad. I told him I would probably be sent to Warwick the next day. Turk said he had run into Bucky in Bellevue. He told me that he and Tito had voted Bucky out of the clique. I told him that I wasn't going for it because Bucky was my man from short-pants days. Turk said he liked him too, but what else could he do after Bucky had let a white boy beat him in the nutbox? When I heard this, there was nothing I could do but agree with Turk. Bucky had to go. That kind of news spread fast, and who wanted to be in a clique with a stud who let a paddy boy beat him?

The next day, I went to the Youth House to wait for Friday and the trip to Warwick. As I lay in bed that night trying to think of a way out, I began to feel sorry for myself. I began to blame Danny, Butch and Kid for my present fate. I told myself, that I wouldn't be going to Warwick if they hadn't taught me how to steal, play hookey, make homemades, and stuff like that. But then, I thought, aw, hell, it wasn't their fault—as a matter of fact, it was a whole lotta fun.

I remembered sitting on the stoop with Danny, years before, when a girl came up and started yelling at him. She said that her mother didn't want her brother to hang out with Danny any more, because Danny had taught her brother how to play hookey. When the girl had gone down the street, I asked Danny what hookey was. He said it was a game he would teach me as soon as I started going to school.

Danny was a man of his word. He was my next-door neighbor, and he rang the doorbell about 7:30 A. M. on the second day of school. Mama thanked him for volunteering to take me to school. Danny said that he would have taught me to play hookey the day before, but he knew that Mama would have to take me to school on the first day. As we headed toward the backyard to hide our books, Danny began to explain the great game of hookey. It sounded like lots of fun to me. Instead of going to school, we would go all over the city stealing, sneak into a movie, or go up on a roof and throw bottles down into the street. Danny suggested that we start the day off by waiting for Mr. Gordon to put out his vegetables; we could steal some sweet potatoes and cook them in the backyard. I was sorry I hadn't started school sooner, because hookey sure was a lot of fun.

Before I began going to school, I was always in the streets with Danny, Kid, and Butch. Sometimes, without saying a word they would all start to run like hell, and a white man was always chasing them. One morning as I entered the backyard where all the hookey players went to draw up an activity schedule for the day, Butch told me that Danny and Kid had been caught by Mr. Sands the day before. He went on to warn me about Mr. Sands, saying Mr. Sands was that white man who was always chasing somebody and that I should try to remember what he looked like and always be on the lookout for him. He also warned me not to try to outrun Mr. Sands, "because that cat is fast." Butch said, "When you see him, head for a backyard or a roof. He won't follow you there."

During the next three months, I stayed out of school twenty-one days. Dad was beating the hell out of me for playing hookey, and it was no fun being in the street in the winter, so I started going to school regularly. But when spring rolled around, hookey became my favorite game again. Mr. Sands was known to many parents in the neighborhood as the truant officer. He never caught me in the street, but he came to my house many mornings to escort me to class. This was one way of getting me to school, but he never found a way to keep me there. The moment my teacher took her eyes off me, I was back on the street. Every time Dad got a card from Mr. Sands, I got bruises and welts from Dad. The beatings had only a temporary effect on me. Each time, the beatings got worse; and each time, I promised never to play hookey again. One time I kept that promise for three whole weeks.

The older guys had been doing something called "catting" for years. That catting was staying away from home all night was all I knew about the term. Every time I asked one of the fellows to teach me how to cat, I was told I wasn't old enough. As time went on, I learned that guys catted when they were afraid to go home and that they slept everywhere but in comfortable places. The usual places for catting were subway trains, cellars, unlocked cars, under a friend's bed, and in vacant newsstands.

One afternoon when I was eight years old, I came home after a busy day of running from the police, truant officer, and storekeepers. The first thing I did was to look in the mailbox. This had become a habit with me even though I couldn't read. I was looking for a card, a yellow card. That yellow card meant that I would walk into the house and Dad would be waiting for me with his razor strop. He would usually be eating and would pause just long enough to say to me, "Nigger, you got a ass whippin' comin'." My sisters, Carole and Margie, would cry almost as much as I would while Dad was beating me, but this never stopped him. After each beating I got, Carole, who was two years older than I, would beg me to stop playing hookey. There were a few times when I thought I would stop just to keep her and Margie, my younger sister, from crying so much. I decided to threaten Carole and Margie instead, but this didn't help. I continued to play hookey, and they continued to cry on the days that the yellow card got home before I did.

Generally, I would break open the mailbox, take out the card, and throw it away. Whenever I did this, I'd have to break open two or three other mailboxes and throw away the contents, just to make it look good.

This particular afternoon, I saw a yellow card, but I couldn't find anything to break into the box with. Having some matches in my pockets, I decided to burn the card in the box and not bother to break the box open. After I had used all the matches, the card was not completely burned. I stood there getting more frightened by the moment. In a little while, Dad would be coming home; and when he looked in the mailbox, anywhere would be safer than home for me.

This was going to be my first try at catting out. I went looking for somebody to cat with me. My crime partner, Buddy, whom I had played hookey with that day, was busily engaged in a friendly rock fight when I found him in Colonial Park. When I suggested that we go up on the hill and steal some newspapers, Buddy lost interest in the rock fight.

We stole papers from newsstands and sold them on the subway trains until nearly 1 A. M. That was when the third cop woke us and put us off the train with the usual threat. They would always promise to beat us over the head with a billy and lock us up. Looking back, I think the cops took their own threats more seriously than we did. The third cop put us off the Independent Subway at Fifty-ninth Street and Columbus Circle. I wasn't afraid of the cops, but I didn't go back in the subway—the next cop might have taken me home.

In 1945, there was an Automat where we came out of the subway. About five slices of pie later, Buddy and I left the Automat in search of a place to stay the night. In the center of the Circle, there were some old lifeboats that the Navy had put on display.

Buddy and I slept in the boat for two nights. On the third day, Buddy was caught ringing a cash register in a five-and-dime store. He was sent to Children's Center, and I spent the third night in the boat alone. On the fourth night, I met a duty-conscious cop, who took me home. That ended my first catting adventure.

Dad beat me for three consecutive days for telling what he called "that dumb damn lie about sleeping in a boat on Fifty-ninth Street." On the fourth day, I think he went to check my story out for himself. Anyhow, the beating stopped for a while, and he never mentioned the boat again.

Before long, I was catting regularly, staying away from home for weeks at a time. Sometimes the cops would pick me up and take me to a Children's Center. The Centers were located all over the city. At some time in my childhood I must have spent at least one night in all of them except the one on Staten Island.

The procedure was that a policeman would take me to the Center in the borough where he had picked me up. The Center would assign someone to see that I got a bath and was put to bed. The following day, my parents would be notified as to where I was and asked to come and claim me. Dad was always in favor of leaving me where I was and saying good riddance. But Mama always made the trip. Although Mama never failed to come for me, she seldom found me there when she arrived. I had no trouble getting out of Children's Centers, so I seldom stayed for more than a couple of days.

When I was finally brought home—sometimes after weeks of catting—Mama would hide my clothes or my shoes. This would mean that I couldn't get out of the house if I should take a notion to do so. Anyway, that's how Mama had it figured. The truth of the matter is that these measures only made getting out of the house more difficult for me. I would have to wait until one of the fellows came around to see me. After hearing my plight, he would go out and round up some of the gang, and they would steal some clothes and shoes for me. When they had the clothes and shoes, one of them would come to the house and let me know. About ten minutes later, I would put on my sister's dress, climb down the back fire escape, and meet the gang with the clothes.

If something was too small or too large, I would go and steal the right size. This could only be done if the item that didn't fit was not the shoes. If the shoes were too small or large, I would have trouble running in them and probably get caught. So I would wait around in the backyard while someone stole me a pair.

Mama soon realized that hiding my clothes would not keep me in the house. The next thing she tried was threatening to send me away until I was twenty-one. This was only frightening to me at the moment of hearing it. Every so often, either Dad or Mama would sit down and have a heart-to-heart talk with me. These talks were very moving. I always promised to mend my bad ways. I was always sincere and usually kept the promise for about a week. During these weeks, I went to school every day and kept my stealing at a minimum. By the beginning of the second week, I had reverted back to my wicked ways, and Mama would have to start praying all over again.

The neighborhood prophets began making prophecies about my life-span. They all had me dead, buried, and forgotten before my twenty-first birthday. These predictions were based on false tales of policemen shooting at me, on truthful tales of my falling off a trolley car into the midst of oncoming automobile traffic while hitching a ride, and also on my uncontrollable urge to steal. There was much justification for these prophecies. By the time I was nine years old, I had been hit by a bus, thrown into the Harlem River (intentionally), hit by a car, severely beaten with a chain. And I had set the house afire.

While Dad was still trying to beat me into a permanent conversion, Mama was certain that somebody had worked roots on me. She was writing to all her relatives in the South for solutions, but they were only able to say, "that boy must been born with the devil in him." Some of them advised Mama to send me down there, because New York was no place to raise a child. Dad thought this was a good idea, and he tried to sell it to Mama. But Mama wasn't about to split up her family. So I stayed in New York, enjoying every crazy minute.

Mama's favorite question was, "Boy, why you so bad?" I tried many times to explain to Mama that I wasn't "so bad." I tried to make her understand that it was trying to be good that generally got me into trouble. I remember telling her that I played hookey to avoid getting into trouble in school. It seemed that whenever I went to school, I got into a fight with the teacher. The teacher would take me to the principal's office. After I had fought with the principal, I would be sent home and not allowed back in school without one of my parents. So to avoid all that trouble, I just didn't go to school. When I stole things, it was only to save the family money and avoid arguments or scoldings whenever I asked for money.

Mama seemed silly to me. She was bothered because most of the parents in the neighborhood didn't allow their children to play with me. What she didn't know was that I never wanted to play with them. My friends were all daring like me, tough like me, dirty like me, ragged like me, cursed like me, and had a great love for trouble like me. We took pride in being able to hitch rides on trolleys, buses, taxicabs and in knowing how to steal and fight. We knew that we were the only kids in the neighborhood who usually had more than ten dollars in their pockets. There were other people who knew this too, and that was often a problem for us. Somebody was always trying to shake us down or rob us. This was usually done by the older hustlers in the neighborhood or by storekeepers or cops. At other times, older fellows would shake us down, con us, or Murphy us out of our loot. We accepted this as the ways of life. Everybody was stealing from everybody else. And sometimes we would shake down newsboys and shoeshine boys. So we really had no complaints coming. Although none of my sidekicks was over twelve years of age, we didn't think of ourselves as kids. The other kids my age were thought of as kids by me. I felt that since I knew more about life than they did, I had the right to regard them as kids....

DAISY BATES
(1919?–)

From *The Long Shadow of Little Rock*

*"If Jesus is like the white people, I don't want any part of him!"
cries young Daisy Gatson in the following selection. In the context
of the highly religious black community in southern Arkansas,
and coming from a child, this is a shocking declaration, indeed.
But it gives evidence to the depth of the bitterness and disillu-
sionment a black child can reach when confronted with reality.
With a child's simplicity but a quite adult steadfastness, she
launches her drive to gain revenge for her mother's murder. The
story of her gradual destruction of the guilty "Drunken Pig" is so
passionately elemental and somehow distinctively Southern that
it seems to belong in the pages of a William Faulkner novel.*

*Daisy Lee Gatson was told by her stepfather when she was a
child to "hate discrimination that eats away at the soul of every
black man and woman. Hate the insults and then try to do something bout it or your hate won't spell a thing." She followed his
advice and as Mrs. L. C. Bates, Arkansas State President of the
NAACP, was largely responsible for the successful integration of
Little Rock High School in 1957.*

I was born Daisy Lee Gatson in the little sawmill town of Huttig, in
southern Arkansas. The owners of the mill ruled the town. Huttig
might have been called a sawmill plantation for everyone worked for
the mill, lived in houses owned by the mill, and traded at the general
store run by the mill.

The hard, red clay streets of the town were mostly unnamed. Main

Street, the widest and longest street in town, and the muddiest after a rain, was the site of our business square. It consisted of four one-story buildings which housed a commissary and meat market, a post office, an ice cream parlor, and a movie house. Main Street also divided "White Town" from "Negra Town." However, the physical appearance of the two areas provided a more definite means of distinction.

The Negro citizens of Huttig were housed in rarely painted, drab red "shotgun" houses, so named because one could stand in the front yard and look straight through the front and back doors into the back yard. The Negro community was also provided with two church buildings of the same drab red exterior, although kept spotless inside by the Sisters of the church, and a two-room schoolhouse equipped with a potbellied stove that never quite succeeded in keeping it warm.

On the other side of Main Street were white bungalows, white steepled churches and a white spacious school with a big lawn. Although the relations between Negro and white were cordial, the tone of the community, as indicated by outward appearances, was of the "Old South" tradition.

As I grew up in this town, I knew I was a Negro, but I did not really understand what that meant until I was seven years old. My parents, as do most Negro parents, protected me as long as possible from the inevitable insult and humiliation that is, in the South, a part of being "colored."

I was a proud and happy child—all hair and legs, my cousin Early B. used to say—and an only child, although not blessed with the privilege of having my own way. One afternoon, shortly after my seventh birthday, my mother called me in from play.

"I'm not feeling well," she said. "You'll have to go to the market and get the meat for dinner."

I was thrilled with such an important errand. I put on one of my prettiest dresses and my mother brushed my hair. She gave me a dollar and instructions to get a pound of center-cut pork chops. I skipped happily all the way to the market.

When I entered the market, there were several white adults waiting to be served. When the butcher had finished with them, I gave him my order. More white adults entered. The butcher turned from me and took their orders. I was a little annoyed but felt since they were grownups it was all right. While he was waiting on the adults, a little white girl came in and we talked while we waited.

The butcher finished with the adults, looked down at us and asked, "What do you want, little girl?" I smiled and said, "I told you before, a pound of center-cut pork chops." He snarled, "I'm not talking to you," and again asked the white girl what she wanted. She also wanted a pound of center-cut pork chops.

"Please may I have my meat?" I said, as the little girl left. The butcher took my dollar from the counter, reached into the showcase, got a handful of fat chops and wrapped them up. Thrusting the package at me, he said, "Niggers have to wait 'til I wait on the white people. Now take your meat and get out of here!" I ran all the way home crying.

When I reached the house, my mother asked what had happened. I started pulling her toward the door, telling her what the butcher had said. I opened the meat and showed it to her. "It's fat, Mother. Let's take it back."

"Oh, Lord, I knew I shouldn't have sent her. Stop crying now, the meat isn't so bad."

"But it is. Why can't we take it back?"

"Go on out on the porch and wait for Daddy." As she turned from me, her eyes were filling with tears.

When I saw Daddy approaching, I ran to him, crying. He lifted me in his arms and smiled. "Now, what's wrong?" When I told him, his smile faded.

"And if we don't hurry, the market will be closed," I finished.

"We'll talk about it after dinner, sweetheart." I could feel his muscles tighten as he carried me into the house.

Dinner was distressingly silent. Afterward my parents went into the bedroom and talked. My mother came out and told me my father wanted to see me. I ran into the bedroom. Daddy sat there, looking at me for a long time. Several times he tried to speak, but the words just wouldn't come. I stood there, looking at him and wondering why he was acting so strangely. Finally he stood up and the words began tumbling from him. Much of what he said I did not understand. To my seven-year-old mind he explained as best he could that a Negro had no rights that a white man respected.

He dropped to his knees in front of me, placed his hands on my shoulders, and began shaking me and shouting.

"Can't you understand what I've been saying?" he demanded. "There's nothing I can do! If I went down to the market I would only cause trouble for my family."

As I looked at my daddy sitting by me with tears in his eyes, I blurted out innocently, "Daddy, are you afraid?"

He sprang to his feet in an anger I had never seen before. "Hell, no! I'm not afraid for myself, I'm not afraid to die. I could go down to that market and tear him limb from limb with my bare hands, but I'm afraid for you and your mother."

That night when I knelt to pray, instead of my usual prayers, I found myself praying that the butcher would die. After that night we never mentioned him again.

Shortly after my eighth birthday I was playing with other children on a neighbor's steps. An older boy, whom I didn't happen to like, came up and began pulling my braids. I said I was going home. The boy said, "You always act so uppity. If you knew what happened to your mother, you wouldn't act so stuck up."

"Nothing's wrong with my mother," I retorted. "I just left her."

"I'm talking about your *real* mother, the one the white man took out and killed."

"That's a story and you're a mean and nasty old boy!" I began to cry.

"It ain't. I heard my folks talking about it."

Just then the mother of one of my playmates came out on the porch and yelled at the boy. "Shut up! You talk too much. I'm going to tell your mother, and you'll get the beating of your life."

"Honey," she said to me, "don't believe nothing that no-good boy says." Still, I wondered what if he was telling me the truth?

At dinner that evening I looked intently at my parents, all the while trying to decide whether I looked like them. I could see no resemblance or likeness to myself in either of them. I remembered many little things, like the day Mother was talking to a salesman when I came in. He glanced at me, then turned to my mother.

"Have you heard from her father?" he had asked her.

When my mother said she hadn't, the salesman nodded toward me. "Does she know?"

"We haven't told her," my mother had said.

During the next few weeks I kept so much to myself that my parents decided that I must be sick. So I was "dosed" up with little pink pills. My cousin Early B. came to visit us. He was several years older than I, but I was glad to see him because he protected me from the boys who liked to taunt and tease me.

One afternoon as we walked along the millpond, I asked Early B. to tell me about my mother. He looked at me puzzled.

"Your mother?" he said guardedly, and pointed in the direction of my house. We could see her sitting on the porch.

"No. I mean my *real* mother."

"You know?"

"Yes."

"Everything?"

"Well, almost."

"Who told you? I'll knock his block off! Have you told your mamma and papa?"

"No."

We walked on in silence until we stood on the bank that divided the millpond from the town's fishing hole. Large logs floated in the water. The smell of fresh-cut lumber mixed with the odor of dead fish. As we stood there, Early B. told me of my parents.

"One night when you were a baby and your daddy was working nights at the mill, a man went to your house and told your mother that your daddy had been hurt. She rushed out leaving you alone, but she met a neighbor and asked her to listen out for you while she went to see about your daddy.

"When your daddy got home the next morning, he found you alone. He went around asking the neighbors if they had seen your mother. The neighbor your mother had asked to look after you told him what happened the night before—that she saw a man who looked like he was colored, although she didn't get a good look at him because he was walking in front of your mother.

"The news spread fast around town that your mother couldn't be found. Later in the morning, some people out fishing found her body."

Early B. stopped and sat down on the pond bank. I stood over him, looking into the dark, muddy water.

"Where did they find her?" I asked.

After a long silence Early B. pointed at the water and said, "Right down there. She was half in and half out."

"Who did it?"

"Well," he answered, "there was a lot of talk from the cooks and cleaning women who worked in 'white town' about what they had heard over there. They said that three white men did it."

"What happened to my father?"

"He was so hurt, he left you with the people who have you now, his best friends. He left town. Nobody has heard from him since."

"What did my real parents look like?"

"They were young. Your daddy was as light as a lot of white people. Your mother was very pretty—dark brown, with long black hair."

Early B.'s friends came along and he wandered off with them. I sat there looking into the dark waters, vowing that some day I would get the men who killed my mother. I did not realize that the afternoon had turned into evening and darkness had closed in around me until someone sitting beside me whispered, "It's time to go home, darling." I turned and saw my daddy sitting beside me. He reached out in the darkness and took my hand.

"How long have you known?" he asked.

"A long time," I said.

He lifted me tenderly in his arms and carried me home.

The next morning I had a high temperature. I remember the neighbors coming in, talking in quiet tones. That afternoon a playmate brought me a little box holding three guinea pigs. At first I thought they were rats. Knowing my mother's fear of rats, I hid the box in my bed.

That night the Church Sisters, who met each week at the church or at the home of some sick person to pray, gathered at our home. They knelt around my bed and prayed for my soul. I noticed the fat knees of one praying lady. It gave me an idea I couldn't resist. I eased the box to the floor and released the guinea pigs. One of them ran across the fat lady's leg. Unable to lift her weight up on the chair beside her, she lumbered around the room, screaming hysterically. The other ladies, managing to keep a few paces ahead of her, joined in the wild demonstration.

Above the hubhub I heard my mother's voice sternly demanding to know where those creatures came from. Helpless with laughter, I could not reply. The guinea pigs broke up the prayer meeting and I got my behind properly spanked. The ladies, although convinced that I certainly needed prayer, decided to do their praying for me elsewhere.

In Arkansas, even in the red clay soil of a mill town, flowers grow without any encouragement at all. Everyone's yard had some sort of flowering bush or plant all spring and summer. And in this town of Huttig, where there was so little beauty, I passionately loved all blooming things. In the woods I hunted out the first of the cowslips and spring beauties, and from open fields, the last of the Indian paintbrush. I was always bringing home bouquets.

All of the neighbors knew that the flowers in our yard were my garden, not Mother's. I had no favorites and delighted at each flower in its season. When the last roses and zinnias had died, I knew in a few short months the old lilac bush would start budding, for winter in Arkansas is short-lived. But this year was different. One morning I was out before breakfast looking for flowers to pick. All I found was a single red rose, the dew still wet on it. I can close my eyes today and see exactly how it looked. Unaccountably I turned, leaving it on its stalk, and walked into the house crying.

My mother met me at the door and I saw her face cloud with anxiety. What was the trouble? "All the other flowers were dead," I sobbed, "and my rose will die, too."

That night I heard her say to Daddy, "I can't understand that child, crying over a dying flower." Then I heard my daddy say, "Let her be. It just takes time."

My family had not spoken to me of my real mother since that day the ladies came to pray for me.

Later in the fall, on a Saturday afternoon, my father and I took a walk in the woods. It was a brisk day. Daddy thought we might find some ripe persimmons. Also, some black walnuts might have fallen from a big old tree he knew about. We walked along sniffing the air, sharp with the smell of pine needles, then came out in an open stretch in sight of the persimmon grove. I was always happy on these excursions with Daddy. I guess it was just the feeling that I couldn't be happy now, couldn't let myself be, that made me ask the question.

"Daddy, who killed my mother? Why did they kill her?"

We walked on a little way in silence. Then he pointed to some flat rocks on a slope, and we made our way there and rested. The persimmons and walnuts were forgotten. He began in tones so soft I could barely hear the words.

He told me of the timeworn lust of the white man for the Negro woman—which strikes at the heart of every Negro man in the South. I don't remember a time when this man I called my father didn't talk to me almost as if I were an adult. Even so, this was a difficult concept to explain to an eight-year-old girl; but he spoke plainly, in simple words I could understand. He wanted me to realize that my mother wouldn't have died if it hadn't been for her race—as well as her beauty, her pride, her love for my father.

"Your mother was not the kind of woman to submit," he said, "so they took her." His voice grew bitter. "They say that three white men did it. There was some talk about who they were, but no one knew for sure, and the sheriff's office did little to find out."

He said some other things about the way the Negro is treated in the South, but my mind had stopped, fastening on those three white men and what they had done. They had killed my mother.

When we walked out of the woods, my daddy looked tired and broken. He took my hand and we walked home in silence.

Dolls, games, even my once-beloved fishing, held little interest for me after that. Young as I was, strange as it may seem, my life now had a secret goal—to find the men who had done this horrible thing to my mother. So happy once, now I was like a little sapling which, after a violent storm, put out only gnarled and twisted branches.

School opened. Nothing had changed. We had the same worn-out textbooks handed down to us from the white school. With the first frosts the teacher wrestled with the potbellied stove. Days drifted by as we tried to gain an education in these surroundings. One afternoon my mother sent me to the commissary, where one could purchase anything from a nail to an automobile. Just as I reached the store, I saw some of my friends approaching. I paused on the step to wait for them. As I stood there waiting, I felt someone staring at me. I turned around and looked into the face of a rather young white man sitting on one of the benches on the porch that ran the entire length of the store. We stared at each other for a long time. I have read descriptions of the contest in staring which a bird and a snake will carry on. The two of us must have presented such a picture, although considering my own feelings, I don't know which of us symbolized the snake and which the bird.

Finally my friends called to me. I turned and entered the store with them. Once inside I looked back. The white man's eyes were still fixed on me.

People who knew my mother said I was "the living image of her." As I stood there I saw the white man's expression change from stare to puzzlement to fright. He ran his hands over his eyes as if to blot out an image. My girl friend, Beatrice, nudged me. "Daisy!" I did not move. The man jumped up from the bench and walked away, looking back at me. Beatrice asked, "What was all that? Did he say something bad to you?" I didn't answer.

As we were about to leave the store, Beatrice said, "Wait for me, I must speak to the old man." I followed her and stood back as she talked to the "old man." He was an elderly and retired mill worker who was now nearly crippled with arthritis. When the weather was clear, he always sat on the porch and chatted with the mill workers. He knew all the town's gossip. He knew all the children, both white and Negro, by name. He usually brought a lunch in a paper bag which he kept by his side. Out of this he often produced candy for us kids. Needless to say, he was to the children the most popular person in town.

I heard Beatrice tell him there was a new baby at her house. He reached in the bag and gave her a peppermint stick. He held out another for me. When I refused, he said to Bea, "What's wrong with her? She lost her sweet tooth?" Bea repeated after him, "What's the matter with you?"

I started to walk away. "Nothing," I said.

Bea caught up with me. "What's wrong with you, Daisy? You aren't any fun anymore!"

"If I want candy, I have some money to buy it," I said. "I don't want anything from white people."

The next day, after school, I asked my adopted mother if she needed anything from the commissary. No, she didn't need anything, but our neighbor wanted me to go to the store for her. I ran all the way.

As I neared the store, I saw the same young white man who had stared at me. He was seated on the same bench. I walked slowly until I reached the steps, then stopped. The man glared at me as if to say, "Look at me all you damned please." I didn't take my eyes off him. Suddenly he leaped to his feet and yelled, "Stop staring at me, you bitch!"

He started toward me. I was too frightened to move. I heard the sharp scraping sound of a chair being pushed back. I turned to see the old man standing, holding onto his chair, watching us both. The man who stared also saw him. He stopped. Then in a thin, weak voice, he muttered: "Go away! Haven't I suffered enough?" He walked slowly away.

I watched his back disappear around the corner. I was no longer afraid, for I knew he was more afraid of me than I was of him. I turned to go into the store, and the old man sank back in his chair.

During the following months I would find some way to get to the commissary at least every other day. By now I had a name for the man on the bench. "Drunken Pig." Each time he seemed a little drunker and a little dirtier than the last. At times he would stare back at me; other times he would pretend that he did not see me. But I could tell from the twitching of his mouth and his uneasy glance that he knew I was there.

One day as I was leaving the store, a little white girl about my own age, with whom I had been friends for a long time, ran up behind me and poked me in the back. "Daisy! Daisy!" When I turned around, she said, "Look, Daisy, I have two pennies. Let's buy some candy and I'll tell you about my vacation."

All my hostility and bitterness must have shown on my face, because she pulled back with a frightened look. I slapped her face. "Don't you ever touch me again! I don't want your penny!"

She put her hands to her cheeks and looked at me in disbelief. I jumped down the store steps and ran away, tears streaming from my eyes. When I reached home, my mother was out. I sat on the front porch, crying and waiting for her. I wondered if I should tell my mother and daddy what had happened. How could I ever make my friend understand why I had struck her? I hardly knew the reason myself.

I wanted badly to go back and tell her I was sorry, and that I didn't really hate her. During our friendship we had often met at the store and shared our pennies. We would have so much fun shopping with our pennies. If I bought winding balls, she would buy peppermint sticks and we would divide them. How could I explain to her that . . . Suddenly I was afraid. Suppose she went home and told her people that I had hit her? Suppose they came for me or my daddy that night?

I remembered hearing of a white man who went to the home of a Negro family, carrying a wide leather belt, and made the father beat his son to teach him to "respect white folks." The white man's daughter was said to have told the Negro boy, "Get off the walk, nigger, and let me pass." The Negro boy is said to have replied, "You don't own all the sidewalk. There's plenty of room for you to pass, and if you think I'm going to get off the sidewalk into the muddy street, you're crazy."

The boy did not attend school after that incident, and the family soon moved away.

When my mother arrived home, I decided not to tell her that I had struck my white friend.

Near Christmas, the weather got very cold. The old potbellied stove at the school acted up. Most of the time we sat in class all day with our coats on. One of the boys who worked in the store in the evening with his father told us that the store had put out the Christmas toys on display. I dashed home, then hastened to the store to look at them. I rushed right past Drunken Pig. He was slumped in his usual place on the porch bench. I walked around the store looking at the toys. Three men were leaning on the counter where the dolls were. I was standing behind them, admiring the big colored doll, when the door opened and Drunken Pig came stumbling in. I heard one of the men say, "What's happened to him?"

One of the other men said, "I got an idea what's happened. You heard about that colored woman they found in the millpond a few years ago? I heard he was involved . . . leastwise, he started to drink about then, and he's been getting worse and worse ever since. He's about hit rock bottom. Too bad,'cause he had a good job at that time."

"If he don't work, how does he buy liquor?" one of the men asked.

"He helps the bootleggers clean out their mash barrels."

I stood motionless, listening. Now that I was sure of what I had suspected, I lost all interest in the doll.

Christmas, the happy, exciting anticipation of the magic hour when Santa Claus would come laden with gifts and goodies, had no real meaning for me that year. Our church was preparing for the annual Christmas pageant, depicting the birth of the Christ Child. One of the church ladies came to see Mother to describe the part I was to play—an angel hovering over the straw crib of the Infant Jesus. "She was *so* pretty in her angel costume last Christmas," the lady cooed. Mother was smiling. She was obviously pleased. To everyone's astonishment I snapped, "*No! I won't!*"

"What is it?" Mother exclaimed. "What is it, my dear?"

"I don't want to," I cried. "I don't want no part of that play about a dead white doll!"

Mother was shocked. "I won't have that kind of talk!" she protested. "You stop that kind of talk this minute!"

"All the pictures I ever saw of Jesus were white," I screamed. "If Jesus is like the white people, I don't want any part of Him!" I fled from the room, leaving everyone in a state of consternation.

Nothing more was ever said about my appearing in the Christmas play. While my friends and family attended the Christmas pageant, I spent a lonely evening with my dog and colored doll.

With the coming of spring, I went through the daily routine of school and homework. I had come to enjoy tormenting Drunken Pig. I felt as if I were making him pay for his sin. I also blamed him for the loss of my white girl friend, whom I now missed dreadfully. I remembered how we used to meet at the store and look at magazines and daydream about places we would like to go together. One day we were looking through a magazine and saw a picture of New York, with the Statue of Liberty in the background. How would it be to go there one day, as her seventeen-year-old cousin had done? While we were musing she turned to me and asked, "Do you think it will always be like this? I can't come to your house and you can't come to mine?"

I watched Drunken Pig cringe when he was sober enough to recognize me at the commissary. He sank lower and lower. The old crippled man sitting on the porch was always the silent observer of these encounters. His eyes did not smile as much as they used to. I felt, in a way, that he was suffering along with me and Drunken Pig. The old man had not spoken a word to me since the day I refused his candy.

Spring was everywhere. The trees were budding and people were plowing their gardens. One morning I heard Mother say to my father, "I think we should send Daisy away for a visit with her grandmother. I don't think this town is good for her. She doesn't take an interest in anything around the house anymore. I asked her if she wanted her flower garden spaded. She even refused that. All she wants to do is go to the store. I wish I knew what was going on in that mind of hers. I saw the mother of that little white girl Daisy used to play with. She asked me why her little girl and Daisy weren't friends any more. I didn't know what to say to her."

At that point I ran into the room and screamed, "Not now! Please! I can't go now!"

They looked at me, puzzled. Daddy finally said, "All right, darling, if you don't want to go to Grandma's you don't have to."

March turned damp and windy and cold, but I continued to make almost daily excursions to the commissary. One afternoon I found Drunken Pig asleep. I came closer and looked down at him. When he did not move, I went into the store and bought a winding ball.

Coming out, I saw some men standing around Drunken Pig. They were saying something to one another. After they left I looked all around. Seeing no one but the old man sitting dozing, a blanket around his shoulders, I walked over to Drunken Pig and shook him lightly. When he did not awaken, I shook him again, harder. He opened his eyes slowly. When he saw me, he closed them again, rubbing his hand across his face. Opening his eyes again, he looked at me as I stood staring down at him. I don't know how long we stayed there, staring at each other. Finally he struggled to his feet. In a low, pleading voice, he said, "In the name of God, leave me alone."

Then he turned, half running, half stumbling, and disappeared in the alley behind the store. I walked home happier than I had been in months; yet I was sad, for as I turned away from him, I saw my white friend standing in the door of the store watching me. I smiled and started toward her. She smiled and held out a bag that I knew held candy. I got almost to her, then turned and walked away. I suddenly remembered that she was white.

During several days of rainy weather I caught a cold and had to stay in. When my cold was better and the rains had ceased, my mother allowed me to go to the store again. At the commissary the old man was dozing in the sun. Drunken Pig wasn't around. I looked in the store. I then went next door to the post office. I came out and stood waiting. The old man sat there watching me for a while. Finally he said, "Daisy, he won't be back no more."

Hesitatingly I walked over to him. "He won't be back? Why not?"

"Because they found him in the alley this morning. That's why. He's dead."

"He can't be dead!" I argued.

"He's better off," the old man said quietly, "and so are you."

I could feel the tears come, and I started to turn away lest he see them. But then I started to sob in earnest, and I soon felt the old man's arm about me, holding me close.

"You're the only one in town to cry over that drunkard," the old man whispered in my ear.

When I stopped crying he reached into his bag and pulled out a large stick of peppermint. "I've been saving this for you," he said earnestly. "Now go home and try to forget." He loosened his embrace and I went on my way.

I walked home in a daze, clutching the candy, feeling numb all over. At home I placed the candy and the money on the table. I suddenly realized I had forgotten to make Mamma's purchase. I walked out into the yard and sat on the woodpile.

That night I kept wishing I could die. I wanted to follow Drunken Pig to hell—I was sure that was where he had gone. A few nights later, when I had gone to bed, my daddy heard me crying. He came in to comfort me. He sat on a chair next to my bed, then took my hand in his.

"I know you've been unhappy for a long time," he began. "I talked with the old crippled man who sits by the commissary. He told me about that drunk who died, and he said I should send you away. Do you want to tell me what it was about?"

Slowly between sobs I told him about my episodes with Drunken Pig. When I finished, Daddy withdrew his hand, wiped the tears from my cheeks, and told me to go to sleep and forget it....

MALCOLM X
(1925–1965)

with the assistance of Alex Haley
From *The Autobiography of Malcolm X*

Malcolm Little, the son of the Reverend Earl Little, was born on May 19, 1925, in Omaha, Nebraska. His was a poor family with several children, a father who died when the children were still young, and a mother who left her children to shift for themselves.

Malcolm was in reform school before he was thirteen. Several years later he was arrested for theft, but not before he had been labeled as a dope peddler, hoodlum and pimp.

In prison, Malcolm embraced the Muslim religion and at the same time developed a passionate hatred for the "devil white man." Taking the name of Malcolm X, he became a devout follower of Elijah Muhammad, whose racist doctrine preached the complete segregation of the races.

Before long Malcolm X tempered his views and was dropped from Muhammad's select clique. He formed a splinter group which roused the hostility of his former leader. From that time on, Malcolm X was a man marked for death. On February 21, 1965, while he was speaking in Manhattan, he was gunned down by three members of Elijah Muhammad's Black Muslims.

The Autobiography of Malcolm X was written shortly before his death. It is not hard to understand his bitterness when we read of his boyhood years.

There we were. My mother was thirty-four years old now, with no husband, no provider or protector to take care of her eight children.

But some kind of a family routine got going again. And for as long as the first insurance money lasted, we did all right.

Wilfred, who was a pretty stable fellow, began to act older than his age. I think he had the sense to see, when the rest of us didn't, what was in the wind for us. He quietly quit school and went to town in search of work. He took any kind of job he could find and he would come home, dog-tired, in the evenings, and give whatever he had made to my mother.

Hilda, who always had been quiet, too, attended to the babies. Philbert and I didn't contribute anything. We just fought all the time— each other at home, and then at school we would team up and fight white kids. Sometimes the fights would be racial in nature, but they might be about anything.

Reginald came under my wing. Since he had grown out of the toddling stage, he and I had become very close. I suppose I enjoyed the fact that he was the little one, under me, who looked up to me.

My mother began to buy on credit. My father had always been very strongly against credit. "Credit is the first step into debt and back into slavery," he had always said. And then she went to work herself. She would go into Lansing and find different jobs—in housework, or sewing—for white people. They didn't realize, usually, that she was a Negro. A lot of white people around there didn't want Negroes in their houses.

So she would do fine until in some way or other it got to people who she was, whose widow she was. And then she would be let go. I remember how she used to come home crying, but trying to hide it, because she had lost a job that she needed so much.

Once, when one of us—I cannot remember which—had to go for something to where she was working, and the people saw us, and realized she was actually a Negro, she was fired on the spot, and she came home crying, this time not hiding it.

When the state Welfare people began coming to our house, we would come from school sometimes and find them talking with our mother, asking a thousand questions. They acted and looked at her, and at us, and around our house, in a way that had about it the feeling—at least for me—that we were not people. In their eyesight we were just *things*, that was all.

My mother began to receive two checks—a Welfare check and, I believe, a widow's pension. The checks helped. But they weren't enough, as many of us as there were. When they came, about the first of the month, one always was already owed in full, if not more, to the man at the grocery store. And, after that, the other one didn't last long.

We began to go swiftly downhill. The physical downhill wasn't as quick as the psychological. My mother was, above everything else, a proud woman, and it took its toll on her that she was accepting charity. And her feelings were communicated to us.

She would speak sharply to the man at the grocery store for padding the bill, telling him that she wasn't ignorant, and he didn't like that. She would talk back sharply to the state Welfare people, telling them that she was a grown woman, able to raise her children, that it wasn't necessary for them to keep coming around so much, meddling in our lives. And they didn't like that.

But the monthly Welfare check was their pass. They acted as if they owned us, as if we were their private property. As much as my mother would have liked to, she couldn't keep them out. She would get particularly incensed when they began insisting upon drawing us older children aside, one at a time, out on the porch or somewhere, and asking us questions, or telling us things—against our mother and against each other.

We couldn't understand why, if the state was willing to give us packages of meat, sacks of potatoes and fruit, and cans of all kinds of things, our mother obviously hated to accept. We really couldn't understand. What I later understood was that my mother was making a desperate effort to preserve her pride—and ours.

Pride was just about all we had to preserve, for by 1934, we really began to suffer. This was about the worst depression year, and no one we knew had enough to eat or live on. Some old family friends visited us now and then. At first they brought food. Though it was charity, my mother took it.

Wilfred was working to help. My mother was working when she could find any kind of job. In Lansing, there was a bakery where, for a nickel, a couple of us children would buy a tall flour sack of day-old bread and cookies, and then walk the two miles back out into the country to our house. Our mother knew, I guess, dozens of ways to cook things with bread and out of bread. Stewed tomatoes with bread, maybe that would be a meal. Something like French toast, if we had any eggs. Bread pudding, sometimes with raisins in it. If we got hold of some hamburger, it came to the table more bread than meat. The cookies that were always in the sack with the bread, we just gobbled down straight.

But there were times when there wasn't even a nickel and we would be so hungry we were dizzy. My mother would boil a big pot of dandelion greens, and we would eat that. I remember that some small-minded neighbor put it out, and children would tease us, that we ate "fried grass." Sometimes, if we were lucky, we would have oatmeal or cornmeal mush three times a day. Or mush in the morning and cornbread at night.

Philbert and I were grown up enough to quit fighting long enough to take the .22 caliber rifle that had been our father's and shoot rabbits that some white neighbors up or down the road would buy. I know now that they just did it to help us, because they, like everyone, shot their own rabbits. Sometimes, I remember, Philbert and I would take little Reginald along with us. He wasn't very strong, but he was always so proud to be along. We would trap muskrats out in the little creek in back of our house. And we would lie quiet until unsuspecting bullfrogs appeared, and we would spear them, cut off their legs, and sell them for a nickel a pair to people who lived up and down the road. The whites seemed less restricted in their dietary tastes.

Then, about in late 1934, I would guess, something began to happen. Some kind of psychological deterioration hit our family circle and began to eat away our pride. Perhaps it was the constant tangible evidence that we were destitute. We had known other families who had gone on relief. We had known without anyone in our home ever expressing it that we had felt prouder not to be at the depot where the free food was passed out. And, now, we were among them. At school, the "on relief" finger suddenly was pointed at us, too, and sometimes it was said aloud.

It seemed that everything to eat in our house was stamped Not To Be Sold. All Welfare food bore this stamp to keep the recipients from selling it. It's a wonder we didn't come to think of Not To Be Sold as a brand name.

Sometimes, instead of going home from school, I walked the two miles up the road into Lansing. I began drifting from store to store, hanging around outside where things like apples were displayed in boxes and barrels and baskets, and I would watch my chance and steal me a treat. You know what a treat was to me? Anything!

Or I began to drop in about dinner time at the home of some family that we knew. I knew that they knew exactly why I was there, but they never embarrassed me by letting on. They would invite me to stay for supper, and I would stuff myself.

Especially, I liked to drop in and visit at the Gohannas' home. They were nice, older people, and great churchgoers. I had watched them lead the jumping and shouting when my father preached. They had, living with them—they were raising him—a nephew whom everyone called "Big Boy," and he and I got along fine. Also living with the Gohannas was old Mrs. Adcock, who went with them to church. She was always trying to help anybody she could, visiting anyone she heard was sick, carrying them something. She was the one who, years later, would tell me something that I remembered a long time: "Malcolm, there's one thing I like about you. You're no good, but you don't try to hide it. You are not a hypocrite."

The more I began to stay away from home and visit people and steal from the stores, the more aggressive I became in my inclinations. I never wanted to wait for anything.

I was growing up fast, physically more so than mentally. As I began to be recognized more around the town, I started to become aware of the peculiar attitude of white people toward me. I sensed that it had to do with my father. It was an adult version of what several white children had said at school, in hints, or sometimes in the open, which really expressed what their parents had said—that the Black Legion or the Klan had killed my father, and the insurance company had pulled a fast one in refusing to pay my mother the policy money.

When I began to get caught stealing now and then, the state Welfare people began to focus on me when they came to our house. I can't remember how I first became aware that they were talking of taking me away. What I first remember along that line was my mother raising a storm about being able to bring up her own children. She would whip me for stealing, and I would try to alarm the neighborhood with my yelling. One thing I have always been proud of is that I never raised my hand against my mother.

In the summertime, at night, in addition to all the other things we did, some of us boys would slip out down the road, or across the pastures and go "cooning" watermelons. White people always associated watermelons with Negroes, and they sometimes called Negroes "coons" among all the other names, and so stealing watermelons became "cooning" them. If white boys were doing it, it implied that they were only acting like Negroes. Whites have always hidden or justified all of the guilts they could by ridiculing or blaming Negroes.

One Halloween night, I remember that a bunch of us were out tipping over those old country outhouses, and one old farmer—I guess he had tipped over enough in his day—had set a trap for us. Always, you sneak up from behind the outhouse, then you gang together and push it, to tip it over. This farmer had taken his outhouse off the hole, and set it just in *front* of the hole. Well, we came sneaking up in single file, in the darkness, and the two white boys in the lead fell down into the outhouse hole neck deep. They smelled so bad it was all we could stand to get them out, and that finished us all for that Halloween. I had just missed falling in myself. The whites were so used to taking the lead, this time it had really gotten them in the hole.

Thus, in various ways, I learned various things. I picked strawberries, and though I can't recall what I got per crate for picking, I remember that after working hard all one day, I wound up with about a dollar, which was a whole lot of money in those times. I was so hungry, I didn't know what to do. I was walking away toward town with visions of buying something good to eat, and this older white boy I knew, Richard Dixon, came up and asked me if I wanted to match nickels. He had plenty of change for my dollar. In about a half hour, he had all the change back, including my dollar, and instead of going to town to buy something, I went home with nothing, and I was bitter. But that was nothing compared to what I felt when I found out later that he had cheated. There is a way that you can catch and hold the nickel and make it come up the way you want. This was my first lesson about gambling; if you see somebody winning all the time, he isn't gambling; he's cheating. Later on in life, if I were continuously losing in any gambling situation, I would watch very closely. It's like the Negro in America seeing the white man win all the time. He's a professional gambler; he has all the cards and the odds stacked on his side, and he has always dealt to our people from the bottom of the deck.

About this time, my mother began to be visited by some Seventh Day Adventists who had moved into a house not too far down the road from us. They would talk to her for hours at a time, and leave booklets and leaflets and magazines for her to read. She read them, and Wilfred, who had started back to school, after we had begun to get the relief food supplies, also read a lot. His head was forever in some book.

Before long, my mother spent much time with the Adventists. It's my belief that what mostly influenced her was that they had even more diet restrictions than she always had taught and practiced with us. Like us, they were against eating rabbit and pork; they followed the Mosaic dietary laws. They ate nothing of the flesh without a split hoof, or that didn't chew a cud. We began to go with my mother to the Adventist meetings that were held further out in the country. For us children, I know that the major attraction was the good food they served. But we listened, too. There were a handful of Negroes, from small towns in the area, but I would say that it was ninety-nine percent white people. The Adventists felt that we were living at the end of time, that the world soon was coming to an end. But they were the friendliest white people I had ever seen. In some ways, though, we children noticed, and, when we were back at home, discussed that they were different from us—such as the lack of enough seasoning in their food, and the different way that white people smelled.

J. SAUNDERS REDDING

(1906–)

From *No Day of Triumph*

So great is the pride of some men that when confronted by a gross injustice they take upon their own shoulders the entire burden of righting the wrong. Such a man was Jay Redding's father, who spent every working day of his life trying to undo the many falsehoods generally circulated about African-Americans. This beautiful vignette illustrates the fierce determination with which an individual can seek to vindicate his race—and the clearly inspiring impact of his behavior upon his son.

Jay S. Redding was born on the fringe of the South in Wilmington, Delaware, in 1906. His story is unusual in the sense that he and the other children in his family received their education without too much financial struggle. All were graduated from Northern colleges and one brother received his LL.D. from Harvard Law School. Jay Redding went to Brown. He is recognized as an eminent sociologist, historian and novelist.

As far back as I can remember, it was necessary for my father to eke out his small government salary by doing all sorts of odd jobs after his regular hours and his vacations. He belonged to a waiters' association, and frequently he served at dinners, banquets, and parties from early evening until dawn. On these occasions he wore the swallow-tailed coat in which he had been married and the black broadcloth trousers which he had picked up at a secondhand shop. This outfit always amused us, for the trousers did not cover his ankles and his big feet spread beneath them in a truly monumental fashion. The coat had a greenish tinge and fitted across his thick shoulders like a harness. My mother had to sew up the shoulder seams after every

188

use. My father cared little about the appearance of his clothes. "So long as they're clean, children," he used to say, when for reasons of pride we used to fidget with his tie, fold down his collars, and see to it that he was wearing a proper belt in his trousers. Our attentions amused him, and he would wink at our mother and say, "Girl, they've all got your side's pride."

Sometimes he would bring from these parties a satchel bulging with steaks, chicken, butter, rolls, and ice cream; and then we feasted—not because we ever went hungry, but because all this was extra and had to be eaten before it spoiled.

My father always took his annual vacation in the late summer or early fall, for then he could find employment among the farmers a few miles outside the city. He would contract to cut corn or harvest potatoes. Sometimes he stayed in the country, but when he did not, he was always back long after we were in bed and gone again before dawn. Often my brother and I, in the room next the bathroom, would wake up in the night and hear my father thrashing about in the tub and murmuring wearily to my mother, who always waited for him late in the night.

As I look back upon it now, I know that my father was driven by more than the necessity to provide a living for his family. Surrounded by whites both at home and at work, he was driven by an intangible something, a merciless, argus-eyed spiritual enemy that stalked his every movement and lurked in every corner. It goaded him every waking hour, but he could not get at it, though he felt it to be embodied in almost every white man he met. Because of this, he moved with defensive caution, calculating the effect of every action and every utterance upon his unseen enemy. Every day he won defensive victories, but every day the final victory seemed more impossible. He was up at dawn, painting the trim, repairing the roof, putting out ashes, shoveling snow from the sidewalk. In fifteen years he was never late for his work, and only once did he allow an illness to keep him home. His endurance was a thing of spirit.

But the other necessity was there too, the physical need to provide for a family that soon increased to seven. We were a problem. We helled through our clothes, and especially our shoes. My father mended our shoes with thick leather patches that balled clumsily on the soles. He trimmed our hair. When it seemed safe, he avoided doctors' bills by purging us with castor oil, plastering us with goose grease, and swathing us in flannel. I myself was often sick with ruinous colds that threatened a serious illness. I was almost constantly under the care of Dr. Elbert, who spent his time thumping my chest and giving me nauseating medicines. But no saving was too trifling, no economy too stringent for my father to make. Sometimes it was a joking matter. Our garbage pail seldom contained anything but vegetable parings and bones, for my mother, too, knew the value of a penny. Indeed, her thrift was generally more effective and yet less severe than my father's. She had a reasonableness in the matter which he lacked. Sometimes she raised objections—futilely, for instance, to my father's spending his vacation harvesting for potatoes or cutting corn. She argued the point of his health, but my father's answer was always the same: "Work wouldn't hurt a man."

When I was fourteen or fifteen, I spent a Saturday on one of these corn-cutting expeditions with him. It was the last weekend of his two-weeks vacation, and he had been working on a farm eight miles out of the city. We left home before daylight and reached the farm just at dawn. It was a large farm, and only a part of it was under cultivation. Before we set to work, the farmer joined us. He was a buck-toothed post of a man, with a skin raw and peeled-looking by the sun. The corn field lay some distance from the house and the land sloped away gently to a flat, rocky strip beyond which the corn field rose abruptly. The brown corn stood in marching rows on the side of the hill. The field had not been cared for. High weeds tangled the rows.

"Well, you overstretched yourself, looks like," the farmer said, looking at the uncut corn on the hill.

My father took off his coat and drew his corn knife from the ground, where he had left it the evening before. I saw his jaw tighten like a fist.

"I'll need a knife for my boy here," he said. "We'll get it done. The weeds will hamper us some, but we'll get it done."

"Maybe you will at that," the farmer said, kicking in a mat of weeds. "Didn' have no time to do nothin' with this crop out here myself. Had another colored feller workin' for me, but he ups an' quits 'bout the time I needed him most. Wasn' much of a loss to me, I don't reckon. He sure was a lazy one. This your boy, hunh?"

"Yes," my father said. He looked past the man. "We'll get it done all right."

"I'm from Missouri," the farmer said.

When he came back with the long-bladed corn knife, he stood for a while and watched us work. I had never cut corn before but it was simply a matter of bending one's back and swinging one's blade as close to the roots as one could. When an armful of stalks was cut, we bound them together and stood them up to finish drying for fodder. The weeds were already giving us trouble. They were wet and tough with dew and they tied themselves around our ankles. But for a while the work did not seem hard to me. My father worked easily, making of bending, swinging, grasping one flowing, rhythmic action.

"The other colored feller sure was a lazy one," the farmer said after a while.

My father did not look up, but I watched the farmer spraddle down the hill and across the rocky gully.

"Damn him," my father said. "Damn him!" It was the only time I ever heard him curse. "Sure. That other colored fellow was lazy. Come on, son. Do you want him to think we're lazy too?"

It began to be hard work cutting uphill, and pretty soon the sun was at us. The weeds grabbed at our blades and we had to hack through them to get at the corn. My father cut very fast and determinedly, paying no attention to me. By nine o'clock my legs were rubbery with fatigue. I could hear my father working the dry, screeching corn somewhere ahead and to the left of me. He made an aspirant sound every time he swung his blade, and this came to me quite distinctly. "Hac. Hac. Hac." I seemed to be floating. My head felt enormously swollen. Bending to the corn, I could feel myself falling, but I had no strength to prevent it. I fell face down in the weeds, struggled up. Then suddenly the earth exploded in my face with blackening, sickening force.

When I came around again, my father was kneeling beside me. His face was gray and hard and his eyes and mouth were like Grandma Redding's. My nose was still bleeding a little and blood was on my shirt and smeared on the damp rag with which my father was stroking my face. He had stuck a twig under my upper lip.

"What's the matter, son?" my father asked. "Feel all right now?"

I spit out the twig. "I can't keep up."

"That's all right. I shouldn't have brought you." He was still stroking my face with the wet, blood-smeared rag. It was unpleasant. I smelled and tasted blood. He looked across the gully toward the house that stood naked and ugly in the broad stroke of the sun. "I'll give that farmer a piece of my mind yet," he said.

"When he said, 'I'm from Missouri,' that's slang," I said. "People say I'm from Missouri when they don't believe you can do something. They say, 'Show me.'"

"I'll show him," my father said.

After lunch I felt strong enough to work again, but my father made me lie under the lip of the hill out of the sun, and all afternoon I listened to the sound of his working moving farther and farther away from me. He finished the field just before dark.

IV

The Twentieth Century:
1951 to the Present—

After We Have Overcome

THE TIME BETWEEN THE EMANCIPATION PROCLAMATION AND BROWN VS. the Board of Education was not quite a hundred years. From 1954 to 1984 when Jesse Jackson ran for president was thirty short years. In historic terms, the change in the status of black Americans is revolutionary, but in social terms, the change is slow and often painful.

These selections tell us about children who knew the Sixteenth Street Baptist Church bombing, Rosa Parks, Martin Luther King, Jr., the march to Selma, the march on Washington, the summer of love, Malcolm X, Vietnam War protests, Kent State, Huey Newton, "Black Power," naturals, and integrated schools. The messages of the time were confusing and conflicting: cultural integration *vs.* cultural separatism, acceptance *vs.* fear, nonviolence *vs.* armed revolution. This section captures that confusion and pain.

ELIZABETH ECKFORD

(1942–)

as told to Daisy Bates
From *The Long Shadow*
of Little Rock

Elizabeth Eckford was one of the black pupils to whom Little Rock's Central High School reluctantly opened its doors in the now famous integration showdown of 1957. The children had originally planned to enter the school in a group, but with racial tensions beyond the danger level, plans were suddenly changed. Eckford somehow was never notified of this change. Thus it came to pass that she was left completely alone to face the full fury of the rabid mob that had gathered outside the school. The experience left her near hysteria and it was a long time before she was able to recount the episode. The following selection is her account of the near-tragic incident as told to Daisy Bates

Eckford graduated from Central High School in 1960. She attended Knox University in Galesburg, Illinois, for one year, then transferred to Central State College in Wilberforce, Ohio.

"The day before we were to go in, we met Superintendent Blossom at the school board office. He told us what the mob might say and do but he never told us we wouldn't have any protection. He told our parents not to come because he wouldn't be able to protect the children if they did.

"That night I was so excited I couldn't sleep. The next morning I was about the first one up. While I was pressing my black and white dress—I had made it to wear on the first day of school—my little brother turned on the TV set. They started telling about a large crowd

195

gathered at the school. The man on TV said he wondered if we were going to show up that morning. Mother called from the kitchen, where she was fixing breakfast. 'Turn that TV off!' She was so upset and worried. I wanted to comfort her, so I said, 'Mother, don't worry.'

"Dad was walking back and forth, from room to room, with a sad expression. He was chewing on his pipe and he had a cigar in his hand, but he didn't light either one. It would have been funny, only he was nervous.

"Before I left home Mother called us into the livingroom. She said we should have a word of prayer. Then I caught the bus and got off a block from the school. I saw a large crowd of people standing across the street from the soldiers guarding Central. As I walked on, the crowd suddenly got very quiet. Superintendent Blossom had told us to enter by the front door. I looked at all the people and thought, 'Maybe I will be safer if I walk down the block to the front entrance behind the guards.'

"At the corner I tried to pass through the long line of guards around the school so as to enter the grounds behind them. One of the guards pointed across the street. So I pointed in the same direction and asked whether he meant for me to cross the street and walk down. He nodded 'yes.' So I walked across the street conscious of the crowd that stood there, but they moved away from me.

"For a moment all I could hear was the shuffling of their feet. Then someone shouted, 'Here she comes, get ready!' I moved away from the crowd on the sidewalk and into the street. If the mob came at me I could then cross back over so the guards could protect me.

"The crowd moved in closer and then began to follow me, calling me names. I still wasn't afraid. Just a little bit nervous. Then my knees started to shake all of a sudden and I wondered whether I could make it to the center entrance a block away. It was the longest block I ever walked in my whole life.

"Even so, I still wasn't too scared because all the time I kept thinking that the guards would protect me.

"When I got right in front of the school, I went up to a guard again. But this time he just looked straight ahead and didn't move to let me pass him. I didn't know what to do. Then I looked and saw that the path leading to the front entrance was a little further ahead. So I walked until I was right in front of the path to the front door.

"I stood looking at the school—it looked so big! Just then the guards let some white students go through.

"The crowd was quiet. I guess they were waiting to see what was going to happen. When I was able to steady my knees, I walked up to the guard who had let the white students in. He too didn't move. When I tried to squeeze past him, he raised his bayonet and then the other guards closed in and they raised their bayonets.

"They glared at me with a mean look and I was very frightened and didn't know what to do. I turned around and the crowd came toward me.

"They moved closer and closer. Somebody started yelling, 'Lynch her! Lynch her!'

"I tried to see a friendly face somewhere in the mob—someone who maybe would help. I looked into the face of an old woman and it seemed a kind face, but when I looked at her again, she spat on me.

"They came closer, shouting, 'No nigger bitch is going to get in our school. Get out of here!'

"I turned back to the guards, but their faces told me I wouldn't get help from them. Then I looked down the block and saw a bench at the bus stop. I thought, 'If I can only get there I will be safe.' I don't know why the bench seemed a safe place to me, but I started walking toward it. I tried to close my mind to what they were shouting, and kept saying to myself, 'If I can only make it to that bench I will be safe.'

"When I finally got there, I don't think I could have gone another step. I sat down and the mob crowded up and began shouting all over again. Someone hollered, 'Drag her over to this tree! Let's take care of this nigger.' Just then a white man sat down beside me, put his arm around me and patted my shoulder. He raised my chin and said, 'Don't let them see you cry.'

"Then, a white lady—she was very nice—she came over to me on the bench. She spoke to me but I don't remember now what she said. She put me on the bus and sat next to me. She asked me my name and tried to talk to me but I don't think I answered. I can't remember much about the bus ride, but the next thing I remember I was standing in front of the School for the Blind, where Mother works.

"I thought, 'Maybe she isn't here. But she has to be here!' So I ran upstairs, and I think some teachers tried to talk to me, but I kept running until I reached Mother's classroom.

"Mother was standing at the window with her head bowed, but she must have sensed I was there because she turned around. She looked as if she had been crying, and I wanted to tell her I was all right. But I couldn't speak. She put her arms around me and I cried."

ITABARI NJERI

(1955–)

From *Every Good-bye Ain't Gone*

Descending from a Harvard-educated, Marxist historian and a nurse of West Indian ancestry, Itabari Njeri was bound to have an interesting childhood. She grew up in Brooklyn and Harlem surrounded by family, a colorful family with tragedy and history. One of her aunts was a gangster's moll in Harlem. Her great-great-great grandfather was a pirate. Her grandfather was killed under suspicious circumstances in an automobile wreck with a white driver in Georgia.

If her childhood was colorful, it was sometimes unhappy. Her father and mother were separated but occasionally reunited. Her father was aloof and bitter, sometimes abusive, and often drunk. Barred from prestigious teaching positions because of his leftist political leanings, he taught at a Jersey City high school. While she hated and was intimidated by her father, his brilliance attracted her. At the same time, she resented her mother's acceptance of his abuse.

Njeri, a graduate of Boston University and the Columbia University School of Journalism, is an award-winning journalist on staff with the Los Angeles Times. *She captured the characters of her life in this well-received autobiography in 1990, and the following piece is excerpted from it.*

By the time I'd hit the kitchen she was in high gear: burning sugar, dicing currants, pouring out the extra-proof rum—sipping the extra-proof rum. Be aware: The cake my grandmother made bore no resemblance to the pale, dry, maraschino cherry–pocked fruitcakes most Americans know. This was a traditional West Indian fruitcake

198

and an exquisite variation of it at that.

As a little girl and since, I've been to more than a few West Indian celebrations where the host served a dry, crumbling, impotent confection and dared to call it fruitcake. Only good manners prevented me from going *spittooey* on the floor, like some animated cartoon character. Instead, the members of my family would take a bite, control themselves, then exchange smug glances: Nothing like Ruby's, we'd agree telepathically.

What Ruby Hyacinth Duncombe Lord created was the culmination of a months-long ritual. The raisins, the prunes, the currants and the citron were soaked in a half gallon of port wine and a pint of rum for three months in a cool, dark place. Even after the cake was baked, liquor was poured on it regularly to preserve it and keep it moist for months. When you finally bit into a piece, the raisins spat back rum.

On the special occasions the cake was served—holidays, birthdays, weddings—I was often outfitted in some party frock my mother, or one of the West Indian seamstresses on the block, had made. Sometimes a bit of hem or a snap required last-minute adjustments. My grandmother would run for the sewing tin and make the alterations with me still in the dress. Her mending done, the needle and thread poised in her upheld hand, she grabbed my wrist.

"Grandmaaaaaah," I squealed extravagantly. She sucked her teeth at my absurd resistance.

"Stop that noise before I knock you into oblivion. Are you insane? Do you actually wish to walk around in your burial shroud?" she asked incredulously. And then she pricked the inside of my wrist, breaking the spell of death that fell when cloth was sewn on a living soul.

I do not know the origins of the practice. Perhaps it was African, as were many things, I later learned, we did and said without realizing it. But such things were not unusual in that place, at that time.

I lived in a country one Brooklyn block long. It was an insular world of mostly West Indians who dwelled in both stately and sagging brownstones, and the occasional wood house that dotted the street.

Scattered among them were Afro-American immigrants from the South. Most mornings, the elder members of these extended families could be seen sweeping and hosing down the sidewalk in front of their row or wood-frame homes. Many of them had come north during the first great migration of blacks from the South around World War I. They were escaping the neoslavery of the post-Reconstruction period. At the same time, my maternal grandparents were sailing from the Caribbean to the United States, fleeing the social prison of British colonialism.

Many of these early Afro-British and Afro-American migrants had saved enough money to buy homes in this Clinton Hill enclave and the surrounding Fort Greene neighborhood in the 1940s when the area opened up to blacks.

Our landlady, and hairdresser, too—she operated a discreet salon on the ground floor of her 1860 Italianate row house—was from Barbados. For years, beginning with my mother, she rented the tree-shaded second floor of her home to members of my family before they bought houses of their own.

The block's most recent arrivals seemed to live in the one tenement I recall on our street, a sturdy, pre–World War II structure whose communal corridors were as tidy as the foyers in the block's private homes.

Like most immigrants, those on our street seemed to possess a drive, tenacity and pride that often set them apart from their countrymen. The social ravages of northern, urban life had yet to engulf the citizens of St. James Place. And the American century, a little past its midpoint, had not fully become what it is—vulgar and dangerous without respite.

As I prepared to leave this country each morning, boarding the bus to the Adelphi Academy nursery school, the old man hosing down the street would wave to me and say, "Be good now." I do not remember his name, if I ever knew it. The people outside of my immediate family and their intimate circle of friends were of fleeting significance to me then. My first seven years on earth were dominated by island voices, resounding in narrow brownstone parlors where all that was wood was perfumed by lemon oil, and parquet floors glowed with the reflected light of chandeliers. It was here, in this world, that we cut the fruitcake.

"Love doll, come give Mariella a kiss," my brother's godmother called to me at one of these house parties, extending her arms and jiggling her bosom. She lived across the street and ran a boarding-house with a crew of mostly male students from Africa, the Middle East and the Caribbean. She was a good friend to my mother and a second grandmother to me. Ruby took her latter status as a personal insult, an offense compounded by Mariella's looks (pretty), size (petite), manner (flirtatious), and age (ten to fifteen years off my grandmother's).

Among her other sins, Mariella was from St. Croix, and her musical accent and speech tended to be as informal and coquettish as Ruby's were imperial and bellicose.

"Y'know," said Mariella, pointing to me, "I raise her since she was this high." She bent down and measured about a foot off the floor. I was five and looked at her strangely. Even then I could figure out she'd probably had too much rum.

Ruby sucked her teeth disgustedly at Mariella's familial claims, and my mother shot her a don't-start-anything glance. Later, I'd hear my grandmother mutter, "Old gypsy pussy," and label anything Mariella said "Anansi story anyway."

"Gypsy pussy" went right over my head at the time, and it took years of repeated hearings—my grandmother sticking the label on any woman she considered flighty—before its meaning dawned on me.

As for "Anansi story," I always thought she was talking about Nancy, some lady I'd never met. I didn't know Anansi was the famed character of West African folklore, the spider who spun tales, his stories still told by the descendants of Africans who'd been brought to Jamaica.

With my two grandmothers in the room—the monarch an the gypsy—someone offered a toast. All raised their glasses but no one drank before a bit of liquor had been flicked with fingers to the floor. Ruby had already sprinkled spirits over the threshold when my mother moved into the apartment. Both gestures were a blessing and an ancestral offering.

While I did spend a lot of time with Mariella, who had two grand-children my age, it was Ruby who was waiting for me after a hard half day at nursery school, then kindergarten, then the first and second grades. I'd tarry with my friends at the candy store before coming home, stocking up on red licorice, candy lipsticks and peppermint sticks. But Ruby and the whole block knew when I was approaching home; my voice came around corners before I did. I knew the Hit Parade by heart, a fact that did not always please my grandmother.

"You too forward," she'd call down to me, her voice floating from our kitchen window above the limestone stairs where I'd planted myself with my bag of candy. Elbows on the stoop, legs dangling the length of three stone steps, I ignored my grandmother and kept singing.

"Oh the wayward wind is a restless wind, a restless wind that yearns to wander, and I was born—"

"What you know about a wayward wind, child? Come upstairs." I loved the regal lilt of my grandmother's accent, her tickled tone, despite the firmness of her call. But I pretended not to hear.

"Sixteen tons and whadiya get, another day older and deeper in—"

"Jill Stacey!" she bellowed, as I began "Blueberry Hill."

Still stretched along the steps, I bent my long neck back, looked toward the sky and saw my grandmother's head sticking out the kitchen window. "Grandma, you want me?" I asked, my scuffed saddle shoes still beating time against the pavement.

"I found my thrill . . ."

"Eh-eh," Ruby uttered quickly, then sucked her teeth. "Yes, it's you that I want. Come and don't try me. Ya know I old and fricasseed."

"What's fricasseed?"

"It's what you do to a tough old bird like me. Now come," she shouted, pulled her head in, then shut the window.

Most afternoons, after I climbed the stairs, we listened to *Our Gal Sunday* and *Helen Trent* during the waning days of radio melodramas. And when my mother bought a television set, we became equally avid fans of *As the World Turns*. As we stared at the tube, I rubbed my grandmother's thickly callused feet with a pumice stone. It was the ritual that accompanied our afternoon entertainment.

Grandma would put down her washboard, wipe her hands on the skirt of her white apron, then sit with her feet in the basin of hot water I had prepared. These were no longer the feet of a pampered, Creole, island princess. And from my spot on the floor, I could smell the Clorox on her hands.

As I tended her crusty feet, I had only the faintest notion then of what life had been like for her in Jamaica. The details of her past came in fragments over the years—a long snatch from her every now and then, a snippet from my mother, a revelation from a cousin or an aunt.

I'd seen only one picture of her back in Jamaica. It was taken in Kingston, where she was born in 1897, shortly before she came to America, circa 1917. The photograph captured her standing regally erect, her buxom, hourglass figure wrapped in an ankle-length white dress. Her cotton-soft hair was pulled tightly into a bun, stretching her taupish-brown skin taut across her cheekbones.

I've often entertained the idea of putting that picture on a round, ruby-red tin that held my grandmother's fruitcake and selling it. The label would read:

DUNCOMBE-LORD

"The World's Finest Traditional West Indian Fruitcake"

You'd have to order it through Bloomingdale's or Neiman-Marcus. Grandma would like that. But the recipe would have to be kept a secret.

When my grandmother came to the United States, she promised her brother, James Vincent Duncombe, that she would never give the coveted formula to anyone outside the family. He was a lawyer and probably realized a mint could be made from these cakes if Ruby ever had the capital and opportunity to go into business. In fact, wealthy Americans for whom she had worked as a housekeeper and cook tried to buy it from her so they could sell it commercially. "Never," she told them. But it wasn't just the pact with her brother. The measure and the manner of her culinary alchemy was one of the few family treasures she still possessed in America. Her middle-class, multiracial background meant next to nothing here. And given the reality of colonial Jamaica, her place of privilege there was severely circumscribed by an odious color-caste system. The island's lighter-hued, mixed-race population may have isolated itself from the black majority, but its members remained second-class citizens under British colonial rule.

There was a gate in front of my grandmother's house in Kingston, she once told me. She was forbidden to go beyond it to play with certain children.

"Why?" I asked her when I was an adult.

Her response was vague but firm. "We just could not."

"What reason did your mother give?"

She looked at me as if I were stupid, then sucked her teeth. "We did not question our parents."

I suspected her lack of candor came from embarrassment. She did not want to admit that color and class differences were the probable reasons she was forbidden to play with the children. In America, she had become a follower of Marcus Garvey. His wife, Amy, had been one of her childhood friends.

Nonetheless, I've always suspected my grandmother of being an ambivalent black nationalist, drawn to the Garveyites because there was no caste to insulate her from the rawness of American racism.

But I can't be certain; she never offered any clear ideological argument for her "Back to Africa" sympathies.

On the one hand, to this day, if she could she would stand for the Queen of England if Elizabeth appeared on TV and the British national anthem were played. She did so when I was growing up. But if you asked her if she wanted to go back to Jamaica, she'd ask you emphatically, "For what? There's nothing in Jamaica I want to go back to."

Otherwise, she did display a certain nationalist consistency. She proudly quoted the King James Bible: "Princes shall come out of Egypt; and Ethiopia shall soon stretch out her hands unto God." She would always say it dramatically, her arms reaching out to me, ending the quote with a booming *"Yes!"*

She joined the African Orthodox Church, too, renouncing her family's Catholicism in the 1930s because the Pope, she said, had blessed the ammunition the Italians used to kill the Ethiopians.

And she made it plain that her father was a Haitian, proudly declaring his complexion "black, black, black," to make a clear distinction between him and the European father of her half sister, Marie.

More about her father I couldn't say. On this matter, Ruby was also curiously vague. In her day, she insisted again, children didn't press their parents about such matters as paternity.

But I do know something about her mother, Alice Dacre Duncombe. My oldest first cousin, Karen, saw a picture of her and described her as a pretty woman with pale, nearly white skin and long dark hair that she wore in two braids, each one draped over a shoulder. Exactly how my great-grandmother Alice managed to own so much property and run her own business, a dry goods store, in the late nineteenth century is a mystery to me. Shopkeeping had long been a common occupation for free men and women of color in Jamaica. But whether she inherited her property from her well-to-do mixed-race and European relatives, or from her husbands, remains a puzzle.

Though I've heard the stories of the servants and the grand house the Duncombes had in Jamaica and have seen some of the exquisite jewelry and silverware they owned, I suspect Ruby was at best shakily middle-class in Kingston. If not, why did her brother, my uncle Vin, have to come to Detroit and work in Henry Ford's factory to make enough money to finish law school? And he chose to stay in the States after receiving his degree, maintaining a marginal law practice under American apartheid in the 1930s, 1940s and 1950s. (His grandchildren did much better. One granddaughter, Beth Duncombe, is part of a flourishing law practice in Detroit. Her sister, Trudy Duncombe Archer, was assistant dean of the Detroit College of Law, where her grandfather got his degree, and is now a district court judge in Michigan. Her husband, Dennis Archer, is Michigan's second black supreme court justice.)

But in early twentieth-century Jamaica, the Duncombe family's position was precarious. They were mixed-race but dominantly African, and the real nonwhite, middle-class power brokers in colonial Jamaica were the East Indians and Chinese.

There couldn't have been many available men in my grandmother's class to choose from. My aunt Rae, confirming this one day, laughed and said, "You think Mama would have come here if they had any prospects for her in Jamaica?"

Fresh from Ellis Island, Ruby joined her brother, my uncle Vin, in Detroit. In the motor city, she met my granddaddy, and pinned her hopes on this soon-to-be physician from Guyana.

Earl Lord defined arrogance. He truly was tall, dark and handsome, the product of a New World mixture of African, English, East Indian and Amer-Indian. The black Lords of the New World were the descendants of a notorious pirate named Sam Lord. He was my great-great-great-grandfather, and you can spend a few nights in his castle if you go to Barbados. The Marriott hotel chain has turned the place into a popular resort hotel.

This pirate, so the story goes (his life was fictionalized in a 1980 novel called *A Regency Rascal* by W. P. Drury), was actually a landlubbing one. With the aid of slaves from his plantation, he lured ships to a nearby reef by hanging lanterns in the coconut trees. Mariners seeing them thought they were the lights of ships anchored in a safe harbor. When the ships ran aground on the shoals, Lord took possession of the cargo, dispatching the sailors who had not drowned.

The castle he had built in Barbados in 1820 was constructed entirely by slave labor. And though he and his wife had only one child that lived, Samuel Lord had twenty children by four enslaved African women. I wish my family knew as much about those anonymous women, one of whom was my great-great-great-grandmother, as they do about this bandit who allegedly stole money entrusted to him by his nieces and nephews and regularly threw his wife into the dungeon till she fled back to England. He returned to England, too, eventually, and died there in 1845.

The black branch of the Lord clan migrated to Guyana toward the end of the last century, and the men, true to the Lord tradition, were tyrannical patriarchs and womanizers. Though my grandfather didn't deviate from that pattern in his youth, he had mellowed considerably, my mother said, by the time I was born.

To this day, I don't know for certain how many children he had, but there were nine "legitimate" ones, as well as my mother's "twin," at last count. Just as Granddaddy was ending years of financial struggle and starting his medical practice, he left the first four of those children and my grandmother to marry Madelyn Parsons. It was the middle of the Depression, and my grandmother was ill prepared to support a family alone—being a foreign dignitary without portfolio here.

But it seems that Earl Lord was not an irresponsible father, just a dictatorial one. He attempted to bring his children to the South, where he'd established his medical practice. But by that time, his first set of offspring were in their teens, and they apparently didn't want to cross the Mason-Dixon line.

Uncle Alex had to drop out of school to support the family. Always a hard worker, he was never without a job. But there are few good jobs any man, especially a black man, can get without a high school diploma.

My aunt Rae, thought to have the brains of the bunch and destined for law school, married too young and spent her working life in dead-end clerical jobs.

Aunt Glo, the youngest, had theatrical aspirations. She decided to be "hep" till she dropped. Her fast life finally made a few newspapers, I understand, the shame of which compelled my mother to move to Brooklyn after college instead of Harlem, where Aunt Glo was the moll of a well-known gangster. Like Thomas Wolfe, I guess my mom thought only the dead knew Brooklyn.

Vivien, my mother, was the only one who escaped the destructive economic and social consequences of my grandfather's absence. She was beautiful, the oldest, very practical and sickly. She went south for the warm weather and lived with Granddaddy while she was in high school. She wanted to be a social worker. Granddaddy wanted her to be a nurse and he made it clear that if he was paying her college tuition, she was going to be a nurse.

Meanwhile, my grandmother was not entirely without resources of her own. She had a good education and spoke with a refined, Afro-British accent. The former was of no particular value in America. But the latter, combined with her color and talent in the kitchen, qualified her as an exotic variation of the colored housekeeper/cook. After moving from Detroit to Washington, D.C., where Granddaddy was enrolled at Howard University, Ruby moved to New York to be with other members of her family. In Greenwich Village, she was welcomed into the homes of doctors and lawyers for a while as head cook and bottle washer. But rich people fall on hard times, too. Grandma was out of work. She and her children went on the relief rolls. To make extra money, she sold her fruitcakes for weddings and holidays.

I never saw my grandmother in a place of her own. Perhaps she could have done more with her life despite the profound and pervasive racism that defined America most of her eighty-nine years. Some of her children seemed to think so. "Spoiled" and "lazy" were words family members often used to describe Ruby. "A con artist," too. As an adult, I have seen my grandmother play both ends against the middle, with cash as the reward. But as a child, I thought she could do no wrong.

When the Oxydol commercial ended the half-hour television drama we'd been watching, I dried her feet and smoothed on the almond-scented lotion we both loved. These concluding actions overlapped seamlessly each day and were ceremoniously sealed by the *clang-clang* of the junk man's belled cart and the *clip-clop* of his horse down St. James Place.

If I recall this time and this place too idyllically, do not blame it on a child's naive rendering of reality, or an adult's wistful longing alone. St. James Place, now part of a landmark district because of its unique architecture and social history, was a haven. My mother sought a more genteel existence and found it there. My recollections are testimony to her determination to insulate me from the certain cruelty that lay just beyond the borders of the block. For contrary to what I felt, the world was a dangerous place for black people.

As I sat tending my grandmother's feet that afternoon in 1957, another year would have to pass before the NAACP could report, for the first time in its history, that there had been *no* lynchings in America. Just an avenue away, my mother couldn't rent an apartment because "No Negroes" were allowed. And I know the block I loved was not held together by culture and class alone. Segregation was the glue, too. It was, after all, just a genteel ghetto.

The junk man's changing bell became faint music as he rolled south toward Fulton Street. Her feet soothed, my grandmother dozed in the parlor, her elbow propped on the arm of the chair, her chin and jowls resting in the palm of her hand. I crept toward the TV to turn it off.

She stirred. "What you doing?" she asked, her voice phlegm-filled and hoarse. "Leave that set alone," she said, squinting at me. "Every shut eye ain't sleep. Every good-bye ain't gone." Indeed, the earth has ears. The night has eyes. "And put *that* in your pipe and smoke it," she instructed.

Several years later, circumstances would compel us to leave St. James Place and I would eventually cease to think of myself as a West Indian first and foremost.

We would buy fifteen-cent tokens, take the A train north of there to 125th, and move into the apartment my father had rented since the waning days of the Harlem renaissance. There, I would discover a new kind of beauty, a new kind of brilliance, a new kind of pain.

ANGELA DAVIS

(1941–)

From *Angela Davis: An Autobiography*

Angela Davis came to national attention in 1970 when she was wanted by the FBI on charges of murder, kidnapping, and conspiracy, because a gun registered in her name was used in a politically charged courtroom kidnapping and murder. She was found not guilty on all charges. What made a caring, bookish young woman from Birmingham, Alabama, into a revolutionary activist in Los Angeles, California?

When she was four years old, Davis and her family became the first black family in an all-white neighborhood. Soon after her family came to the neighborhood, other black families followed. Resentful whites fought the integration and so often resorted to violence and bombings that the area become known as Dynamite Hill.

At her segregated school, Carrie A. Tuggle Elementary School, Davis learned Negro history, honored Negro History Week, and sang the "Negro National Anthem" along with "My Country tis of Thee" or the "Star Spangled Banner."

An exceptionally compassionate child, she stole change from her father to give to hungry children at her school. Davis developed a strong sense of justice and a tendency to intervene in conflicts. Summer visits to New York City, where her mother was studying for her master's degree at New York University, exposed Davis to a world where blacks could sit anywhere on the bus. She hated the racist rules of the South and those that enforced them.

The excerpt describes events in Davis's teen years.

My childhood friends and I were bound to develop ambivalent attitudes toward the white world. On the one hand there was our instinctive aversion toward those who prevented us from realizing our grandest as well as our most trivial wishes. On the other, there was the equally instinctive jealousy which came from knowing that they had access to all the pleasurable things we wanted. Growing up, I could not help feeling a certain envy. And yet I have a very vivid recollection of deciding, very early, that I would never—and I was categorical about this—never harbor or express the desire to be white. This promise that I made to myself did nothing, however, to drive away the wishdreams that filled my head whenever my desires collided with a taboo. So, in order that my daydreams not contradict my principles, I constructed a fantasy in which I would slip on a white face and go unceremoniously into the theater or amusement park or wherever I wanted to go. After thoroughly enjoying the activity, I would make a dramatic, grandstand appearance before the white racists and with a sweeping gesture, rip off the white face, laugh wildly and call them all fools.

Years later, when I was in my teens, I recalled this childish daydream and decided, in a way, to act it out. My sister Fania and I were walking downtown in Birmingham when I spontaneously proposed a plan to her: We would pretend to be foreigners and, speaking French to each other, we would walk into the shoe store on 19th Street and ask, with a thick accent, to see a pair of shoes. At the sight of two young Black women speaking a foreign language, the clerks in the store raced to help us. Their delight with the exotic was enough to completely, if temporarily, dispel their normal disdain for Black people.

Therefore, Fania and I were not led to the back of the store where the one Black clerk would normally have waited on us out of the field of vision of the "respectable" white customers. We were invited to take seats in the very front of this Jim Crow shop. I pretended to know no English at all and Fania's broken English was extremely difficult to make out. The clerks strained to understand which shoes we wanted to try on.

Enthralled by the idea of talking to foreigners—even if they did happen to be Black—but frustrated about the communication failure, the clerks sent for the manager. The manager's posture was identical. With a giant smile he came in from his behind-the-scenes office saying, "Now, what can I do for you pretty young ladies?" But before he let my sister describe the shoes we were looking for, he asked us about our background—where were we from, what were we doing in the States and what on earth had brought us to a place like Birmingham, Alabama? "It's very seldom that we get to meet people like you, you know." With my sister's less than elementary knowledge of English, it required a great effort for her to relate our improvised story. After repeated attempts, however, the manager finally understood that we came from Martinique and were in Birmingham as part of a tour of the United States.

Each time this man finally understood something, his eyes lit up, his mouth opened in a broad "Oh!" He was utterly fascinated when she turned to me and translated his words. The white people in the store were at first confused when they saw two Black people sitting in the "whites only" section, but when they heard our accents and conversations in French, they too seemed to be pleased and excited by seeing Black people from so far away they could not possibly be a threat.

Eventually I signaled to Fania that it was time to wind up the game. We looked at him: his foolish face and obsequious grin one eye-blink away from the scorn he would have registered as automatically as a trained hamster had he known we were local residents. We burst out laughing. He started to laugh with us, hesitantly, the way people laugh when they suspect themselves to be the butt of the joke.

"Is something funny?" he whispered.

Suddenly I knew English, and told him that he was what was so funny. "All Black people have to do is pretend they come from another country, and you treat us like dignitaries." My sister and I got up, still laughing, and left the store.

I had followed almost to the *t* the scenario of my childhood daydream.

In September 1949, Fania had just turned one, and my brother Benny was about to turn four. Having spent three years playing the same games in nursery school and visiting the hospital next door, I was ready for something different and had pleaded to go early to elementary school. On the Monday after Labor Day, wearing my stiff new red plaid dress, I jumped into my father's truck, eager to begin my first day at "big" school.

The road to school took us down Eleventh Court across the overpass above the railroad tracks, through the street dividing the Jewish Cemetery in half and three blocks up the last hill. Carrie A. Tuggle School was a cluster of old wooden frame houses, so dilapidated that they would have been instantly condemned had they not been located in a Black neighborhood. One would have thought that this was merely a shoddy collection of houses built on the side of a grassless hill if it had not been for the children milling around or the fenced-in grave out front, bearing a sign indicating that Carrie A. Tuggle, founder of the school, was buried there.

Some of the houses were a motley whitewashed color. Others were covered with ugly brownish-black asphalt siding. That they were spread throughout an area of about three square blocks seemed to be proof of the way the white bureaucracy had gone about establishing a "school" for Black children. Evidently, they had selected a group of rundown houses and, after evicting the inhabitants, had declared them to be the school. These houses stood all along a steep incline; at the bottom of the hill, there was a large bowl-shaped formation in the earth, covered with the red clay that is peculiar to Alabama. This empty bowl had been designated the playground. Houses similar to the school buildings were located around the other sides of the bowl, houses whose outsides and insides were falling to pieces.

My mother, a primary school teacher herself, had already taught me how to read, write and do simple arithmetic. The things I learned in the first grade were far more fundamental than school learning. I learned that just because one is hungry, one does not have the right to a good meal; or when one is cold, to warm clothing, or when one is sick, to medical care. Many of the children could not even afford to buy a bag of potato chips for lunch. It was agonizing for me to see some of my closest friends waiting outside the lunchroom silently watching the other children eating.

For a long time, I thought about those who ate and those who watched. Finally I decided to do something about it. Knowing that my father returned from his service station each evening with a bag of coins, which he left overnight in a kitchen cabinet, one night I stayed awake until the whole house was sleeping. Then, trying to overcome my deep fear of the dark, I slipped into the kitchen and stole some of the coins. The next day I gave the money to my hungry friends. Their hunger pangs were more compelling than my pangs of conscience. I would just have to suffer the knowledge that I had stolen my father's money. My feelings of guilt were further appeased by reminding myself that my mother was always taking things to children in her class. She took our clothes and shoes—sometimes even before we had outgrown them—and gave them to those who needed them. Like my mother, what I did, I did quietly, without any fanfare. It seemed to me that if there were hungry children, something was wrong and if I did nothing about it, I would be wrong too.

This was my first introduction to class differences among my own people. We were the not-so-poor. Until my experiences at school, I believed that everyone else lived the way we did. We always had three good meals a day. I had summer clothes and winter clothes, everyday dresses and a few "Sunday" dresses. When holes began to wear through the soles of my shoes, although I may have worn them with pasteboard for a short time, we eventually went downtown to select a new pair.

The family income was earned by both my mother and father. Before I was born, my father had taken advantage of his hard-earned college degree, from St. Augustine's in Raleigh, North Carolina, to secure a position teaching history at Parker High School. But life was especially difficult during those years; his salary was as close to nothing as money could be. So with his meager savings he began to buy a service station in the Black section of downtown Birmingham.

My mother, who, like my father, came from a very humble background, also worked her way through college and got a job teaching in the Birmingham elementary school system. The combined salaries were nothing to boast about, yet enough to survive on, and much more than was earned by the typical Southern Black family. They had managed to save enough to buy the old house on the hill, but they had to rent out the upstairs for years to make the mortgage payments. Until I went to school I did not know that this was a stunning accomplishment.

The prevailing myth then as now is that poverty is a punishment for idleness and indolence. If you had nothing to show for yourself, it meant that you hadn't worked hard enough. I knew that my mother and father had worked hard—my father told us stories of walking ten miles to school each day, and my mother had her collection of anecdotes about the difficult life she had led as a child in the little town of Sylacauga. But I also knew that they had had breaks.

My preoccupation with the poverty and wretchedness I saw around me would not have been so deep if I had not been able to contrast it with the relative affluence of the white world. Tuggle was all the shabbier when we compared it to the white school nearby. From the top of the hill we could see an elementary school for white children. Solidly built of red brick, the building was surrounded by a deep-green lawn. In our school, we depended on potbellied coal stoves in winter, and when it rained outside, it rained inside. By the time a new building was constructed to replace the broken-down old one, I was too old to spend more than a year or so in its classrooms, which were reserved for the lower grades.

There were never enough textbooks to go around, and the ones that were available were old and torn, often with the most important pages missing. There was no gym for sports periods—only the "bowl." On rainy days when the bowl's red clay was a muddy mess, we were cooped up somewhere in one of the shacks.

Tuggle was administered and controlled as a section of the "Birmingham Negro Schools" by an all-white Board of Education. Only on special occasions did we see their representatives face to face—during inspections or when they were showing off their "Negro schools" to some visitor from out of town. Insofar as the day-to-day activities were concerned, it was Black people who ran the school.

Perhaps it was precisely these conditions that gave us a strong positive identification with our people and our history. We learned from some of our teachers all the traditional ingredients of "Negro

History." From the first grade on, we all sang the "Negro National Anthem" by James Weldon Johnson when assemblies were convened—either along with or sometimes instead of "The Star Spangled Banner" or "My Country,'Tis of Thee." I recall being very impressed with the difference between the official anthems, which insisted that freedom was a fact for everybody in the country, and the "Negro National Anthem," whose words were of resistance. And although my singing voice was nothing I wanted to call attention to, I always sang the last phrases full blast: "Facing the rising sun, till a new day is born, let us march on till victory is won!"

As we learned about George Washington, Thomas Jefferson and Abraham Lincoln, we also became acquainted with Black historical figures. Granted, the Board of Education would not permit the teachers to reveal to us the exploits of Nat Turner and Denmark Vesey. But we were introduced to Frederick Douglass, Sojourner Truth and Harriet Tubman.

One of the most important events each year at Tuggle was Negro History Week. Special events were planned for assembly, and in all grades each child would be responsible for a project about a Black historical or contemporary figure. Throughout those years, I learned something about every Black person "respectable" enough to be allotted a place in the history books—or, as far as contemporary people were concerned, who made their way into "Who's Who in Negro America" or *Ebony* magazine. The weekend before Negro History Week each year, I was always hard at work—creating my poster, calling on the assistance of my parents, clipping pictures, writing captions and descriptions.

Without a doubt, the children who attended the de jure segregated schools of the South had an advantage over those who attended the de facto segregated schools of the North. During my summer trips to New York, I found that many of the Black children there had never heard of Frederick Douglass or Harriet Tubman. At Carrie A. Tuggle Elementary School, Black identity was thrust upon us by the circumstances of oppression. We had been pushed into a totally Black universe; we were compelled to look to ourselves for spiritual nourishment. Yet while there were those clearly supportive aspects of the Black Southern school, it should not be idealized. As I look back, I recall the pervasive ambivalence at school, an ambivalence which I confronted in virtually every classroom, and every school-related event. On the one hand, there was a strong tendency affirming our identity as Black people that ran through all the school activities. But on the other hand, many teachers tended to inculcate in us the official, racist explanation for our misery. And they encouraged an individualistic, competitive way out of this torment. We were told that the ultimate purpose of our education was to provide us with the skills and knowledge to lift ourselves singly and separately out of the muck and slime of poverty by "our own bootstraps." This child would become a doctor, this one a lawyer; there would be the teachers, the engineers, the contractors, the accountants, the businessmen—and if you struggled extraordinarily hard, you might be able to approach the achievements of A. G. Gaston, our local Black millionaire.

This Booker T. Washington syndrome permeated every aspect of the education I received in Birmingham. Work hard and you will be rewarded. A corollary of this principle was that the road would be harder and rockier for Black people than for their white counterparts. Our teachers warned us that we would have to steel ourselves for hard labor and more hard labor, sacrifices and more sacrifices. Only this would prove that we were serious about overcoming all the obstacles before us. It often struck me they were speaking of these obstacles as if they would always be there, part of the natural order of things, rather than the product of a system of racism, which we could eventually overturn.

I continued to have my doubts about this "work and ye shall be rewarded" notion. But, I admit, my reaction was not exactly straightforward. On the one hand, I did not entirely believe it. It didn't make sense to me that all those who had not "made it" were suffering for their lack of desire and the defectiveness of their will to achieve a better life for themselves. If this were true, then, great numbers of our people—perhaps the majority—had really been lazy and shiftless, as white people were always saying.

But on the other hand, it seemed that I was modeling my own aspirations after precisely that "work and be rewarded" principle. I had made up my mind that I was going to prove to the world that I was just as good, just as intelligent, just as capable of achieving as any white person. At that time—and until my high school years in New York—I wanted to become a pediatrician. Never once did I doubt that I would be able to execute my plans—after elementary school, high school, then college and medical school. But I had a definite advantage: my parents would see to it that I attended college, and would help me survive until I could make it on my own. This was not something that could be said for the vast majority of my schoolmates.

The work-and-be-rewarded syndrome was not the only thing which seemed to fly in the face of the positive sense of ourselves. We knew, for example, that whenever the white folks visited the school we were expected to "be on our P's and Q's," as our teachers put it. I could not understand why we had to behave better for them than we behaved for ourselves, unless we really did think they were superior. The visitors from the Board of Education always came in groups— groups of three or four white men who acted like they owned the place. Overseers. Sometimes if the leader of the group wanted to flaunt his authority he looked us over like a herd of cattle and said to the teacher, "Susie, this is a nice class you have here." We all knew that when a white person called a Black adult by his or her first name it was a euphemism for "Nigger, stay in your place." When this white assault was staged, I tried to decipher the emotions on the teacher's face: acquiescence, obsequiousness, defiance, or the pain of realizing that if she did fight back, she would surely lose her job.

Once a Black teacher did fight back. When the white men called him "Jesse" in front of his class, he replied in a deep but cold voice, "In case you have forgotten, my name is Mr. Champion." He knew, as the words left his lips, that he had just given up his job. Jesse Champion was a personal friend of my parents, and I was appalled by the silence that reigned among the Black community following his act. It probably stemmed from a collective sense of guilt that his defiance was the exception and not the norm.

Nothing in the world made me angrier than inaction, than silence. The refusal or inability to do something, say something when a thing needed doing or saying, was unbearable. The watchers, the head shakers, the back turners made my skin prickle. I remember once when I was seven or eight, I went along with my friend Annie Laurie and her family on a trip to the country. At the house we visited, a dog was running around in the yard. Soon another dog appeared. Without any warning the two animals were tearing at each other's throats. Saliva was flying and blood gushed from the wounds. Everyone was just standing, looking, doing nothing. It seemed we would stand there all day watching the hot Alabama sun beat down on the stupid, pointless fight of two dogs gnawing out each other's guts and eyes I couldn't stand it any longer; I rushed in and tried to pull the dogs apart. It wasn't until after the screaming adults had dragged me away that I thought about the danger. But then it didn't matter; the fight had been stopped.

The impulse I felt then was with me at other fights. Fights not between animals but between people, but equally futile and meaningless. All through school there were absurd battles—some brief, but many sustained and deadly. I frequently could not keep from stepping in.

The children fought over nothing—over being bumped, over having toes stepped on, over being called a name, over being the target of real or imagined gossip. They fought over everything—split shoes, and cement yards, thin coats and mealless days. They fought the meanness of Birmingham while they sliced the air with knives and punched Black faces because they could not reach white ones.

It hurt me. The fight in which my girl friend Olivia got stabbed with a knife. It hurt to see another friend, Chaney—furious when a teacher criticized her in front of the class—stand up, grab the nearest chair and fly into the teacher with it. The whole class turned into one great melee, some assisting Chaney, others trying to rescue the teacher, and the rest of us trying to break up the skirmish.

It hurt to see us folding in on ourselves, using ourselves as whipping posts because we did not yet know how to struggle against the real cause of our misery.

Time did not cool the anger of the white people who still lived on the hill. They refused to adapt their lives to our presence. Every so often a courageous Black family moved or built on the white side of Center Street, and the simmering resentment erupted in explosions and fires. On a few such occasions, Police Chief Bull Conner would announce on the radio that a "nigger family" had moved in on the white side of the street. His prediction "There will be bloodshed tonight" would be followed by a bombing. So common were the bombings on Dynamite Hill that the horror of them diminished.

On our side, old houses abandoned by their white inhabitants were gradually bought up, and the woods where we picked blackberries were giving way to new brick houses. By the time I was eight or nine, we had a whole neighborhood of Black people. When the weather was warm, all the children came out after dark to play hide and go seek. There were many hiding places within our boundaries, which were not less than one or two square blocks. The night made the game more exciting, and we could pretend we were outsmarting the white folks.

Sometimes we actually dared to penetrate their turf. "I dare you to go up on the Montees' porch," one of us would say. Whoever took him up would leave us on our side of the street as he hesitantly crossed over into enemy territory, tiptoed up the Montees' cement steps, touched the wooden porch with one shoe as if he were testing a hot stove, then raced back to us. When it was my turn, I could virtually hear the bombs going off as I ran up the steps and touched the Montee porch for the first time in my life. When this game began to lose its aura of danger, we made it more challenging. Instead of just touching the porch, we had to run to the door, ring the bell and hide in the bushes around their house, while the old woman or old man came out, trying to figure out what was going on. When they finally caught on to our game, even though they could seldom find us, they stood on the porch screaming, "You little niggers better leave us alone!"

In the meantime my playmates and school friends were learning how to call each other "nigger," or what, unfortunately, was just as bad in those days, "black" or "African," both of which were considered synonymous with "savage." My mother never allowed anyone to say the word "nigger" in the house. (For that matter, no "bad words"— "shit," "damn," not even "hell" could be uttered in her presence.) If we wanted to describe an argument we had had with someone, we had to say, "Bill called me that bad word that starts with an *n*."

Eventually, my mouth simply refused to pronounce those words for me, regardless of how hard I might want to say them.

If, in the course of an argument with one of my friends, I was called "nigger" or "black," it didn't bother me nearly so much as when somebody said, "Just because you're bright and got good hair, you think you can act like you're white." It was a typical charge laid against light-skinned children.

Sometimes I used to secretly resent my parents for giving me light skin instead of dark, and wavy instead of kinky hair. I pleaded with my mother to let me get it straightened, like my friends. But she continued to brush it with water and rub vaseline in it to make it lie down so she could fix the two big wavy plaits which always hung down my back. On special occasions, she rolled it up in curlers made out of brown paper to make my Shirley Temple Curls.

One summer when our Brownie troop was at Camp Blossom Hill, it started to rain as we were walking from the mess hall to our cabins, and the girls' hands immediately went for their heads. The water was no threat to my unstraightened hair, so I paid no attention to the rain. One of the girls switched out and said, "Angela's got good hair. She can stroll in the rain from now to doomsday." I know she wasn't intentionally trying to hurt me, but I felt crushed. I ran back to my cabin, threw myself on the bunk sobbing.

My cousins Snookie, Betty Jean and their mother, Doll, lived in Ketona, Alabama. I always loved to spend the weekend with them, because I knew they would put the hot comb over the wood fire and run it through my hair until it was straight as a pin. If I begged my mother long enough, she would let me wear it to school for a few days before she made me wash it out.

Downtown near the post office was the Birmingham Public Library. It was open only to white people, but in a hidden room in the building, accessible only through a secret back entrance, a Black librarian had her headquarters. Black people could pass lists of books to her, which she would try to secure from the library.

As a result of my mother's encouragement and prodding, books became a gratifying diversion for me. Mother taught me how to read when I had hardly reached my fourth year and eventually, when I was a little older, we both established a quota system for the number of books I should be reading per week. My mother or father picked up my books downtown, or else the Black librarian, Miss Bell, would bring them by the house.

Later a new Black library was built down the hill, on the corner of Center Street and Eighth Avenue. The new red brick library, with its shiny linoleum floors and varnished tables, became one of my favorite hangouts. For hours at a time, I read avidly there—everything from *Heidi* to Victor Hugo's *Les Misérables*, from Booker T. Washington's *Up From Slavery* to Frank Yerby's lurid novels.

Reading was far more satisfying than my weekly piano lessons and Saturday morning dance classes. For my fifth Christmas, my mother and father had gotten enough money together to buy me a full-sized piano. Once a week I trudged over to Mrs. Chambliss' house, dutifully played my scales and compositions, suffering the humiliation of being screamed at if I made a mistake. When the lesson was over, I paid her seventy-five cents and, if it was dark, waited for Mother or Daddy to pick me up so I wouldn't have to walk by the cemetery alone. On the other six days, I had to practice before I went out in the neighborhood with my friends. Around the end of May each year, Mrs. Chambliss' recital took place either at St. Paul's Methodist Church or the 16th Street Baptist Church two blocks away from my father's service station. With my hair in curls, wearing a ruffled organdy dress, rigid with nervousness, I tapped out the piece I had been practicing for months. The reward for the ordeal was three whole months without the pressure of piano lessons.

Saturday mornings I joined scores of leotard-clad girls at the Smithfield Community Center in the projects where we used to live. There Mrs. Woods and her helpers made sure we did our pliés and arabesques. Ballet during the first part of the class, then tap, soft shoe. My natural clumsiness defied the delicate ballet steps, so I always tried to find a place to hide in one of the back rows. For a while, my little brother, Benny, was coming along, so I had the added responsibility of taking care of him. One morning as we were walking down Center Street, he ran out in front of me—straight across Ninth Avenue. A bus came screeching to a stop, practically knocking him down. Trembling violently, I ran to rescue him. He was totally oblivious to the fact that he had almost been killed. During the warm-up exercises, I was still shaking. Suddenly I felt something warm streaming down my legs. I dropped to the floor, into the puddle of my urine, so humiliated I couldn't bear to look up at the staring faces of the other pupils. A girl named Emma came over and put her arms around my shoulder. Saying, "Angela, don't worry. Let's go outside," she led me away. She never knew how much her gesture meant to me. Still, having to face this same crowd every Saturday filled me with shame.

Some years back, Black visitors to Birmingham had all of three post cards from which to choose if they wanted a souvenir of the Black section of the city. Sixteenth Street Baptist Church. Parker High School. A. G. Gaston's Funeral Home. Perhaps the white people who made the photographs and retouched them in bright reds and yellows had decided that our lives could be summarized by church, school and funerals. Once we were born, we got religion and a sprinkling of learning; then there was nothing left to do but die.

They tried to make this sprinkling of learning appear to come from the most impressive institution of education around. On the picture post card, Parker looked brand new, whiter than if it had been white-washed the day before, and had bright-green grass painted in front, where the dry dust refused to yield even a weed. Above the picture, stamped in bold black print, were the words: "A. H. Parker High School, Largest in the World for Colored Pupils"—as if there should have been tourists from every region of the globe coming to get a glimpse of this wonder.

Perhaps, on its face, the statement was true—I don't think anyone ever did the research to confirm or contradict it. But whatever truth it contained rested squarely on the miserable conditions of Black people. If Parker was the "largest high school for colored pupils," it was for the same reason that there was not a single public high school in Harlem and the same reason that the education of Black youth in South Africa doesn't merit a grain of consideration. When my mother was high school age, the "world's largest" had been called Industrial High School, and it was the only Black high school for hundreds of miles around. She lived in the small town of Sylacauga, at least seventy-five miles from the city. The only way she could hope to get an education beyond the eighth grade was to leave her family and move to Birmingham.

My friends and I were not overly eager to enter high school. When we graduated from Carrie A. Tuggle Elementary School, we had to enter Parker Annex, several blocks away from the main building. This was a cluster of beaten-up wooden huts not much different from what we had just left.

When we arrived on the first day we discovered that the inside of these structures was even more dilapidated than the outside. Unpainted wooden floors, ancient walls covered with graffiti no one ever bothered to remove. We realized that when the season began to turn, we would have to depend on the archaic potbellied stove in the corner of each house—we called them Shack I, Shack II, etc.

Very few of my classes were stimulating—biology, chemistry, mathematics were the subjects that interested me most. My history classes were a farce. Farcical not so much because of the teachers' deficiency as the deficiency of the textbooks assigned by the Board of Education. In our American History book I discovered that the Civil War was the "War for Southern Independence" and that Black people much preferred to be slaves than to be free. After all, the books pointed out, the evidence of our ancestors' cheerful acceptance of their plight was the weekly Saturday night singing and dancing sessions. In elementary school, we had already been taught that many of the songs by slaves had a meaning understood only by them. "Swing Low, Sweet Chariot" for instance also referred to the journey toward freedom in *this* life. But there was nothing about this in our high school textbooks. The teachers either had too much on their hands keeping the classes orderly or else they were not as concerned as our elementary-school teachers were about presenting us with an accurate picture of Black history.

The inner-directed violence which was so much a part of our school lives at Tuggle accelerated at Parker to the point where it verged on fratricide. Hardly a day would pass without a fight—in class or outside. And on one warm and wind-swept day—right there in the schoolyard—one of my schoolmates actually succeeded in knifing all life from another.

We seemed to be caught in a whirlpool of violence and blood from which none of us could swim away.

About the time I entered high school, the civil rights movement was beginning to awaken some Black Alabamians from their deep but fretful sleep. But judging from the general inactivity at Parker High School, you never would have known that Rosa Parks had refused to move to the back of the bus in Montgomery on December 4, 1955, or that Martin Luther King was leading a full-scale bus boycott there, just a hundred miles away, or that, in fact, there was supposed to be a budding bus movement in Birmingham.

Some of us were affected by the boycott, however. On a few occasions, a small group of my schoolmates and I spontaneously decided to sit in the front of the bus to show our support of our sisters and brothers. Inevitably, a shouting match ensued between us and the bus driver. The Black people on the bus were forced to take sides. Because there was no extensive organized movement at that time in Birmingham, some of them were afraid of our audacity and implored us to do what the white man said.

Around this time, the NAACP was declared illegal in Alabama, and its members were threatened with imprisonment. My parents were both members and determined not to allow Bull Conner and company to scare them into submission. Like others who related to the movement, my parents received bomb threats, but they continued to pay their dues until the NAACP was officially dissolved and replaced by the Alabama Christian Movement for Human Rights, headed by Reverend Fred Shuttlesworth.

On the day after Christmas in 1956, the bus protest in Birmingham was scheduled to be launched by the ACMHR. Having decided to crush it before it had a chance to gather momentum, the racists, encouraged by Bull Conner, pulled out of the closet their old trusty weapons: the sticks of dynamite we had come to know so well. Christmas night, a roaring explosion ripped through the home of Reverend Shuttlesworth. They had planted the bomb beneath the house, directly under the bed where the minister was sleeping. People said that it was a miracle of God that everything around him was blown to pieces, yet the minister escaped without a scratch. We learned the next day that he had taken a neighbor who had been hurt during the explosion to the hospital and had returned home by bus, riding in the front.

Later that day quite a number of people followed Reverend Shuttlesworth's example and were subsequently arrested.

I was very agitated during those days. Something was happening which could change our lives. But I was too young, so I was told (I was twelve), and a girl at that, to be exposed to the billy clubs and violence of the police. As the years passed, however, and the needs of the movement increased, it became necessary to incorporate every man, woman and child who was willing into all levels of protest activity. In fact, shortly thereafter, the Shuttlesworth children began to play leading roles in ACMHR's work.

While these upheavals were exploding in the streets of Birmingham, little of it penetrated Parker's campus. Over the next three years, the movement reached high points and then lulled. The daily schedule of classes, complemented by football and basketball games, went on. The off-campus social life of the Black middle class continued undisturbed—except for the usual, routine racist incidents.

For instance, one Sunday some friends and I were driving home from the movies. Among those in the car was Peggy, a girl who lived down the street. She was very light-skinned, with blond hair and green eyes. Her presence usually provoked puzzled and hostile stares because white people were always misidentifying her as white. This time it was a policeman who mistook her for a white person surrounded by Black people. And just as my friends were about to drop me off in front of the house, he forced us over to the side, demanding to know what we niggers were doing with a white girl. He ordered us out of the car and searched all of us, except Peggy, whom he separated from the group. In Alabama at that time, there was a state statute which prohibited all except economic intercourse between Blacks and whites. The cop threatened to throw all of us in jail, including Peggy, whom he called a "nigger lover."

When Peggy angrily explained that she was Black like all the rest of us, the cop was obviously embarrassed. He worked off his embarrassment by harassing us with foul language, hitting some of the boys and searching every inch of the car for some excuse to take us to jail. This was a routine incident, perhaps even milder than most, but no less enraging because it was typical.

At fourteen, in my junior year, I felt restless and exceedingly limited. The provincialism of Birmingham bothered me, and I had not yet been swept up into the Civil Rights Movement to the extent that it could forge for me a solid raison d'être. I could not define or articulate the dissatisfaction I felt. I simply had the sensation of things closing in on me—and I wanted to get out. The time was fast approaching when, in order not to be outcasts, girls my age in middle-class circles had to play an active role in the established social life of the Black community. I hated the big formal dances and felt very awkward and out of place at the one or two such events I attended. I had to get away. One way or another, I was going to leave Birmingham.

I discovered two avenues of escape: the early entrance program at Fisk University in Nashville and an experimental program developed by the American Friends Service Committee, through which Black students from the South could attend integrated high schools in the North. I applied for both and, after some months, learned that I had been accepted by both.

With medical school in mind, at first I had a strong inclination toward the Fisk alternative. Fisk would not only be an escape from the provincialism I detested, it would also mean that I could more easily pursue my plans to become a pediatrician; Meharry Medical School was right on its campus. And Fisk was among the most academically prestigious Black universities in the country. It was the Fisk of W. E. B. DuBois. But it was also the University of the Black Bourgeoisie par excellence, and I could predict that my disinclination to become involved in purely social affairs would create enormous personal problems. Probably if I did not pledge a sorority, I would remain an outsider.

As far as the American Friends' program was concerned, I had been able to gather only the most rudimentary information. I knew that the school I would attend, Elisabeth Irwin High School, was in New York and that I would live with a white family in Brooklyn. Though I knew nothing about the school, New York still fascinated me. I thought of all the things I had not been able to do for the first fifteen years of my life. I could do them in New York. I had a very undeveloped appreciation of music or the theater; I could look forward to exploring a whole new cultural universe.

Ready and willing to accept the challenge of the unknown, I was only a little frightened. My mother thought more about the dangers I might confront, and though she wanted me to receive a fuller education, she was distressed about my having to leave home. I was only fifteen and she feared that a year on a university campus, surrounded by men and women much older than I, would rob me of the rest of my childhood and make me mature before my time. I don't think she quite realized that any Black child growing up in the South is forced to mature "before her time" anyway. But when she considered New York, all she could see was a gigantic house of horrors. Elisabeth Irwin was located in Greenwich Village, which, to her, was the haven of weird beatniks.

My own preference was Elisabeth Irwin High School, New York City, where I would live in the home of W. H. Melish. But because of Mother's misgivings, I was willing to content myself with Fisk. We telephoned the Melishes in New York and informed them with regret of our decision. I tried to think about the positive side of Fisk: In four years, I would be nineteen and could attend Meharry Medical School; a few years later I would be curing children.

With my suitcases packed and my mind snapped shut, I was ready to go (even if I had not bought all the suggested clothes on the list, such as formals for various occasions). One or two days before I was to leave, my father, my dear father, broke out of his normal reticence and asked me to tell him frankly what I wished to do. But before I could answer, he said he wanted to tell me about some of his own experiences during his brief stay at Fisk. (He had graduated from St. Augustine College in Raleigh, North Carolina, but had done some graduate work at Fisk.) It was a very good school, he said. But to accomplish anything there you had to enter the place with an unwavering conception of what you were going to do. I had to see both sides of Fisk, he said, its historical significance to Black people—and its problems as well.

By the time we wound up the conversation, I knew that I would not be attending Fisk University, at least not that year. I would just have to persuade my mother that I was capable of defending myself against whatever dangers might be lurking in the streets of New York.

BEBE MOORE CAMPBELL

(1950–)

From *Sweet Summer*

Bebe Moore Campbell divided her childhood. Mother-Father. North-South. Integrated-Segregated. During the winter, she lived with her mother and grandmother in Philadelphia, where she was a good pupil at an integrated school. Every summer, she went to live with her father in North Carolina, where she could not check books out of the local library.

When Campbell returned home each fall, her social worker mother would have to coach her not to use the "Negro colloquialisms" she picked up down South, the words used by her father, grandmother, and uncles in North Carolina. She learned from both her parents. Her mother, who attended the University of Pennsylvania on a full scholarship, taught her to seize opportunity, to be better than "them"—a credit to her race. From her father, a paraplegic from a car accident, she learned of determination and dignity.

Campbell, recipient of a National Endowment for the Arts Literature Grant, is a journalist living in Los Angeles. This excerpt comes from the memoirs of her childhood.

The blare of Monday's late bell jolted the last vestiges of torpor from my bones. In September I had entered 5A. In January 1961 I skipped 5B and went to the sixth grade. Most of my fifth-grade classmates accompanied me to Miss Tracy's room. The Philadelphia school system, in order to end midyear graduations, had abandoned the A/B grade levels. In January most students were skipped into the next grade, although some were retained.

Miss Tracy nodded her head and held out her hands, letting her palms face her students; she drew her hands upward. I rose with the rest of the class and placed my hand over my heart, shifting my weight from foot to foot and staring straight ahead at the bulletin boards, which were still covered with red and green construction-paper Santa Clauses and Christmas trees. I acted as if I were speaking, but when the rest of the class said, "I pledge allegiance to the flag..." I only mouthed the words. Months before, Reverend Lewis had told the congregation that Negroes in the South were being beaten by white people because they wanted to integrate lunch counters at drugstores. A few weeks earlier, while Mommy, Nana, Michael and I were sitting in the living room watching television, the show was interrupted; the announcer showed colored people trying to march and white policemen coming after them with giant German shepherds.

"Now you know that ain't right," Nana had said angrily.

The day after I saw that news bulletin I was saying the Pledge of Allegiance in class and right in the middle of it my head started hurting so bad I thought it was gonna fall off and I felt so mad I wanted to punch somebody. I didn't want to say the pledge, that was the problem. I was afraid not to say anything, so I just kept opening my mouth, but nothing came out. After that I only pretended to say the words. If they were gonna sic dogs on Negroes then I wasn't gonna say some pledge and I wasn't gonna sing "The Star-Spangled Banner" neither. Not for them, I wasn't.

Sixth grade was rough. In the first place, I didn't like Miss Tracy. None of my friends liked her either. She was the meanest teacher I ever had, so full of rules and ultimatums. No talking. No erasures on spelling tests. No going to the bathroom except at recess. No this, no that. Always use her name when addressing her. No, Miss Frankenstein. Yes, Miss Frankenstein. She sent Linda out of the room just because she said "Excuse me" to me when she dropped my spelling paper. I mean...really. I could see Linda through the small glass window in the door, standing outside in the hall crying while we graded the spelling papers. Causing my best friend's tears was enough for me to start hating Miss Tracy, but I had other reasons.

It was a year of hot breathing and showdowns at Logan. We were sixth-graders, on our way out the door and feeling our oats every step of the way. Some of the boys began to sound a little bit like men, their upper lips darkened and their chests expanded. Among the girls, an epidemic of hard little bumps popped out on our chests. First Carol, then Linda, then me. We were embarrassed; we were proud. But the little band of Negroes at Logan felt something more than puberty. Fierce new rhythms—bam de bam de *bam bam bam!*—were welling up inside us. We were figuring things out. At home in the living room with our parents we watched the nightly news—the dogs, the hoses and nightsticks against black flesh—and we seethed; we brought our anger to school. The rumor flew around North Philly,

West Philly and Germantown that Elvis Presley had said, "All colored people can do for me is buy my records and shine my shoes." In the schoolyard and the classroom we saw the sea of white surrounding us and we drew in closer. We'd been fooling ourselves. It didn't matter how capable we were: it was *their* school, *their* neighborhood, *their* country, *their* planet. We were the outsiders and they looked down on us. Our bitterness exploded like an overdue time bomb.

"Miss Tracy doesn't like Negroes," I announced to Carol and Linda when we sat under the poplar tree at recess.

Linda got excited. "How do you know that?"

"You ever notice how she never picks us to do anything? And she's always putting our names on the board for talking and she doesn't ever put David's name on the board and all he does is run his mouth and eat boogers."

"And try to act like his Elvis Presley," Carol added. "Miss Tracy's always calling us 'you people.' And remember that time she sent Wallace to the office when that white boy stepped on his foot?"

"That doesn't mean she doesn't like Negroes," Linda said doubtfully. Carol and I looked at each other and shook our heads. What a baby.

"Well, what does it mean, then?" I asked Linda sarcastically.

"It means she doesn't like the Negroes in her room," Carol said dryly.

The skirmishes were slight affairs, nothing anyone could really put a finger on. A black boy pushed a white boy in line. A black girl muttered "cracker" when a white girl touched her accidentally. One afternoon when David was walking past our tree Carol yelled, "Elvis Presley ain't doing nothing but imitating colored people. And he can't even sing." David looked at her in astonishment. She put her hands on her hips and declared, "I ain't buying his records and I ain't shining his shoes neither!"

"Boys and girls, you're growing up," Miss Tracy said to the class one afternoon. Yes, we were. Something hot and electric was in the air.

The winter before I graduated from Logan Elementary, there was a disturbance in my class. Miss Tracy was absent and we had a substitute, a small, pretty woman named Mrs. Brown. She had taught us before, and all of us liked her because if we finished our work she would let us play hangman. We were spelling that day, going through our list of words in the usual, boring way. Mrs. Brown picked someone and the person had to go to the blackboard and write a sentence using the spelling word. We had three more words to go and I'd already been picked, so my interest in the whole process was waning. Hurry up, I thought. I was only half listening when I heard Mrs. Brown ask Clarence, who was wearing his everyday uniform, a suit and a tie, to stop talking. Clarence turned a little in his chair and frowned. He continued to talk.

"Did you hear me, Clarence?" Mrs. Brown asked.

"No."

Everybody turned to stare at Clarence and to check him for any outward signs of mental instability. Nobody talked back to teachers at Logan. Mrs. Brown coughed for a full minute, then stood up and asked Clarence to go to the board. Her voice was sharp. Clarence slouched in his seat. "No," he said almost lazily. Nobody breathed. Mrs. Brown said he would have to go to the principal's office if he wouldn't behave. All of us in class shuddered as if we were one body. Was Clarence crazy? I thought of my own dark trek to the principal's office. Nobody wanted to visit Jennie G. Clarence glared at Mrs. Brown so forcefully that she turned away from him. Clarence said slowly, "Later for the principal. Later for you. Later for all y'all white people. Send me to the principal. That don't cut no cheese with me."

Everything happened fast after that, after it was clear that Clarence had lost his mind. Mrs. Brown quickly dispatched one of the boys to bring Mr. Singer, who appeared moments later at the door. Mrs. Brown conferred with Mr. Singer hastily and then he took Clarence by the arm and ushered him out of the room. Clarence did a diddy-bop hoodlum stroll and showed not one bit of remorse as he left.

As soon as he was gone, Mrs. Brown leaned back in her chair and put the sides of her hands to her temples. The small diamond on her finger glittered in the sunlight. "Why would he say such awful things to me? Why?" she demanded, looking at the class. "Why?" she repeated, her eyes now focusing on every dark face in the class as if we alone knew the answer. Everyone was looking at Linda, Carol, Wallace and me, I realized. And they were . . . scared. Their eyes asked: Are you like Clarence? Are you angry too? Mrs. Brown tried to start the lesson again, but nobody was concentrating. Linda, Carol and I looked at each other cautiously. It was silently agreed: we wouldn't explain anything.

"That nigger's crazy!" Wallace whispered as we filed outside for recess. There was no more that could be said.

In the schoolyard, in our compact circle, we whooped like renegades. "He sure told Mrs. Brown off!" we exclaimed, falling all over each other in our excitement. "Later for all y'all white people," we repeated that single line, giggling as we slapped each other's thighs. I thought not of the dogs and the nightsticks, but of the ponytails and poodle skirts on *Bandstand*, bobbing and swishing off beat, twisting and turning so happily. Carol, Linda and I nodded at each other. The single vein of anger that was growing in us all had been acknowledged this day. We had a crazy nigger in our midst, close enough for comfort.

Clarence, of course, was suspended. A much more subdued boy returned to school flanked by his mother and father. The grapevine said that Jennie G. had said sternly to his parents, "We will not tolerate that kind of rude, uncivilized behavior at Logan. Is that clear?" When it was all over, Clarence had to apologize to Mrs. Brown and tell her he didn't know what on earth had gotten into him. But I knew.

I turned eleven in February. My father drove to Philadelphia to celebrate, and he took my mother and me to dinner at Horn & Hardart because the aisles were wide enough for his wheelchair. After we ate I got behind Daddy and pushed him, and we all went around the corner to the movies. The usher stared when Daddy came in, and said, "Now you aren't gonna block up the aisle, are you?"

Mommy looked straight ahead past the man. Daddy stuck out his chin a little, laughed and said, "Where would you like me to sit, mister?" I could tell he was mad. We ended up sitting in the back. Daddy hopped into the aisle chair and folded up his chair and leaned it against the outside of his seat. I sat next to him and every time something funny or exciting happened, I squeezed Daddy's hand until I was sure he wasn't angry anymore.

We came straight home after the movie. After my father parked the car in front of our house, my parents handed me a small box. Inside was a thin Timex watch with a black strap. I gasped with happiness and excitement. I was sitting between my mother and father, admiring my watch, basking in their adoration. I'd forgotten all about the usher. This is the way it should always be, I thought. When my mother said it was time for us to go in I said, "Kiss Daddy."

Mommy paused for a moment. My father looked awkward. He leaned toward my mother. She pecked him on the cheek.

"No. Not like that," I chided them. "Kiss on the lips."

They obeyed me and gave each other another brief, chaste peck. Why couldn't they kiss better than that? Mr. Johnston wasn't my mother's boyfriend anymore. He hadn't been around for several months. Why couldn't she love my daddy again? My mother and father didn't look at each other as they moved away.

I wanted magic from them, a kiss that would ignite their love, reunite all three of us. As my father drove off I looked down at my watch and stared at the minute hand ticking away.

Miss Tracy worked our butts off until just before graduation. She assigned us a health report and an arithmetic project, and we had to write a creative story using all the spelling words we'd had since January. On top of everything else, she gave us a book report.

Miss Tracy took our class to the school library and told us to find the book we wanted to do a report on and to make sure we told her what it was. I turned the library inside out trying to find a book I liked. The problem was, I'd read all the good stuff. So I asked Miss Tracy if I could get my book from the public library; she said that was fine with her.

Michael, Mommy and I went to the downtown library one Sunday after church. I searched in the young adult section for an interesting title. Then I went to where the new books were displayed and picked up one with a picture of an earnest-looking black boy in the foreground and a small town in the background. I started leafing through some of the pages and I couldn't put it down. The book was about Negroes trying to win their rights in a small southern town and how they struggled against bad white people and were helped by good ones. There weren't any bad Negroes and that fit my mood perfectly. As I was reading it, the thought hit me instantly: Miss Tracy wouldn't want me to do my report on *South Town*. She'd tell me it wasn't "suitable." I decided I wouldn't tell Miss Tracy; I'd just do the report.

The day I stood in front of the class to give my report, my mouth was dry and my hands were moist. "My book is called *South Town*," I said, holding the book up so everybody could see the cover. The whole class got quiet as they studied the black boy's serious face; Miss Tracy's head jerked up straight. "This was a very exciting, dramatic book, and I liked it a lot, because every summer I live in a place exactly like the town that was described in this book," I said, my voice rising. I had my entire book report memorized and after a while everything came easily. I walked across the room, raising my hand for dramatic flair, feeling like a bold renegade telling my people's struggle to the world. I whispered when I described a sad part of the book. I finished with a flourish. "I recommend this book for anyone interested in the struggle for Negroes to gain equal rights in America. Thank you."

As soon as I sat down I could feel Miss Tracy's breath on my neck. "You didn't ask my permission to do that report," she said. Her hazel eyes were as cold as windowpanes in February. I had forgotten how terrifying Miss Tracy's rage could be. What if she gave me an F? Or sent me to the principal's office? Oh, Lordy.

"I'm sorry," I said, my voice drained of dramatic flair. I didn't feel like such a bold renegade anymore. I was scared.

Miss Tracy turned away without saying a word. Three days later she returned the reports. At the bottom in the right-hand corner of mine there was a small B. Emblazoned across the top in fierce red ink were the words: "Learn to follow directions."

I took the report home and gave it to my mother who, of course, asked, "What directions didn't you follow?" I told her the whole story; then I held my breath. The last thing I wanted to hear was, "Bebe, I'm disappointed in you." Mommy didn't say that; she just looked at Miss Tracy's comments again. Then she said, "Sometimes you eat the bear; sometimes the bear eats you," which sounded kinda strange coming from her, because Mommy wasn't one for a lot of down-home sayings. She put the report in the bottom drawer of her bureau, where she kept my school papers and grades. "Don't worry about it," Mommy said.

Three weeks later I sat on the stage of the school auditorium in the green chiffon dress my mother made me, underneath it a brand-new Littlest Angel bra identical to the one Linda's mother had bought her. The straps cut into my shoulders, but my mind was too crowded with thoughts for me to feel any pain. As Nana, Mommy, Michael and Pete watched, I walked across the stage to receive my certificate. Pete took pictures. I wanted my father to be there, but at least I could show him the photos.

Two weeks later I kissed Mommy, Nana and Michael good-bye and climbed into my father's newest acquisition, a blue Impala convertible. "BebebebebebebebebeMoore," Daddy sang out when he saw me, then, "I guess you're getting too big for that stuff, huh?" His eyes were questioning, searching. I didn't know what to say, afraid that if I said yes, Daddy would never again make a song of my name, and if I said no, he'd think of me as a baby forever. So I leaned my head back against the seat and smiled. The wind was in my face and I was heading toward a North Carolina summer that would deliver a heartbreak and a promise.

ANNE MOODY
(1940–)

From *Coming of Age in Mississippi*

Anne Moody was born in Centreville, Mississippi. She attended
local public schools and even went to college in state—Natchez
Junior College and Tougaloo College, where she received her
bachelor of science degree in 1963. She was active in the civil
rights movement as a student, taking part in voter registration
projects and desegregation of Woolworth's lunch counter in Jackson.

In 1964 Moody became a fund raiser and public speaker for
the Council on Racial Equality (CORE). From 1964 to 1965 she
was on Cornell Campus as civil rights project coordinator, and
she worked with New York City's poverty programs in 1967. In
the early 1970s, Moody moved to Europe to study and write, a
little disillusioned with the movement. When her vision of civil
rights broadened to include a more global view of the exploited
and powerless, she left the movement, which she saw moving to
a splintered and narrowly nationalistic path. She currently lives
in New York City working as a teacher, lecturer, and writer.

In 1968, Moody wrote Coming of Age in Mississippi. The book
was received with great critical acclaim and was awarded the
American Library Association "Best Book of the Year Award" and
the Gold Medal Award" from the National Council of Catholics
and Jews. Today the book is in its eighteenth printing, has been
translated into seven languages, and is used extensively as a high
school and college text. This excerpt comes from the book.

*   *   *

CHILDHOOD

That white lady Mama was working for worked her so hard that she always came home griping about backaches. Every night she'd have to put a red rubber bottle filled with hot water under her back. It got so bad that she finally quit. The white lady was so mad she couldn't get Mama to stay that the next day she told Mama to leave to make room for the new maid.

This time we moved two miles up the same road. Mama had another domestic job. Now she worked from breakfast to supper and still made five dollars a week. But these people didn't work Mama too hard and she wasn't as tired as before when she came home. The people she worked for were nice to us. Mrs. Johnson was a schoolteacher. Mr. Johnson was a rancher who bought and sold cattle. Mr. Johnson's mother, an old lady named Miss Ola, lived with them.

Our house, which was separated from the Johnsons' by a field of clover, was the best two-room house we had been in yet. It was made out of big new planks and it even had a new toilet. We were also once again on paved streets. We just did make those paved streets, though. A few yards past the Johnsons' house was the beginning of the old rock road we had just moved off.

We were the only Negroes in that section, which seemed like some sort of honor. All the whites living around there were well-to-do. They ranged from schoolteachers to doctors and prosperous businessmen. The white family living across the street from us owned a funeral home and the only furniture store in Centreville. They had two children, a boy and a girl. There was another white family living about a quarter of a mile in back of the Johnsons who also had a boy and a girl. The two white girls were about my age and the boys a bit younger. They often rode their bikes or skated down the little hill just in front of our house. Adline, Junior and I would sit and watch them. How we wished Mama could buy us a bike or even a pair of skates to share.

There was a wide trench running from the street alongside our house. It separated our house and the Johnsons' place from a big two-story house up on the hill. A big pecan tree grew on our side of the trench, and we made our playhouse under it so we could sit in the trench and watch those white children without their knowing we were actually out there staring at them. Our playhouse consisted of two apple crates and a tin can that we sat on.

One day when the white children were riding up and down the street on their bikes, we were sitting on the apple crates making

Indian noises and beating the tin can with sticks. We sounded so much like Indians that they came over to ask if that was what we were. This was the beginning of our friendship. We taught them how to make sounds and dance like Indians and they showed us how to ride their bikes and skate. Actually, I was the only one who learned. Adline and Junior were too small and too scared, although they got a kick out of watching us. I was seven, Adline five, and Junior three, and this was the first time we had ever had other children to play with. Sometimes, they would take us over to their playhouse. Katie and Bill, the children of the whites that owned the furniture store, had a model playhouse at the side of their parents' house. That little house was just like the big house, painted snow white on the outside, with real furniture in it. I envied their playhouse more than I did their bikes and skates. Here they were playing in a house that was nicer than any house I could have dreamed of living in. They had all this to offer me and I had nothing to offer them but the field of clover in summer and the apple crates under the pecan tree.

The Christmas after we moved there, I thought sure Mama would get us some skates. But she didn't. We didn't get anything but a couple of apples and oranges. I cried a week for those skates, I remember.

Every Saturday evening Mama would take us to the movies. The Negroes sat upstairs in the balcony and the whites sat downstairs. One Saturday we arrived at the movies at the same time as the white children. When we saw each other, we ran and met. Katie walked straight into the downstairs lobby and Adline, Junior, and I followed. Mama was talking to one of the white women and didn't notice that we had walked into the white lobby. I think she thought we were at the side entrance we had always used which led to the balcony. We were standing in the white lobby with our friends, when Mama came in and saw us. "C'mon! C'mon!" she yelled, pushing Adline face on into the door. "Essie Mae, um gonna try my best to kill you when I get you home. I told you 'bout running up in these stores and things like you own 'em!" she shouted, dragging me through the door. When we got outside, we stood there crying, and we could hear the white children crying inside the white lobby. After that, Mama didn't even let us stay at the movies. She carried us right home.

All the way back to our house, Mama kept telling us that we couldn't sit downstairs, we couldn't do this or that with white children. Up until that time I had never really thought about it. After all, we were playing together. I knew that we were going to separate schools and all, but I never knew why.

After the movie incident, the white children stopped playing in front of our house. For about two weeks we didn't see them at all. Then one day they were there again and we started playing. But things were not the same. I had never really thought of them as white before. Now all of a sudden they were white, and their whiteness made them better than me. I now realized that not only were they better than me because they were white, but everything they owned and everything connected with them was better than what was available to me. I hadn't realized before that downstairs in the movies was any better than upstairs. But now I saw that it was. Their whiteness provided them with a pass to downstairs in that nice section and my blackness sent me to the balcony.

Now that I was thinking about it, their schools, homes, and streets were better than mine. They had a large red brick school with nice sidewalks connecting the buildings. Their homes were large and beautiful with indoor toilets and every other convenience that I knew of at the time. Every house I had ever lived in was a one- or two-room shack with an outdoor toilet. It really bothered me that they had all these nice things and we had nothing. "There is a secret to it besides being white," I thought. Then my mind got all wrapped up in trying to uncover that secret.

One day when we were all playing in our playhouse in the ditch under the pecan tree, I got a crazy idea. I thought the secret was their "privates." I had seen everything they had but their privates and it wasn't any different than mine. So I made up a game called "The Doctor." I had never been to a doctor myself. However, Mama had told us that a doctor was the only person that could look at children's naked bodies besides their parents. Then I remembered the time my Grandma Winnie was sick. When I asked her what the doctor had done to her she said, "He examined me." Then I asked her about "examined" and she told me he looked at her teeth, in her ears, checked her heart, blood and privates. Now I was going to be the doctor. I had all of them, Katie, Bill, Sandra, and Paul plus Adline and Junior take off their clothes and stand in line as I sat on one of the apple crates and examined them. I looked in their mouths and ears, put my ear to their hearts to listen for their heartbeats. Then I had them lie down on the leaves and I looked at their privates. I examined each of them about three times, but I didn't see any differences. I still hadn't found that secret.

That night when I was taking my bath, soaping myself all over, I thought about it again. I remembered the day I had seen my two uncles Sam and Walter. They were just as white as Katie them. But Grandma Winnie was darker than Mama, so how could Sam and Walter be white? I must have been thinking about it for a long time because Mama finally called out, "Essie Mae! Stop using up all that soap! And hurry up so Adline and Junior can bathe 'fore that water gits cold."

"Mama," I said, "why ain't Sam and Walter white?"

"'Cause they mama ain't white," she answered.

"But you say a long time ago they daddy is white."

"If the daddy is white and the mama is colored, then that don't make the children white."

"But they got the same hair and color like Bill and Katie them got," I said.

"That still don't make them white! Now git out of that tub!" she snapped.

Every time I tried to talk to Mama about white people she got mad. Now I was more confused than before. If it wasn't the straight hair and the white skin that made you white, then what was it?

HIGH SCHOOL

About two weeks after school opened, all my plans were in operation. I was busy for a total of eighteen hours a day. Each day I spent the last two periods of school on the band or on basketball. Then I would go straight to work. I was never home until eight or nine at night and as soon as I entered the house, I'd begin helping Adline and them with their lessons so I wouldn't even have to talk to Mama or Raymond. On Wednesday and Friday nights I took piano lessons. On Sundays I taught Sunday school and B.T.U.

I was so busy now that I could work for Mrs. Burke and not think of her or her guild meetings. I would fall asleep at night without dreaming old, embedded, recurring dreams. I had to keep a lot of things in the back of my mind until I finished high school.

When our mid-semester grades were released, I discovered I had made A's in all my subjects. Everything seemed so easy now. Sometimes I got scared because things were moving along too smoothly. Things had always seemed hard before. But now I was doing three times as much and I felt as if I could take on the whole world and not be tired by it. I was even better in basketball than I had ever been. In fact, I was the number one girl on the team.

Mr. Hicks, our new coach, was a nut for physical fitness—especially for girls. He hated women who were dumb about sports and he used to practice us until we were panting like overplowed mules. Sometimes he'd even take us out to play touch football with the boys so that we could learn that game. All the girls who didn't go along with his physical fitness program or who were fat and lazy he dismissed immediately. He was determined to have a winning team and was interested only in tall, slim girls who were light and fast on their feet. I think I worked harder than almost anyone else.

Shortly after mid-semester, Mr. Hicks organized a gymnastic and tumbling team. All the basketball players were required to participate. Running and heaving a ball on that open basketball court wasn't so bad, but falling on it when we did somersaults, handsprings, and rolls was like falling on steel.

Mr. Hicks was the most merciless person I had ever met. The first few weeks some of the girls could hardly walk, but he made them practice anyhow. "The only way to overcome that soreness and stiffness is to work it out," he would say. We all learned to like Mr. Hicks, in spite of his cruelty, because in the end he was always right. After three weeks our stiffness was completely gone and we all felt good. Now I took in all the activities without even getting shortwinded. And I finished the semester with straight A's.

One Wednesday, I was ironing in Mrs. Burke's dining room as usual when she came to me looking very serious.

"Essie, I am so tired and disgusted with Wayne," she said, sitting down in one of the dining room chairs. "He almost flunked out of school last semester. At this rate he won't finish high school. I don't know what to do. He's in algebra now and he just can't manage it. I've tried to find someone to tutor him in math, but I haven't been able to. How is *your* math teacher?" she asked me.

"Oh, he is very good, but he hardly ever teaches our class. Most of the time he lets me take over," I said.

"Are you that good in algebra?" she asked.

"Yes, I make all A's in algebra, and he thinks I am one of his best students."

She looked at me for a moment as if she didn't believe me. Then she left the dining room.

"Look, Essie," she said, coming back with a book. "These are the problems Wayne is having trouble with. Can you work them?"

"Yes, we've passed these in my book. I can do them all," I said.

"See if you can work these two," Mrs. Burke said to me. "I'll press a couple of these shirts for you meanwhile."

I sat down at the dining room table and began working the two problems. I finished them before she finished the first shirt.

When I gave her the paper, she looked at me again like she didn't believe me. But after she had studied it and checked my answers against the ones given in the back of the book, she asked me if I would tutor Wayne a few evenings a week. "I'll pay you extra," she said. "And I can also help you with your piano lessons sometimes."

Within a week I was helping Wayne and a group of his white friends with their algebra every Monday, Tuesday, and Thursday night. While Mrs. Burke watched television in the living room, we would all sit around the dining room table—Wayne, Billy, Ray, Sue, Judy and me. They were all my age and also in the tenth grade. I don't think Mrs. Burke was so pleased with the even proportion of boys to girls in the group. Neither did she like the open friendship that was developing between Wayne and me. She especially didn't like that Wayne was looking up to me now as his "teacher." However, she accepted it for a while. Often Wayne would drive me home after we had finished the problems for the night.

Then, one Tuesday, she came through the dining room just as Wayne was asking me a question. "Look Essie," he said, "how do we do this one?" He asked this as he leaned over me with his arms resting on the back of my chair, his cheek next to mine.

"*Wayne!*" Mrs. Burke called to him almost shouting. Wayne and I didn't move, but the others turned and stared at her. "Listen to what Essie is saying," she said, trying to get back her normal tone of voice.

"Mother, we *were* listening," Wayne said very indignantly, still cheek to cheek with me.

The room was extremely quiet now. I felt as if I should have said something. But I couldn't think of anything to say. I knew Wayne was purposely trying to annoy his mother so I just sat there, trying to keep from brushing my cheek against his, feeling his warm breath on my face. He stared at her until she looked away and went hurriedly into the kitchen.

Wayne straightened up for a moment and looked at each of his friends as they looked to him for an explanation. His face was completely expressionless. Then he leaned over me again and asked the same question he had asked before. At that point, Mrs. Burke came back through the dining room.

"Wayne, you can take Billy them home, now," she said.

"We haven't done this problem, Mother. If you would stop interrupting maybe we could finish."

"Finish the problem then and take Billy them home, but drop Essie off first," Mrs. Burke said and left the room.

I explained the problem. But I was just talking to the paper. Everyone had lost interest now.

When we left the house Mrs. Burke watched us get into the car and drive off. Didn't anyone say a word until Wayne stopped in front of my house. Then Billy said, "See you Thursday, Essie," as cheerfully as he could. "O.K.," I said, and Wayne drove away.

The following evening when I went to work, Mrs. Burke wasn't home and neither was Wayne. Mrs. Burke had left word with Mrs. Crosby that I was to do the ironing and she had put out so many clothes for me to do that by the time I finished I was late for my piano lesson. I ran out of the house and down the front walk with my music books in my hand just as Mrs. Burke and Wayne were pulling into the driveway.

"Did you finish the ironing already, Essie?" Mrs. Burke asked me, as she got out of the car.

"I just finished," I said.

"Where are you going in such a hurry?" Wayne asked.

"I'm late for my piano lesson."

"Let me drive you then," he said.

"I'm going to use the car shortly, Wayne," Mrs. Burke snapped.

"It's not far from here. I can walk," I said, rushing down the sidewalk.

The next evening Sue and Judy didn't show up. Only the boys came. Mrs. Burke kept passing through the dining room every few minutes or so. The moment we finished doing the problems, she came in and said, "Essie, I gotta stop in and see Mrs. Fisher tonight. I'll drop you off."

I had begun to get tired of her nagging and hinting, but I didn't know what to do about it. In a way I enjoyed helping Wayne and his friends. I was learning a lot from them, just as they were from me. And I appreciated the extra money. Mrs. Burke paid me two dollars a week for helping Wayne and Wayne's friends paid me a dollar each. I was now making twelve dollars a week, and depositing eight dollars in my savings account. I decided not to do anything about Mrs. Burke. "She will soon see that I won't mess with Wayne," I thought.

The Saturday afternoon I was out in the backyard hanging clothes on the line while Wayne was practicing golf.

"Essie, you want to play me a round of golf?" he asked as I finished and headed for the back door.

"I don't know how to play," I said.

"It's easy. I'll teach you," he said. "Come, let me show you something."

He gave me the golf club and tried to show me how to stand, putting his arms around me and fixing my hands on the club.

"Essie, the washing machine stopped long ago!" Mrs. Burke suddenly yelled out of the house.

"I'll show you when you finish the wash," Wayne said as I walked away. I didn't even look back at him. Walking into the house, I felt like crying. I could feel what was happening inside Wayne. I knew that he was extremely fond of me and he wanted to do something for me because I was helping him and his friends with their algebra. But the way he wanted to do it put me up tight. By trying to keep him from doing it, Mrs. Burke only made him want to do it more. I knew Wayne respected me and wouldn't have gotten out of his place if I'd remained distant and cool. Now I wanted to tell him that he didn't have to do anything for me—but I didn't know how.

Wayne, Billy, and Ray received B's on the mid-semester exams. They were so happy about their marks they brought their test papers over for me to see. I shall never forget that night. The four of us sat around the table after we had corrected the mistakes on their papers.

"Gee, Essie, we love you," Billy said. "And just think, Wayne, we could have gotten A's, and if we make an A on the final exam we will get a B for a final grade." Wayne didn't say anything for a while. He just looked at Billy, then at me. When he looked at me he didn't have to speak.

"Boy, let's call Sue and Judy and see what they got," he finally said. He ran to the phone in the hall, followed by Billy and Ray.

When they left me sitting there, I began to wonder how it was that Wayne and his friends were so nice and their parents so nasty and distasteful.

Sue and Judy came back to me for help because they almost flunked the exam. Mrs. Burke seemed more relaxed once the girls were back. However, they were not relaxed at all. They felt guilty for leaving in the first place. For a week or so they brought me little gifts and it made me nervous. But after that we were again one little happy family.

The dining room in Mrs. Burke's house had come to mean many things to me. It symbolized hatred, love, and fear in many variations. The hatred and the love caused me much anxiety and fear. But courage was growing in me too. Little by little it was getting harder and harder for me not to speak out. Then one Wednesday night it happened.

Mrs. Burke seemed to discuss her most intimate concerns with me whenever I was ironing. This time she came in, sat down, and asked me, "Essie, what do you think of all this talk about integrating the schools in the South?"

At first I looked at her stunned with my mouth wide open. Then Mama's words ran through my head: "Just do your work like you don't know nothin'." I changed my expression to one of stupidity.

"Haven't you heard about the Supreme Court decision, and all this talk about integrating the schools?" she asked.

I shook my head no. But I lied.

"Well, we have a lot of talk about it here and people seemingly just don't know what to do. But I am not in favor of integrating schools. We'll move to Liberty first. I am sure that they won't stand for it there. You see, Essie, I wouldn't mind Wayne going to school with *you*. But all Negroes aren't like you and your family. You wouldn't like to go to school with Wayne, would you?" She said all this with so much honesty and concern, I felt compelled to be truthful.

"I don't know, Mrs. Burke. I think we could learn a lot from each other. I like Wayne and his friends. I don't see the difference in me helping Wayne and his friends at home and setting in a classroom with them. I've learned a lot from Judy them. Just like all Negroes ain't like me, all white children I know ain't like Wayne and Judy them. I was going to the post office the other day and a group of white girls tried to force me off the sidewalk. And I have seen Judy with one of them. But I know Judy ain't like that. She wouldn't push me or any other Negro off the street."

"What I asked you, Essie, is if you wanted to go to school with Wayne," Mrs. Burke said stiffly. "I am not interested in what Judy's friends did to you. So you are telling me you want to go to school with Wayne!" She stormed out of the dining room, her face burning with anger.

After she left I stood at the ironing board waiting—waiting for her to return with my money and tell me she didn't need me any more. But she didn't. She didn't confront me at all before I left that evening. And I went home shaking with fear.

The next evening when I came to work I found a note from Mrs. Burke stating she was at a guild meeting and telling me what to do. That made things even worse. As I read the note my hand shook. My eyes lingered on "the Guild." Then when Wayne and his friends didn't show up for their little session with me, I knew something was wrong. I didn't know what to do. I waited for an hour for Wayne and Judy them to come. When they didn't, I went to Mrs. Crosby's room and knocked.

When Mrs. Crosby didn't answer my heart stopped completely. I knew she was in there. She had been very ill and hadn't been out in a month. In fact, I hadn't even seen her because Mrs. Burke had asked me not to go to her room. At last I put my hand on the knob of her door and slowly turned it. "She can't be dead, she can't be dead," I thought. I opened the door slowly.

"Mrs. Crosby," I called. She was sitting up in bed as white as a ghost. I saw that she must have been sleeping. Her long, long hair was not braided as usual. It was all over the pillow everywhere.

"How do you feel, Mrs. Crosby?" I asked, standing at the foot of her bed. She beckoned for me to come closer. Then she motioned for me to sit on her bed. As I sat on the bed, she took my hands and held them affectionately.

"How do you feel?" I repeated.

"Weak but better," she said in a very faint voice.

"I was suppose to help Wayne them with their algebra this evening, but they didn't come," I said.

"I know," she said. "I heard Wayne and his mother fighting last night. Wayne is a nice boy, Essie. He and his friends like you very much. However, his mother is a very impatient woman. You study hard in school, Essie. When you finish I am going to help you to go to college. You will be a great math teacher one day. Now you go home. Wayne and his friends aren't coming tonight." She squeezed my hands.

The way she talked scared me stiff. When it was time to go home and I walked out on the porch, it was dark. I stood there afraid to move. "I can't go through the project now," I thought. "Mrs. Burke them might have someone out there to kill me or beat me up like they beat up Jerry. Why did I have to talk to Mrs. Burke like that yesterday?" I took the long way home that went along the lighted streets. But I trembled with fear every time a car drove past. I just knew that out of any car five or six men could jump and grab me.

The following day, I didn't go to work. I didn't even go to school. I told Mama I had a terrible headache and I stayed in bed all day.

"Essie Mae, it's four o'clock. You better git up from there and go to work," Mama called.

"My head's still hurting. I ain't going to work with my head hurting this bad," I whined.

"Why is you havin' so many headaches? You been lazin' in bed all day. Miss Burke gonna fire you. Junior, go up there and tell Miss Burke Essie Mae is sick."

I lay in bed thinking I had to find some other ache because Mama was getting wise to my headaches. If I could only tell her about Mrs. Burke, I wouldn't have to lie to her all the time. I really missed Mrs. Rice. Mrs. Rice would have told me what to do. I couldn't talk to any of the other teachers. "What can I do?" I thought. "I can't just quit, because she'll fix it so I can't get another job."

When Junior came back, I called him into my room.

"What did Mrs. Burke say?" I asked him.

"She ain't said nothing but for you to come to work tomorrow,'cause the house need a good cleanin'. She want me to come with you to mow the yard."

I felt a little better after Junior told me that. But I couldn't understand Mrs. Burke's actions. It worried me that she was still going to keep me on. What if she was doing that just to try and frame me with something? "I'll see how she acts tomorrow," I finally decided.

At seven o'clock on Saturday morning Junior and I headed through the project for Mrs. Burke's house. Usually I took advantage of my walk through the project to think about things and compose myself before I got to work, but today I didn't have a single thought in my head. I guess I had thought too much the day before. When I walked up on her porch and saw her standing in the hall smiling it didn't even register. I was just there. I realized at that point I was plain tired of Mrs. Burke.

I went about the housecleaning like a robot until I got to the dining room. Then I started thinking. I stood there for some time thinking about Mrs. Burke, Wayne, and his friends. It was there I realized that when I thought of Wayne my thoughts were colored by emotions. I liked him more than a friend. I stood softly looking down at the table and the chair where Wayne sat when I helped him with his lessons.

When I looked up Mrs. Burke was standing in the doorway staring at me. I saw the hatred in her eyes.

"Essie," she said, "did you see my change purse when you cleaned my room?"

"No," I answered, "I didn't see it."

"Maybe I dropped it outside in the yard when I was showing Junior what to do," she said.

"So, that's how she's trying to hurt me," I thought, following her to the back door. "She better not dare." I stood in the back door and watched her walk across the big backyard toward Junior. First she stood talking to him for a minute, then they walked over to a corner of the yard and poked around in the grass as though she was looking for her purse. After they had finished doing that, she was still talking to Junior and he stood there trembling with fear, a horrified look on his face. She shook him down and turned his pockets inside out. I opened the door and ran down the steps. I didn't realize what I was about to do until I was only a few paces away from them.

"Did you find it out here, Mrs. Burke?" I asked her very coldly, indicating that I had seen her shake Junior down.

"No, I haven't found it," she answered. She looked at Junior as if she still believed he had it."

"Did you see Mrs. Burke's purse, Junior?" I asked him.

"No, I ain't saw it." He shook his head and never took his eyes off Mrs. Burke.

"Junior hasn't seen it, Mrs. Burke. Maybe we overlooked it in the house."

"You cleaned my bedroom, Essie, and you said you didn't see it," Mrs. Burke said, but she started back to the house, and I followed her.

When we got inside, she went in the bedroom to look for her purse and I went back to housecleaning. About thirty minutes later she interrupted me again.

"I found it, Essie," she said, showing me the change purse in her hand.

"Where was it?" I asked.

"I had forgotten. Wayne and I watched TV in his room last night." She gave me a guilty smile.

"I am glad you found it." I picked up the broom and continued sweeping.

"I'll just find me another job," I thought to myself. "This is my last day working for this bitch. School will be out soon and I'll go back to Baton Rouge and get a job. Ain't no sense in me staying on here. Sooner or later something might really happen. Then I'll wish I had quit."

"Essie, I don't have enough money to pay you today," Mrs. Burke said, sitting at the big desk in the hallway. She was looking through her wallet. "I'll pay you on Monday. I'll cash a check then."

"You can give me a check, now, Mrs. Burke. I won't be back on Monday."

"Do you go to piano lessons on Monday now?" she asked.

"I am not coming back, Mrs. Burke," I said it slowly and deliberately, so she didn't misunderstand this time.

She looked at me for a while, and then said, "Why?"

"I saw what you did to Junior. Junior don't steal. And I have worked for white people since I was nine. I have worked for you almost two years, and I have never stole anything from you or anybody else. We work, Mrs. Burke, so we won't have to steal."

"O.K., Essie, I'll give you a check," Mrs. Burke said angrily. She hurriedly wrote one out and gave it to me.

"Is Junior still here?" I asked.

"No, I paid him and he's gone already. Why?" she asked.

I didn't answer. I just slowly walked to the front door. When I got there, I turned around and looked down the long hallway for the last time. Mrs. Burke stood at the desk staring at me curiously as I came back toward her again.

"Did you forget something?" she asked as I passed her.

"I forgot to tell Mrs. Crosby I am leaving," I said, still walking.

"Mama doesn't pay you. I do! I do!" she called to me, as I knocked gently and opened Mrs. Crosby's door.

Mrs. Crosby was propped up on pillows in bed as usual. But she looked much better than she had the last time I was in her room.

"How are you feeling, Mrs. Crosby?" I asked, standing by the side of her bed.

"Much better, Essie," she answered. She motioned for me to sit down.

"I just came to tell you this is my last day working for Mrs. Burke, Mrs. Crosby."

"What happened? Did she fire you, Essie?" she asked.

"She didn't fire me. I just decided to leave."

"I understand, Essie," she said. "And you take care of yourself. And remember when you are ready for college let me know, and I'll help you." She squeezed my hand.

"I gotta go, Mrs. Crosby," I said. "I hope you'll be up soon."

"Thanks, Essie, and please take care of yourself," she said.

"I will, Mrs. Crosby. 'Bye."

" 'Bye, Essie," she said. She squeezed my hand again and then I left her room.

When I walked out of Mrs. Crosby's room, Mrs. Burke was still standing in the hallway by the desk.

"Maybe you would like to come back tonight and say good-bye to Wayne, too," she said sarcastically.

I didn't say anything to her. I walked past her and out of that house for good. And I hoped that as time passed I could put not only Mrs. Burke but all her kind out of my life for good.

THE MOVEMENT

During my senior year at Tougaloo, my family hadn't sent me one penny. I had only the small amount of money I had earned at Maple Hill. I couldn't afford to eat at school or live in the dorms, so I had gotten permission to move off campus. I had to prove that I could finish school, even if I had to go hungry every day. I knew Raymond and Miss Pearl were just waiting to see me drop out. But something happened to me as I got more and more involved in the Movement. It no longer seemed important to prove anything. I had found something outside myself that gave meaning to my life.

I had become very friendly with my social science professor, John Salter, who was in charge of NAACP activities on campus. All during the year, while the NAACP conducted a boycott of the downtown stores in Jackson, I had been one of Salter's most faithful canvassers and church speakers. During the last week of school, he told me that sit-in demonstrations were about to start in Jackson and that he wanted me to be the spokesman for a team that would sit-in at Woolworth's lunch counter. The two other demonstrators would be classmates of mine, Memphis and Pearlena. Pearlena was a dedicated NAACP worker, but Memphis had not been very involved in the Movement on campus. It seemed that the organization had had a rough time finding students who were in a position to go to jail. I had nothing to lose one way or the other. Around ten o'clock the morning of the demonstrations, NAACP headquarters alerted the news services. As a result, the police department was also informed, but neither the policemen nor the newsmen knew exactly where or when the demonstrations would start. They stationed themselves along Capitol Street and waited.

To divert attention from the sit-in at Woolworth's, the picketing started at J. C. Penney's a good fifteen minutes before. The pickets were allowed to walk up and down in front of the store three or four times before they were arrested. At exactly 11 A.M., Pearlena, Memphis, and I entered Woolworth's from the rear entrance. We separated as soon as we stepped into the store, and made small purchases from various counters. Pearlena had given Memphis her watch. He was to let us know when it was 11:14. At 11:14 we were to join him near the lunch counter and at exactly 11:15 we were to take seats at it.

Seconds before 11:15 we were occupying three seats at the previously segregated Woolworth's lunch counter. In the beginning the waitresses seemed to ignore us, as if they really didn't know what was going on. Our waitress walked past us a couple of times before she noticed we had started to write our own orders down and realized we wanted service. She asked us what we wanted. We began to read to her from our order slips. She told us that we would be served at the back counter, which was for Negroes.

"We would like to be served here," I said.

The waitress started to repeat what she had said, then stopped in the middle of the sentence. She turned the lights out behind the counter, and she and the other waitresses almost ran to the back of the store, deserting all their white customers. I guess they thought that violence would start immediately after the whites at the counter realized what was going on. There were five or six other people at the counter. A couple of them just got up and walked away. A girl sitting next to me finished her banana split before leaving. A middle-aged white woman who had not yet been served rose from her seat and came over to us. "I'd like to stay here with you," she said, "but my husband is waiting."

The newsmen came in just as she was leaving. They must have discovered what was going on shortly after some of the people began to leave the store. One of the newsmen ran behind the woman who spoke to us and asked her to identify herself. She refused to give her name, but said she was a native of Vicksburg and a former resident of California. When asked why she had said what she had said to us, she replied, "I am in sympathy with the Negro movement." By this time a crowd of cameramen and reporters had gathered around us taking pictures and asking questions, such as Where were we from? Why did we sit-in? What organization sponsored it? Were we students? From what school? How were we classified?

I told them that we were all students at Tougaloo College, that we were represented by no particular organization, and that we planned to stay there even after the store closed. "All we want is service," was my reply to one of them. After they had finished probing for about twenty minutes, they were almost ready to leave.

At noon, students from a nearby white high school started pouring in to Woolworth's. When they first saw us they were sort of surprised. They didn't know how to react. A few started to heckle and the newsmen became interested again. Then the white students started chanting all kinds of anti-Negro slogans. We were called a little bit of everything. The rest of the seats except the three we were occupying had been roped off to prevent others from sitting down. A couple of the boys took one end of the rope and made it into a hangman's noose. Several attempts were made to put it around our necks. The crowds grew as more students and adults came in for lunch.

We kept our eyes straight forward and did not look at the crowd except for occasional glances to see what was going on. All of a sudden I saw a face I remembered—the drunkard from the bus station sit-in. My eyes lingered on him just long enough for us to recognize each other. Today he was drunk too, so I don't think he remembered where he had seen me before. He took out a knife, opened it, put it in his pocket, and then began to pace the floor. At this point, I told Memphis and Pearlena what was going on. Memphis suggested that we pray. We bowed our heads, and all hell broke loose. A man rushed forward, threw Memphis from his seat, and slapped my face. Then another man who worked in the store threw me against an adjoining counter.

Down on my knees on the floor, I saw Memphis lying near the lunch counter with blood running out of the corners of his mouth. As he tried to protect his face, the man who'd thrown him down kept kicking him against the head. If he had worn hard-soled shoes instead of sneakers, the first kick probably would have killed Memphis. Finally a man dressed in plain clothes identified himself as a police officer and arrested Memphis and his attacker.

Pearlena had been thrown to the floor. She and I got back on our stools after Memphis was arrested. There were some white Tougaloo teachers in the crowd. They asked Pearlena and me if we wanted to leave. They said that things were getting too rough. We didn't know what to do. While we were trying to make up our minds, we were joined by Joan Trumpauer. Now there were three of us and we were integrated. The crowd began to chant, "Communists, Communists, Communists." Some old man in the crowd ordered the students to take us off the stools.

"Which one should I get first?" a big husky boy said.

"That white nigger," the one man said.

The boy lifted Joan from the counter by her waist and carried her out of the store. Simultaneously, I was snatched from my stool by two high school students. I was dragged about thirty feet toward the door by my hair when someone made them turn me loose. As I was getting up off the floor, I saw Joan coming back inside. We started back to the center of the counter to join Pearlena. Lois Chaffee, a white Tougaloo faculty member, was now sitting next to her. So Joan and I just climbed across the rope at the front end of the counter and sat down. There were now four of us, two whites and two Negroes, all women. The mob started smearing us with ketchup, mustard, sugar, pies, and everything on the counter. Soon Joan and I were joined by John Salter, but the moment he sat down he was hit on the jaw with what appeared to be brass knuckles. Blood gushed from his face and someone threw salt into the open wound. Ed King, Tougaloo's chaplain, rushed to him.

At the other end of the counter, Lois and Pearlena were joined by George Raymond, a CORE field worker and a student from Jackson State College. Then a Negro high school boy sat down next to me. The mob took spray paint from the counter and sprayed it on the new demonstrators. The high school student had on a white shirt; the word "nigger" was written on his back with red spray paint.

We sat there for three hours taking a beating when the manager decided to close the store because the mob had begun to go wild with stuff from the other counters. He begged and begged everyone to leave. But even after fifteen minutes of begging, no one budged. They would not leave until we did. Then Dr. Beittel, the president of Tougaloo College, came running in. He said he had just heard what was happening.

About ninety policemen were standing outside the store; they had been watching the whole thing through the windows, but had not come in to stop the mob or do anything. President Beittel went outside and asked Captain Ray to come and escort us out. The captain refused, stating the manager had to invite him in before he could enter the premises, so Dr. Beittel himself brought us out. He had told the police that they had better protect us after we were outside the store. When we got outside, the policemen formed a single line that blocked the mob from us. However, they were allowed to throw at us everything they had collected. Within ten minutes, we were picked up by Reverend King in his station wagon and taken to the NAACP headquarters on Lynch Street.

After the sit-in, all I could think of was how sick Mississippi whites were. They believed so much in the segregated Southern way of life, they would kill to preserve it. I sat there in the NAACP office and thought of how many times they had killed when this way of life was threatened. I knew that the killing had just begun. "Many more will die before it is over with," I thought. Before the sit-in, I had always hated the whites in Mississippi. Now I knew it was impossible for me to hate sickness. The whites had a disease, an incurable disease in its final stage. What were our chances against such a disease? I thought of the students, the young Negroes who had just begun to protest, as young interns. When these young interns got older, I thought, they would be the best doctors in the world for social problems.

AUDRE LORDE
(1934–)

From *Zami: A New Spelling of My Name*

Audre Lorde loved poetry from an early age. When people asked the young girl how her day went, she replied in verse from something she had read. And when she ran out of published works to quote, she had to start writing her own poetry. She published her first poem, a love poem, in Seventeen *magazine when she was still in high school. Both her parents and her school discouraged her romantic inclinations.*

Lorde's parents were West Indian, and she grew up in a strict household. Her father was a real estate broker in New York, where they lived. While her parents sent Audre and her sisters to an integrated Catholic school, they didn't encourage her to socialize with whites and regarded them with suspicion.

As much as for her love poems, Lorde is known for her poems of anger, words that decry acts of racism, the crimes against black Americans. She received National Endowment for the Arts grants in 1981 and 1988. The Cancer Journals, *which chronicled her fight against breast cancer won her a 1981 Book Award from the American Library Association Gay Caucus. She currently teaches English at Hunter College in New York and lectures nationwide.*

The following excerpt comes from her biomythography, a work she wrote as a combination biography, history, and myth.

As a child, the most horrible condition I could contemplate was being wrong and being discovered. Mistakes could mean exposure, maybe even annihilation. In my mother's house, there was no room in which to make errors, no room to be wrong.

I grew Black as my need for life, for affirmation, for love, for sharing—copying from my mother what was in her, unfulfilled. I grew Black as *Seboulisa*, who I was to find in the cool mud halls of Abomey several lifetimes later—and, as alone. My mother's words teaching me all manner of wily and diversionary defenses learned from the white man's tongue, from out of the mouth of her father. She had had to use these defenses, and had survived by them, and had also died by them a little, at the same time. All the colors change and become each other, merge and separate, flow into rainbows and nooses.

I lie beside my sisters in the darkness, who pass me in the street unacknowledged and unadmitted. How much of this is the pretense of self-rejection that became an immovable protective mask, how much the programmed hate that we were fed to keep ourselves a part, apart?

One day (I remember I was still in the second grade) my mother was out marketing, and my sisters were talking about someone being *Colored*. In my six-year-old way, I jumped at this chance to find out what it was all about.

"What does *Colored* mean?" I asked. To my amazement, neither one of my sisters was quite sure.

"Well," Phyllis said. "The nuns are white, and the Short-Neck Store-Man is white, and Father Mulvoy is white and we're Colored."

"And what's Mommy? Is she white or Colored?"

"I don't know," answered Phyllis impatiently.

"Well," I said, "if anybody asks me what I am, I'm going to tell them I'm white same as Mommy."

"Ohhhhhhhhh, girl, you better not do that," they both chorused in horror.

"Why not?" I asked, more confused than ever. But neither of them could tell me why.

That was the first and only time my sisters and I discussed race as a reality in my house, or at any rate as it applied to ourselves.

Our new apartment was on 152nd Street between Amsterdam Avenue and Broadway in what was called Washington Heights, and already known as a "changing" neighborhood, meaning one where Black people could begin to find overpriced apartments out of the depressed and decaying core of Harlem.

The apartment house that we moved into was owned by a small landlord. We moved at the end of the summer, and I began school that year in a new Catholic school which was right across the street from our house.

Two weeks after we moved into the new apartment, our landlord hanged himself in the basement. The *Daily News* reported that the suicide was caused by his despondency over the fact that he finally had to rent to Negroes. I was the first Black student in St. Catherine's School, and all the white kids in my sixth grade class knew about the landlord who had hanged himself in the basement because of me and my family. He had been Jewish; I was Black. That made us both fair game for the cruel curiosity of my pre-adolescent classmates.

Ann Archdeacon, red-headed darling of the nuns and of Monsignor Brady, was the first one to ask me what I knew about the landlord's death. As usual, my parents had discussed the whole matter in patois, and I only read the comics in the daily paper.

"I don't know anything about it," I said, standing in the schoolyard at lunchtime, twisting my front braids and looking around for some friendly face. Ann Archdeacon snickered, and the rest of the group that had gathered around us to hear roared with laughter, until Sister Blanche waddled over to see what was going on.

If the Sisters of the Blessed Sacrament at St. Mark's School had been patronizing, at least their racism was couched in the terms of their mission. At St. Catherine's School, the Sisters of Charity were downright hostile. Their racism was unadorned, unexcused, and particularly painful because I was unprepared for it. I got no help at home. The children in my class made fun of my braids, so Sister Victoire, the principal, sent a note home to my mother asking her to comb my hair in a more "becoming" fashion, since I was too old, she said, to wear "pigtails."

All the girls wore blue gabardine uniforms that by springtime were a little musty, despite frequent drycleanings. I would come in from recess to find notes in my desk saying "You Stink." I showed them to Sister Blanche. She told me that she felt it was her Christian duty to tell me that Colored people *did* smell different from white people, but it was cruel of the children to write nasty notes because I couldn't help it, and if I would remain out in the yard the next day after the rest of the class came in after lunchtime, she would talk to them about being nicer to me!

The head of the parish and the school was Monsignor John J. Brady, who told my mother when she registered me that he had never expected to have to take Colored kids into his school. His favorite pastime was holding Ann Archdeacon or Ilene Crimmons on his lap, while he played with their blonde and red curls with one hand, and slid the other hand up the back of their blue gabardine uniforms. I did not care about his lechery, but I did care that he kept me in every Wednesday afternoon after school to memorize Latin nouns.

The other children in my class were given a cursory quiz to test their general acquaintance with the words, and then let go early, since it was the early release day for religious instruction.

I came to loathe Wednesday afternoons, sitting by myself in the classroom trying to memorize the singular and plural of a long list of Latin nouns, and their genders. Every half-hour or so, Father Brady would look in from the rectory, and ask to hear the words. If I so much as hesitated over any word or its plural, or its gender, or said it out of place on the list, he would spin on his black-robed heel and disappear for another half-hour or so. Although early dismissal was at 2:00 P.M., some Wednesdays I didn't get home until after four o'clock. Sometimes on Wednesday nights I would dream of the white, acrid-smelling mimeograph sheet: *agricola, agricolae*, fem., farmer. Three years later when I began Hunter High School and had to take Latin in earnest, I had built up such a block to everything about it that I failed my first two terms of it.

When I complained at home about my treatment at school, my mother would get angry with me.

"What do you care what they say about you, anyway? Do they put bread on your plate? You go to school to learn, so learn and leave the rest alone. You don't need friends." I did not see her helplessness, nor her pain.

I was the smartest girl in the class, which did nothing to contribute to my popularity. But the Sisters of the Blessed Sacrament had taught me well, and I was way ahead in math and mental arithmetic.

In the spring of the sixth grade, Sister Blanche announced that we were going to hold elections for two class presidents, one boy and one girl. Anyone could run, she said, and we would vote on Friday of that week. The voting should be according to merit and effort and class spirit, she added, but the most important thing would be marks.

Of course, Ann Archdeacon was nominated immediately. She was not only the most popular girl in the school, she was the prettiest. Ilene Crimmons was also nominated, her blonde curls and favored status with the Monsignor guaranteed that.

I lent Jim Moriarty ten cents, stolen from my father's pocket at lunchtime, so Jim nominated me. A titter went through the class, but I ignored it. I was in seventh heaven. I knew I was the smartest girl in the class. I had to win.

That afternoon when my mother came home from the office, I told her about the election, and how I was going to run, and win. She was furious.

"What in hell are you doing getting yourself involved with so much foolishness? You don't have better sense in your head than that? What-the-france do you need with election? We send you to school to work, not to prance about with president-this election-that. Get down the rice, girl, and stop talking your foolishness." We started preparing the food.

"But I just might win, Mommy. Sister Blanche said it should go to the smartest girl in the class." I wanted her to see how important it was to me.

"Don't bother me with that nonsense. I don't want to hear any more about it. And don't come in here on Friday with a long face, and any 'I didn't win, Mommy,' because I don't want to hear that, either. Your father and I have enough trouble to keep among-you in school, never mind election."

I dropped the subject.

The week was a very long and exciting one for me. The only way I could get attention from my classmates in the sixth grade was by having money, and thanks to carefully planned forays into my father's pants pockets every night that week, I made sure I had plenty. Every day at noon, I dashed across the street, gobbled down whatever food my mother had left for my lunch, and headed for the schoolyard.

Sometimes when I came home for lunch my father was asleep in my parents' bedroom before he returned to work. I now had my very own room, and my two sisters shared another. The day before the election, I tiptoed through the house to the closed french doors of my parents' bedroom, and through a crack in the portieres peeked in upon my sleeping father. The doors seemed to shake with his heavy snoring. I watched his mouth open and close a little with each snore, stentorian rattles erupting below his nuzzled moustache. The covers thrown partially back, to reveal his hands in sleep tucked into the top of his drawstring pajamas. He was lying on his side toward me, and the front of his pajama pants had fallen open. I could see only shadows of the vulnerable secrets shading the gap in his clothing, but I was suddenly shaken by this so-human image of him, and the idea that I could spy upon him and he not be aware of it, even in his sleep. I stepped back and closed the door quickly, embarrassed and ashamed of my own curiosity, but wishing his pajamas had gapped more so that I could finally know what exactly was the mysterious secret men carried between their legs.

When I was ten, a little boy on the rooftop had taken off my glasses, and so seeing little, all I could remember of that encounter, when I remembered it at all, was a long thin pencil-like thing that I knew couldn't have any relationship to my father.

Before I closed the door, though, I slipped my hand around the door-curtains to where Daddy's suit hung. I separated a dollar bill from the thin roll which he carried in his pants pocket. Then I retreated back into the kitchen, washed my plate and glass, and hurried back to school. I had electioneering to do.

I knew better than to say another word to my mother about the presidency, but that week was filled with fantasies of how I would break the news to her on Friday when she came home.

"Oh, Mommy, by the way, can I stay later at school on Monday for a presidents' meeting?" Or "Mother, would you please sign this note saying it is all right for me to accept the presidency?" Or maybe even, "Mother, could I have a little get-together here to celebrate the election?"

On Friday, I tied a ribbon around the steel barrette that held my unruly mass of hair tightly at the nape of my neck. Elections were to be held in the afternoon, and when I got home for lunch, for the first time in my life, I was too excited to eat. I buried the can of Campbell's soup that my mother had left out for me way behind the other cans in the pantry and hoped she had not counted how many were left.

We filed out of the schoolyard and up the stairs to the sixth grade room. The walls were still lined with bits of green from the recent St. Patrick's Day decorations. Sister Blanche passed out little pieces of blank paper for our ballots.

The first rude awakening came when she announced that the boy chosen would be president, but the girl would only be vice-president. I thought this was monstrously unfair. Why not the other way around? Since we could not, as she explained, have two presidents, why not a girl president and a boy vice-president? It doesn't really matter, I said to myself. I can live with being vice-president.

I voted for myself. The ballots were collected and passed to the front of the room and duly counted. James O'Connor won for the boys. Ann Archdeacon won for the girls. Ilene Crimmons came in second. I got four votes, one of which was mine. I was in shock. We all clapped for the winners, and Ann Archdeacon turned around in her seat and smiled her shit-eating smile at me. "Too bad you lost." I smiled back. I wanted to break her face off.

I was too much my mother's daughter to let anyone think it mattered. But I felt I had been destroyed. How could this have happened? I was the smartest girl in the class. I had not been elected vice-president. It was as simple as that. But something was escaping me. Something was terribly wrong. It wasn't fair.

A sweet little girl named Helen Ramsey had decided it was her Christian duty to befriend me, and she had once lent me her sled during the winter. She lived next to the church, and after school, that day, she invited me to her house for a cup of cocoa. I ran away without answering, dashing across the street and into the safety of my house. I ran up the stairs, my bookbag banging against my legs. I pulled out the key pinned to my uniform pocket and unlocked the door to our apartment. The house was warm and dark and empty and quiet. I did not stop running until I got to my room at the front of the house, where I flung my books and my coat in a corner and collapsed upon my convertible couch-bed, shrieking with fury and disappointment. Finally, in the privacy of my room, I could shed the tears that had been burning my eyes for two hours, and I wept and wept.

I had wanted other things before that I had not gotten. So much so, that I had come to believe if I really wanted something badly enough, the very act of my wanting it was an assurance that I would not get it. Was this what had happened with the election? Had I wanted it too much? Was this what my mother was always talking about? Why she had been so angry? Because wanting meant I would not get? But somehow this felt different. This was the first time that I had wanted something so badly, the getting of which I was sure I could control. The election was supposed to have gone to the smartest girl in the class, and I was clearly the smartest. That was something I had done, on my own, that should have guaranteed me the election. The smartest, not the most popular. That was me. But it hadn't happened. My mother had been right. I hadn't won the election. My mother had been right.

This thought hurt me almost as much as the loss of the election, and when I felt it fully I shrieked with renewed vigor. I luxuriated in my grief in the empty house in a way I could never have done if anyone were home.

All the way up front and buried in my tears, kneeling with my face in the cushions of my couch, I did not hear the key in the lock, nor the main door open. The first thing I knew, there was my mother standing in the doorway of my room, a frown of concern in her voice.

"What happened, what happened? What's wrong with you? What's this racket going on here?"

I turned my wet face up to her from the couch. I wanted a little comfort in my pain, and getting up, I started moving toward her.

"I lost the election, Mommy," I cried, forgetting her warnings. "I'm the smartest girl in class, Sister Blanche says so, and they chose Ann Archdeacon instead!" The unfairness of it all flooded over me again and my voice cracked into fresh sobs.

Through my tears, I saw my mother's face stiffen with rage. Her eyebrows drew together as her hand came up, still holding her handbag. I stopped in my tracks as her first blow caught me full on the side of my head. My mother was no weakling, and I backed away, my ears ringing. The whole world seemed to be going insane. It was only then I remembered our earlier conversations.

"See, the bird forgets, but the trap doesn't! I warned you! What you think you doing coming into this house wailing about election? If I told you once I have told you a hundred times, don't chase yourself behind these people, haven't I? What kind of ninny raise up here to think those good-for-nothing white piss-jets would pass over some little·jaćabat girl to elect you anything?" Smack! "What did I say to you just now?" She cuffed me again, this time on my shoulders, as I huddled to escape her rain of furious blows, and the edges of her pocketbook.

"Sure enough, didn't I tell you not to come in here bringing down tears over some worthless fool election?" Smack! "What the hell you think we send you to school for?" Smack! "Don't run yourself behind other people's business, you'll do better. Dry up, now, dry up!" Smack! She pulled me to my feet from where I had sunk back onto the couch.

"Is cry you want to cry? I'll give you something hard to cry on!" And she cuffed me again, this time more lightly. "Now get yourself up from there and stop acting like some stupid fool, worrying yourself about these people's business that doesn't concern you. Get-the-france out of here and wipe up your face. Start acting like a human being!"

Pushing me ahead of her, my mother marched back through the parlor and into the kitchen. "I come in here tired from the street and here you, acting like the world is ending. I thought sure enough some terrible thing happened to you, come to find out it's only election. Now help me put away this foodstuff."

I was relieved to hear her tone mollify, as I wiped my eyes. But I still gave her heavy hands a wide berth.

"It's just that it's not fair, Mother. That's all I was crying about," I said, opening the brown paper bags on the table. To admit I had been hurt would somehow put me in the wrong for feeling pain. "It wasn't the election I cared about so much really, just that it was all so unfair."

"Fair, fair, what's fair, you think? Is fair you want, look in God's face." My mother was busily dropping onions into the bin. She paused, and turning around, held my puffy face up, her hand beneath my chin. Her eyes so sharp and furious before, now just looked tired and sad.

"Child, why you worry your head so much over fair or not fair? Just do what is for you to do and let the rest take care of themselves." She smoothed straggles of hair back from my face, and I felt the anger gone from her fingers. "Look, your hair all mess-up behind from rolling around with foolishness. Go wash your face and hands and come help me dress this fish for supper."

JOHN EDGAR WIDEMAN and ROBERT DOUGLAS WIDEMAN

(1941–), (1950–)

From *Brothers and Keepers*

John Edgar Wideman grew up in a ghetto of Pittsburgh, "the wrong side of the tracks—under the tracks, if the truth be told." He worked hard in school and went away on scholarship to the University of Pennsylvania. He excelled—studied at Oxford, was a Rhodes Scholar, received a P.E.N./Faulkner award for fiction, taught literature at universities, and wrote critically acclaimed novels. He distanced himself from his poor background.

Nearly ten years younger than his brother, Robert was in many ways the opposite of John. He embraced all that John rejected: crime, drugs, ignorance; he was rebellious, did poorly in school, used drugs, and stole. In 1975, at age twenty-five, Robert killed a man and was charged with murder. Two years later he was sentenced to life in prison without chance of parole or probation.

In the book from which this excerpt was taken, John Wideman alternates recollections of his life with first-person narrative from Robert. The brothers, separated by years, didn't share their child-hoods. John examines the differences between their personalities and backgrounds that led down two such different paths—and muses how easily his own inner rage and a turn of luck could have landed him in prison as well. The following piece describes Robert's story of the summer of 1968.

Robby was the rebel. He was always testing our parents, seeing how much he could get away with. Hanging on the coattails of his big brother Dave, he hit the streets earlier, harder than the rest of us, partied on weekends, stretched his curfew past midnight. He was grounded countless times, but he ignored the groundings just as he'd ignored the house rules that he'd broken to get himself in trouble in the first place. At thirteen he was a tallish, skinny kid. He began to let his hair grow out into an Afro. Facial hair began to sprout and he logged hours in front of the bathroom mirror, picking his bush, measuring, prodding the curly hairs on his chin, the shadow darkening his upper lip. My mother's warnings, threats, pleas, had no effect on him. He learned to ride out the storms of her anger, to be sullen and stubborn till his hardheaded persistence wore her down. Only so many privileges she could take away before she had no cards to play. Hitting him was a waste of energy. She'd hurt herself on his hard, bony body; neither her hands, nor her words, made dents in the wall he was fashioning around himself.

Daddy could still shake him up. Edgar Wideman was six foot tall and weighed around two hundred hard pounds. Robby knew Daddy could tear up his behind and knew that if he pushed the wrong way at the wrong time, Edgar would punch him out. My father's rage, his fists were the atom bomb, the nuclear deterrent. Robby feared him so he gauged his misconduct with a diplomat's finely honed sensitivity to consequence and repercussion. Yet Robby understood that he had launched himself on a collision course. His determination to become an independent power setting his own rules would bring on a confrontation with Daddy. The shit had to hit the fan sooner or later, so it became a question of biding his time, of marshaling his forces, and convincing himself that he'd survive the holocaust generally intact.

One of the worst parts of being grounded was losing phone privileges. With a stable of young girls to keep happy, a phone was an indispensable tool, especially since Robby's ladies were scattered all over the city and he had neither time nor money to make his rounds in person. When he was stuck in the house the phone was the only pipeline to his world, so when Mom said no calls in or out, Robby was in exile, a monarch languishing while enemies nibbled away at his undefended turf. Predictably, the last great battle between Robby and my father was fought about the phone.

In the house on Marchand Street the phone sat on a three-legged stand just inside the front door. The phone cord would stretch halfway up the front hall steps so you could climb them and stake out a sanctuary, lean your back against the wall or banister, and escape the confines of the house, talk yourself and the one listening into a dreamlike place where you could be whoever you wanted to be. Mom was exactly right when she said, That boy lives on the phone. Like his music, his dancing, the dark basements and street corners, the phone allowed Rob to practice the magic powers he knew he possessed, those powers the world outside his skin denied or threatened.

For a series of trespasses Robby had been absolutely, positively prohibited from using the phone. He observed the ban for most of one day, then the walls started closing in. A particularly sweet thing in Penn Hills had beaucoup hard legs hitting on her day and night. Robby'd laid a mean rap on her and was just starting to get over. But a day without a call might undo his work. He waited till Mom went grocery shopping, then dialed Penn Hills. Everything was beautiful. He was rapping hard and heavy; the lady was coming on strong. In just a few minutes she'd squeeze through the telephone wire. He'd have that fine thing curled lovey-dovey on his lap. The conversation got so good to him he missed the clatter of Mom returning through the front door.

What do you think you're doing? Hang up and get down off those steps. You know you're not supposed to touch the phone.

She stomped straight to the kitchen with her armload of Giant Eagle bags, but the fire in her voice, her eyes said she'd be right back.

Sure enough as soon as the grocery bags hit the kitchen table she was hotfooting it back into the hall. Robby scooted up two more stairs and blocked the stairwell with his leg.

Just a minute, Mom. I'm almost through now. She'd have to knock down the barrier of his outstretched leg and fight through his body before she got to the phone.

Come down off the stairs, boy. Hang up that phone and come down this instant.

He hunched over, cradling, protecting his love. It was difficult to keep his voice soft, insinuating, cool, and still drown out his mother's screeching. He cupped the receiver with his palm. Shielded his love in a corner of the steps, his chest, his heart almost touching the dial.

Mom was screaming and starting up the steps, and Robby stiffened his leg. She'd hit there first, knock his leg down and fight him for the phone. He needed just a little more time. He had this sweet thing's nose wide open. Just a minute now. If Mom could just be cool a minute, he'd finish his business and she could snatch the phone if she wanted it. Beat him over the head with it if she wanted. So he got his leg up and his arm too, a second line of defense to buy another few seconds—time for the three or four good-byes he needed to sew up the fine lady on the other end of the line.

Yeah, baby, I miss you, too. Yeah, it's just somebody, just my mama wants to use the phone, babe, but that's alright. I ain't gon give it up while I got something sweet as you on the wire.

No way he'd kick his mother, but he'd wave that leg and keep it in her path long's he could. He had five or six things going at once. Leg and arm stiffened for protection and heavy breathing and heavy rapping through his fingers so his hand could smother the racket coming up the steps after him. He's so busy he doesn't notice right away the front door swing open again.

He knows something's up when he hears the thump, thumple,

thump of his ass hitting the steps one by one as he's dragged by the leg from his perch. Bram, bram, bram. Then the phone disappears, flies through the air and strikes the floor ringing once, louder than he's ever heard it. His father bends over to recover the phone, picks it up off the hall floor, sets it on the stand, slams the receiver back on the base. That big nigger had snatched the phone out his hand. That was my baby he flattened like a pancake when he bashed the two pieces of black phone together. Robby thinks this while he scrambles to his feet and leaps up the stairs. This is it, he thinks, and for a millisecond he considers jumping on his father's broad back, pummeling, kicking, settling once and for all the matter of who's boss. But that was a lot of hard nigger in the hall. And though his hands ached with fury, with sudden emptiness where a moment before he'd been holding his baby, he grabbed banister instead of his father's tough meat and scatted up the steps three at a time to the room he shared with brother David. He needed an equalizer. Something hard or heavy or sharp in his hand when that herd of elephants pursuing him got to the top of the steps.

Leave him alone. Don't go up there now. His mother's voice, then the steps bending, creaking, sighing, as slowly, in no hurry or rush or nothing, Edgar Wideman mounted them.

Robby slammed the door of his room. To buy time, to muffle the footsteps he hears anyway louder and louder pounding in his ears as he flings open a drawer and pulls out the scissors he knew were there. Long scissors. Black loops and thick, mismatched blades, the longer, wider one rounding to a point, the other tapering like a dagger. How should he hold them? Should he put his fingers through the holes or clutch both round eyes together like the handle of a knife? Cold steel in hand he faces the closed door waiting for it to burst open. How long had the scissors been lying in the drawer? Did he know he was after them when he bounced off his butt in the hall and catapulted up the stairs? Did he know then what he was after? Where he was headed? Had he been the one who had cached the weapon in the top bureau drawer? Did he know when he did it that he'd need them today? Did he know when he dialed Valery Jackson that he'd need the scissors to avenge her honor, his dignity? Was getting in her drawers tied to what he knew he could lay his hands on in the top drawer of the tall, slew-foot bureau?

Somebody was sobbing. The door flies open and it's not his daddy in tears. It's not his mother either, because he can hear her running up the steps shouting for his father to stop, to let him alone, to come back downstairs. The sobbing has something to do with the rhythm of the scissors, the beat shaking his hand so the weapon is a blur of black and silver through his tears. The tears are messing up everything and they go with the sobs, like the trembling goes with somebody sobbing so it's him backed up against the wall, sobbing like a baby, facing the big man who looms in the space where the door used to be.

I'll kill you if you come in here. Swear to God I'll kill you.

And it's him talking, screaming at Edgar Wideman and talking to the scissors, calmly, coolly like he tried to get to Valery Jackson under his mother's shouts. Steady. Steady. Rise up like a weapon. Don't act like something pointed at me. Don't act like I'm the one should be scared of these blades.

I hate you. I hate your guts. You come over here and I'll kill you. Swear I'll kill you if you touch me. You ain't gon whip me no more. It's his voice shaky with sobs. He's spitting tears from his lips. His eyes are rolling down his cheeks. But he's got his hand up and it stabs the air with the points of the scissors.

You ain't gon touch me. You ain't never whipping me again.

Edgar doesn't. He never smacks his son in anger again. He stands in the doorway, a puzzled look on his face. It's like he keeps putting two and two together and it comes out four, but four's wrong so he adds two and two again and gets four but four's wrong again, so he patiently does the sum again, two plus two equals . . . He doesn't hurry, concentrates as hard as he can on getting the answer right even though he knows it's a simple problem, the easiest kind of problem, and he's produced the answer a million times before, everybody in their right mind, everybody with good sense or less knows the answer but he stands in the door staring at his son, staring at the scared kid with the load of scissors in his hand and the snot and tears and trembling lips and thinks, yes, I brought you into the world and, yes, I could take you out, thinks that thought facing his son, watches the pointy scissors bob and thinks, yes, I've faced cold steel before, killed before, and unclenches his fist and feels the air go out of his chest, the cold stinging air that had risen to block his nostrils so they flared for breath, and a sigh goes out of him and memories drain until he's back to the problem, back to the only solution he knows and knows it will be wrong again.

Why are you doing this? Why don't you listen to what anybody tells you? You're just a rebel. A damned rebel. You don't listen to anybody.

He can hear his mother saying his father's name. Softly, rising in the stairwell, filtering into the room, little soft bubbles of his father's name. Edgar, Edgar, then, *Oh, God. Please stop this*, bursting against his father's rage, his father's shouts as he hesitates at the threshold of his son's room. The puzzled, hurt look doesn't leave his father's eyes even though his mouth twists and his lips curl, and his words explode like shots in the little bedroom.

A rebel. A damned rebel.

Then the space is empty. The stairs bend under two people descending.

* * *

I was scared. Scared as I ever been in my life. He could have took those scissors and made me eat them. I didn't know what Ida done if he called my bluff. He must of taked pity on me. He seen I got myself in too far to back away. Had those scissors in my hand but I was wishing I didn't. Wished I'd never hid them in the drawer. Wished I never been born.

Edgar didn't do a thing. He was as mad as I ever seen him but he just stood there yelling at me and didn't take a step until he turned around and went back downstairs. Called me a rebel. Said I wouldn't listen. I guess he decided it wasn't worth it. I guess he told me what he thought of me and didn't have no more to say.

Anyway that's part of the beginning. I can look back now and see it must have been funny in a way. I can laugh at how I must have looked. My scrawny ass quivering and crying so much I must have looked like a drowned rat to Daddy. But he never hit me again. He told me what he thought and let me slide that day. Never mentioned the phone or the scissors or nothing about that day ever.

At about the time I was beginning to teach Afro-American literature at the University of Pennsylvania, back home on the streets of Pittsburgh Robby was living through the changes in black culture and consciousness I was reading about and discussing with my students in the quiet of the classroom. Not until we began talking together in prison did I learn about that side of his rebelliousness. *Black Fire* was a book I used in my course. It was full of black rage and black dreams and black love. In the sixties when the book was published, young black men were walking the streets with, as one of the *Black Fire* writers put it, dynamite growing out of their skulls. I'd never associated Robby with the fires in Homewood and in cities across the land, never envisioned him bobbing in and out of the flames, a constant danger to himself, to everyone around him because "dynamite was growing out of his skull." His plaited naps hadn't looked like fuses to me. I was teaching, I was trying to discover words to explain what was happening to black people. That my brother might have something to say about these matters never occurred to me. The sad joke was, I never even spoke to Robby. Never knew until years later that he was the one who could have told me much of what I needed to hear.

It was a crazy summer. The summer of '68. We fought the cops in the streets. I mean sure nuff punch-out fighting like in them Wild West movies and do. Shit. Everybody in Homewood up on Homewood Avenue duking with the cops. Even the little weeny kids was there, standing back throwing rocks. We fought that whole summer. Cop cars all over the place and they'd come jumping out with nightsticks

and fists balled up. They wore leather jackets and gloves and sometimes they be wearing them football helmets so you couldn't go upside
they heads without hurting your hand. We was rolling. Steady fighting.
All you need to be doing was walking down the avenue and here they
come. Screeching the brakes. Pull up behind you and three or four
cops come busting out the squad car ready to rumble. Me and some
the fellas just minding our business walking down Homewood and
this squad car pulls up. Hey, you. Hold it. Stop where you are, like
he's talking to some silly kids or something. All up in my face. What
you doing here, like I ain't got no right to be on Homewood Avenue,
and I been walking on Homewood Avenue all my life an ain't no jive
police gon get on my case just cause I'm walking down the avenue.
Fuck you, pig. Ain't none your goddamn business, pig. Well, you know
it's on then. Cop come running at Henry and Henry ducks down on
one knee and jacks the motherfucker up. Throw him clean through
that big window of Murphy's five-and-dime. You know where I mean.
Where Murphy's used to be. Had that cop snatched up in the air and
through that window before he knew what hit him. Then it's on for
sure. We rolling right there in the middle of Homewood Avenue.

That's the way it was. Seem like we was fighting cops every day.
Funny thing was, it was just fighting. Wasn't no shooting or nothing
like that. Somebody musta put word out from Downtown. You can
whip the niggers' heads but don't be shooting none of em. Yeah.
Cause the cops would get out there and fight but they never used no
guns. Might bust your skull with a nightstick but they wasn't gon
shoot you. So the word must have been out. Cause you know if it was
left to the cops they would have blowed us all away. Somebody said
don't shoot and we figured that out so it was stone rock 'n' roll and
punch-up time.

Sometimes I think the cops dug it too. You know like it was exercise
or something. Two or three carloads roll up and it's time to get it
on. They was looking for trouble. You could tell. You didn't have to
yell pig or nothing. Just be minding your business and here they come
piling out the car ready to go ten rounds. I got tired of fighting cops.
And getting whipped on. We had some guys go up on the rooves.
Brothers was gon waste the motherfuckers from up there when they
go riding down the street but shit, wasn't no sense bringing guns into
it long as they wasn't shooting at us. Brothers didn't play in those
days. We was organized. Cops jump somebody and in two minutes
half of Homewood out there on them cops' ass. We was organized
and had our own weapons and shit. Rooftops and them old boarded-
up houses was perfect for snipers. Dudes had pistols and rifles and
shotguns. You name it. Wouldna believed what the brothers be firing
if it come to that but it didn't come to that. Woulda been stone war
in the streets. But the shit didn't come down that way. Maybe it woulda
been better if it did. Get it all out in the open. Get the killing done

wit. But the shit didn't hit the fan that summer. Least not that way.

Lemme see. I woulda been in eleventh grade. One more year of Westinghouse left after the summer of '68. We was the ones started the strike. Right in the halls of good old Westinghouse High School. Like I said, we had this organization. There was lots of organizations and clubs and stuff like that back then but we had us a mean group. Like, if you was serious business you was wit us. Them other people was into a little bit of this and that, but we was in it all the way. We was gon change things or die trying. We was known as bad. Serious business, you know. If something was coming down they always wanted us with them. See, if we was in it, it was some mean shit. Had to be. Cause we didn't play. What it was called was Together. Our group. We was so bad we was having a meeting once and one the brothers bust in. Hey youall. Did youall hear on the radio Martin Luther King got killed? One the older guys running the meeting look up and say, We don't care nothing bout that ass-kissing nigger, we got important business to take care of. See, we just knew we was into something. Together was where it was at. Didn't nobody dig what King putting down. We wasn't about begging whitey for nothing and we sure wasn't taking no knots without giving a whole bunch back. After the dude come in hollering and breaking up the meeting we figured we better go on out in the street anyway cause we didn't want no bullshit. You know. Niggers running wild and tearing up behind Martin Luther King getting wasted. We was into planning. Into organization. When the shit went down we was gon be ready. No point in just flying around like chickens with they heads cut off. I mean like it ain't news that whitey is offing niggers. So we go out the meeting to cool things down. No sense nobody getting killed on no humbug.

Soon as we got outside you could see the smoke rising off Homewood Avenue. Wasn't that many people out and Homewood burning already, so we didn't really know what to do. Walked down to Hamilton and checked it out around in there and went up past the A & P. Say to anybody we see, Cool it. Cool it, brother. Our time will come. It ain't today, brother. Cool it. But we ain't really got no plan. Didn't know what to do, so me and Henry torched the Fruit Market and went on home.

Yeah. I was a stone mad militant. Didn't know what I was saying half the time and wasn't sure what I wanted, but I was out there screaming and hollering and waving my arms around and didn't take no shit from nobody. Mommy and them got all upset cause I was in the middle of the school strike. I remember sitting down and arguing with them many a time. All they could talk about was me messing up in school. You know. Get them good grades and keep your mouth shut and mind your own business. Trying to tell me white folks ain't all bad. Asking me where would niggers be if it wasn't for good white folks. They be arguing that mess at me and they wasn't about to hear nothing I had to say. What it all come down to was be a good nigger and the white folks take care of you. Now I really couldn't believe they was saying that. Mommy and Geral got good sense. They ain't nobody's fools. How they talking that mess? Wasn't no point in arguing really, cause I was set in my ways and they sure was set in theirs. It was the white man's world and wasn't no way round it or over it or under it. Got to get down and dance to the tune the man be playing. You know I didn't want to hear nothing like that, so I kept on cutting classes and fucking up and doing my militant thing every chance I got.

I dug being a militant cause I was good. It was something I could do. Rap to people. Whip a righteous message on em. People knew my name. They'd listen. And I'd steady take care of business. This was when Rap Brown and Stokely and Bobby Seale and them on TV. I identified with those cats. Malcolm and Eldridge and George Jackson. I read their books. They was Gods. That's who I thought I was when I got up on the stage and rapped at the people. It seemed like things was changing. Like no way they gon turn niggers round this time.

You could feel it everywhere. In the streets. On the corner. Even in jive Westinghouse High people wasn't going for all that old, tired bullshit they be laying on you all the time. We got together a list of demands. Stuff about the lunchroom and a black history course. Stuff like that and getting rid of the principal. We wasn't playing. I mean he was a mean nasty old dude. Hated niggers. No question about that. He wouldn't listen to nobody. Didn't care what was going on. Everybody hated him. We told them people from the school board his ass had to go first thing or we wasn't coming back to school. It was a strike, see. Started in Westinghouse, but by the end of the week it was all over the city. Langley and Perry and Fifth Avenue and Schenley. Sent messengers to all the schools, and by the end of the week all the brothers and sisters on strike. Shut the schools down all cross the city, so they knew we meant business. Knew they had to listen. The whole Board of Education came to Westinghouse and we told the principal to his face he had to go. The nasty old motherfucker was sitting right there and we told the board, He has to go. The man hates us and we hate him and his ass got to go. Said it right to his face and you ought to seen him turning purple and flopping round in his chair. Yeah. We got on his case. And the thing was they gave us everything we asked for. Yes . . . Yes . . . Yes. Everything we had on the list. Sat there just as nice and lied like dogs. Yes. We agree. Yes. You'll have a new principal. I couldn't believe it. Didn't even have to curse them out or nothing. Didn't even raise my voice cause it was yes to this and yes to that before the words out my mouth good.

We's so happy we left that room with the Board and ran over to the auditorium and in two minutes it was full and I'm up there scream-

ing. We did it. We did it. People shouting back Right on and Work
out and I gets that whole auditorium dancing in they seats. I could
talk now. Yes, I could. And we all happy as could be, cause we thought
we done something. We got the black history course and got us a
new principal and, shit, wasn't nothing we couldn't do, wasn't nothing
could stop us that day. Somebody yelled, Party, and I yelled back,
Party, and then I told them, Everybody come on up to Westinghouse
Park. We gon stone party. Wasn't no plan or nothing. It all just started
in my head. Somebody shouted party and I yelled Party and the next
thing I know we got this all-night jam going. We got bands and lights
and we partied all night long. Ima tell you the truth now. Got more
excited bout the party than anything else. Standing up there on the
stage I could hear the music and see the niggers dancing and I'm
thinking, Yeah. I'm thinking bout getting high and tipping round,
checking out the babes and grooving on the sounds. Got me a little
reefer and sipping out somebody's jug of sweet wine and the park's
full of bloods and I'm in heaven. That's the way it was too. We partied
all night long in Westinghouse Park. Cops like to shit, but wasn't
nothing they could do. This was 1968. Wasn't nothing they could do
but surround the park and sit out there in they cars while we partied.
It was something else. Bands and bongos and niggers singing, *Oh bop
she bop* everywhere in the park. Cops sat out in them squad cars and
Black Marias, but wasn't nothing they could do. We was smoking and
drinking and carrying on all night and they just watched us, just sat
in the dark and didn't do a thing. We broke into the park building to
get us some lectricity for the bands and shit. And get us some light.
Broke in the door and took what we wanted, but them cops ain't
moved an inch. It was our night and they knew it. Knew they better
leave well enough alone. We owned Westinghouse Park that night.
Thought we owned Homewood.

In a way the party was the end. School out pretty soon after that
and nobody followed through. We come back to school in the fall
and they got cops patrolling the halls and locks on every door. You
couldn't go in or out the place without passing by a cop. They had
our ass then. Turned the school into a prison. Wasn't no way to get
in the auditorium. Wasn't no meetings or hanging out in the halls.
They broke up all that shit. That's when having police in the schools
really got started. When it got to be a regular everyday thing. They
fixed us good. Yes, yes, yes, when we was sitting down with the Board,
but when we come back to school in September everything got locks
and chains on it.

We was just kids. Didn't really know what we wanted. Like I said.
The party was the biggest thing to me. I liked to get up and rap. I
was a little Stokely, a little Malcolm in my head but I didn't know
shit. When I look back I got to admit it was mostly just fun and games.
Looking for a way to get over. Nothing in my head. Nothing I could

say I really wanted. Nothing I wanted to be. So they lied through their teeth. Gave us a party and we didn't know no better, didn't know we had to follow through, didn't know how to keep our foot in they ass.

Well, you know the rest. Nothing changed. Business as usual when we got back in the fall. Hey, hold on. What's this? Locks on the doors. Cops in the halls. Big cops with big guns. Hey, man, what's going down? But it was too late. The party was over and they wasn't about to give up nothing no more. We had a black history class, but wasn't nobody eligible to take it. Had a new principal, but nobody knew him. Nobody could get to him. And he didn't know us. Didn't know what we was about except we was trouble. Troublemakers; and he had something for that. Boot your ass out in a minute. Give your name to the cops and you couldn't get through the door cause everybody had to have an I.D. Yeah. That was a new one. Locks and I.D.'s and cops. Wasn't never our school. They made it worse instead of better. Had our chance, then they made sure we wouldn't have no more chances.

It was fun while it lasted. Some good times, but they was over in a minute and then things got worser and worser. Sixty-eight was when the dope came in real heavy too. I mean you could always get dope but in '68 seems like they flooded Homewood. Easy as buying a quart of milk. Could cop your works in a drugstore. Dope was everywhere that summer. Cats ain't never touched the stuff before got into dope and dope got into them. A bitch, man. It come in like a flood.

Me. I start to using heavy that summer. Just like everybody else I knew. The shit was out there and it was good and cheap, so why not? What else we supposed to be doing? It was part of the fun. The good times. The party.

We lost it over the summer, but I still believe we did something hip for a bunch of kids. The strike was citywide. We shut the schools down. All the black kids was with us. The smart ones. The dumb ones. It was hip to be on strike. To show our asses. We had them honkies scared. Got the whole Board of Education over to Westinghouse High. We lost it, but we had them going, Bruh. And I was in the middle of it. Mommy and them didn't understand. They thought I was just in trouble again. The way I always was. Daddy said one his friends works Downtown told him they had my name down there. Had my name and the rest of the ringleaders'. He said they were watching me. They had my name Downtown and I better be cool. But I wasn't scared. Always in trouble, always doing wrong. But the strike was different. I was proud of that. Proud of getting it started, proud of being one the ringleaders. The mad militant. Didn't know exactly what I was doing, but I was steady doing it.

The week the strike started, think it was Tuesday, could have been Monday but I think it was Tuesday, cause the week before was when some the students went to the principal's office and said the student council or some damn committee or something wanted to talk to him about the lunchroom and he said he'd listen but he was busy till next week, so it could have been Monday, but I think it was Tuesday cause knowing him he'd put it off as long as he could. Anyway, Mr. Lindsay sitting in the auditorium. Him and vice-principal Meers and the counselor, Miss Kwalik. They in the second or third row sitting back and the speakers is up on stage behind the mike but they ain't using it. Just talking to the air really, cause I slipped in one the side doors and I'm peeping what's going on. And ain't nothing going on. Most the time the principal whispering to Miss Kwalik and Mr. Meers. Lindsay got a tablet propped up on his knee and writes something down every now and then but he ain't really listening to the kids on stage. Probably just taking names cause he don't know nobody's name. Taking names and figuring how he's gon fuck over the ones doing the talking. You. You in the blue shirt, Come over here. Don't none them know your name less you always down in the office cause you in trouble or you one the kiss-ass, nicey-nice niggers they keep for flunkies and spies. So he's taking names or whatever, and every once in a while he says something like, Yes. That's enough now. Who's next? Waving the speakers on and off and the committee, or whatever the fuck they calling theyselves, they ain't got no better sense than to jump when he say jump. Half of them so scared they stuttering and shit. I know they glad when he wave them off the stage cause they done probably forgot what they up there for.

Well, I get sick of this jive real quick. Before I know it I'm up on the stage and I'm tapping the mike and can't get it turned on so I goes to shouting. Talking trash loud as I can. Damn this and damn that and Black Power and I'm somebody. Tell em ain't no masters and slaves no more and we want freedom and we want it now. I'm stone preaching. I'm chirping. Get on the teachers, get on the principal and everybody else I can think of. Called em zookeepers. Said they ran a zoo and wagged my finger at the chief zookeeper and his buddies sitting down there in the auditorium. Told the kids on the stage to go and get the students. You go here. You go there. Like I been giving orders all my life. Cleared the stage in a minute. Them chairs scraped and kids run off and it's just me up there all by my ownself. I runs out of breath. I'm shaking, but I'm not scared. Then it gets real quiet. Mr. Lindsay stands up. He's purple and shaking worse than me. Got his finger stabbing at me now. Shoe's on the other foot now. Up there all by myself now and he's doing the talking.

Are you finished? I hope you're finished cause your ass is grass. Come down from there this instant. You've gone too far this time, Wideman. Get down from there. I want you in my office immediately.

They's all three up now, Mr. Lindsay and Miss Kwalik and Meers, up and staring up at me like I'm stone crazy. Like I just pulled out my dick and peed on the stage or something. Like they don't believe it. And to tell the truth I don't hardly believe it myself. One minute I'm watching them kids making fools of theyselves, next minute I'm bad-mouthing everything about the school and giving orders and telling Mr. Lindsay to his face he ain't worth shit. Now the whiteys is up and staring at me like I'm a disease, like I'm Bad Breath or Okey Doke the damn fool and I'm looking round and it's just me up there. Don't know if the other kids is gone for the students like I told them or just run away cause they scared.

Ain't many times in life I felt so lonely. I'm thinking bout home. What they gon say when Mr. Lindsay calls and tells them he kicked my ass out for good. Cause I had talked myself in a real deep hole. Like, Burn, baby burn. We was gon run the school our way or burn the motherfucker down. Be our school or wasn't gon be no school. Yeah, I was yelling stuff like that and I was remembering it all. Cause it was real quiet in there. Could of heard a pin drop in the balcony. Remembering everything I said and then starting to figure how I was gon talk myself out this one. Steady scheming and just about ready to cop a plea. I's sorry boss. Didn't mean it, Boss. I was just kidding. Making a joke. Ha. Ha. I loves this school and loves you Mr. Lindsay. My head's spinning and I'm moving away from the mike but just at that very minute I hears the kids busting into the balcony. It's my people. It's sure nuff them. They bust in the balcony and I ain't by myself no more. I'm hollering again and shaking a power fist and I tells Mr. Lindsay:

You get out. You leave.

I'm king again. He don't say a word. Just splits with his flunkies. The mike starts working and that's when the strike begins.

Your brother was out there in the middle of it. I was good, too. Lot of the time I be thinking bout the party afterward, my heart skipping forward to the party, but I was willing to work. Be out front. Take the weight. Had the whole city watching us, Bruh.

NATHAN McCALL

(1954–)

Dispatches from a Dying Generation

Born in Portsmouth, Virginia, Nathan McCall spent much of his time growing up on the streets, where he did drugs, fought, burglarized, and robbed. The turning point in his life came while serving a twelve-year sentence in prison, where he discovered books and began to examine his life and the world beyond.

McCall also began writing in prison, and upon his release in 1978, went to Norfolk State University and graduated with honors with a degree in journalism. He now works as a reporter for The Washington Post. *Soon after the following piece appeared in* The Post, *McCall signed both book and movie contracts to tell his story.*

Revisiting My Violent Past—and the Friends Who Never Escaped —on the Mean Streets of Home

Make me wanna holler, and throw up both my hands,
It make me wanna holler, and throw up both my hands.

> —*From "Inner City Blues" by Marvin Gaye*

Two Christmases ago, I went home to Portsmouth, Va., and some of the boys from my old days on the block—Tony, Nutbrain and Roger—dropped by to check me out. We caught up on the years, and their stories revealed that not much with the old gang had changed: One had just gotten out of jail, he said, "for doing a rain dance" on his estranged girlfriend. Another had lost his house and family to a cocaine habit. A third friend, they said, had recently gotten his front teeth bashed out with a brick in a soured drug deal.

We learned that another old friend was back in town and decided to pay him a surprise visit. We crammed into my car, stopped at a store and bought a bottle of cheap wine—Wild Irish Rose, I think—just like the old days. I slid Marvin Gaye's classic "What's Going On?" into the cassette player and, while cruising along, it struck me: It really *was* like old times—them passing the wine bottle from hand-to-hand; Roger and Nutbrain arguing and elbowing each other in the back seat; and everybody playing the dozens—trading insults left and right.

When our friend answered the door, he seemed surprised but not glad to see us. Within minutes, we knew the reason for his nervousness. There was a knock, followed by whispers and the stealthy entry of a scraggly-bearded man and a disheveled woman. Clearly, the three of them were about to do some drugs, *just like old times*.

What was different was that we left. And though I made a point of not being judgmental, I wondered, like Marvin Gaye had nearly two decades earlier, what *is* going on?

Lately, with the mounting toll of homicides, drug abuse and prison stints threatening to decimate a generation of young black men, I'm still wondering—not as an outsider but as one who came perilously close to becoming a fatal statistic myself.

These days, my visits home have become occasions for mourning, soul-searching and anger. On one recent visit, I saw a story, splashed across the top of the newspaper about the police busting up a $20-million narcotics ring. Listed in the article were several of the people I've known most of my life.

I sighed. It wasn't the first time that day I'd been hit with negative news about the neighborhood. And it wasn't the last. Before that day ended, family members and people I met on the streets told tale after tale of homeboys, young black men like me, living lives mired in lunacy.

Every day in D.C., I read dismal accounts of blacks murdered over trivia—drugs, a coat, a pair of sneakers, pocket change. The people in those stories are faceless to me. I peruse the accounts with detached sadness, then turn the page.

But in my hometown, 200 miles south, the names conjure images of real people who lived down the street, around the corner, on the next block.

Trips to my old neighborhood, a large black community called Cavalier Manor, bring a distressingly close-up view of black America's running tragedy. When I'm there, it dawns on me over and over again that this "endangered species" thing is no empty phrase.

Consider this: Most of the guys I hung out with are either in prison, dead, drug zombies or nickel-and-dime street hustlers. Some are racing full-throttle toward self-destruction. Others already have plunged into the abyss: Kenny Banks got 19 years for dealing drugs. Baby Joe just finished a 15-year bit for a murder beef. Charlie Gregg was in drug rehab. Bubba Majette was murdered. Teddy sleeps in the streets. Sherman is strung out on drink and drugs. Since I began writing this story several weeks ago, two former peers have died from drugs and alcohol.

Many of my former running pals are insane—literally; I'm talking overcoats in August and voices in their heads. Of the 10 families on my street that had young males in their households, four—including my own—have had one or more siblings serve time. One of my best buddies, Shane, was recently sent to prison. He shot a man several times, execution-style. He got life.

Often when I go home, as I did this past Christmas season, I prepare with a pep talk to myself and a pledge to focus on the positive—time spent with family and old friends who are doing well, and opportunities to lend a compassionate ear to those not so well off.

I know I will see former buddies. Some are old hoods, hanging on the same corners where I left them 15 years ago. I see in them how far I've come. I'm not sure what they see in me. In exchanges that are sometimes awkward, they recount their hard knocks. I say little about my establishment job or the new life I've found.

What should I say? Get a job? Go to college? Adopt my middle-class success strategies?

The fact is, I know what they've been through. And I understand what they face. I took the plunge myself, several times.

From a shoplifting charge, to stealing an ice-cream truck, to possession of a sawed-off shotgun and, ultimately, to armed robbery, I've had my share of clashes with the law.

Before I was 20, I'd seen people shot and was shot at myself. When I was 19, in a running rivalry with some other thugs, I shot a man in the chest at point-blank range. He survived, and the following year he shot and killed a man and went to prison.

When I read about the shootings in D.C. and at home, I often flash back to scenes in which I played a part. It's hard for me now to believe I was once very much a part of that world. Yet it's all too easy to understand how it came to be.

Many people are puzzled about the culture of violence pervading black communities; it's so foreign to them. Some wonder if there is something innately wrong with black males. And when all else fails, they reach for the easy responses: "Broken homes?" "Misplaced values?" "Impoverished backgrounds?"

I can answer with certainty only about myself. My background and those of my running partners don't fit all the convenient theories, and the problems among us are more complex than something we can throw jobs, social programs or more policemen at.

Portsmouth, a Navy town of nearly 103,000, is not the blighted big city that D.C. is. And Cavalier Manor is no ghetto or lair of single-parent homes. In fact, my old neighborhood is middle class by black standards and has long symbolized the quest for black upward mobility in Portsmouth. There are sprawling homes, manicured lawns and two-car garages. A scenic lake winds through part of the neighborhood. The homeowners are hardworking people who embrace the American dream and pursue it passionately.

Shane and I and the others in our loosely-knit gang started out like most other kids. Ebullient and naive, we played sandlot football, mowed neighbors' lawns for spending change and went to the movies. We devoured comic books, exchanged baseball cards and attended church.

Yet somewhere between adolescence and adulthood, something inside us changed. Our optimism faded. Our hearts hardened, and many of us went on to share the same fates as the so-called disadvantaged.

I'm not exactly sure why, but I've got a good idea.

A psychologist friend once explained that our fates are linked partly to how we perceive our choices in life. Looking back, the reality may well have been that possibilities for us were abundant. But in Cavalier Manor, we perceived our choices as being severely limited.

Nobody flatly said that. But in various ways, inside our community and out, it was communicated early and often that as black men in a hostile world our options would be few.

The perception was powerfully reinforced by what we saw in our families, where we had inherited a legacy of limited choices. My grandmother's parents were unschooled, and she spent her life as an uneducated domestic, working for white families. My stepfather left school after the 10th grade, and my mother, who dropped out after 11 years, did only slightly better. They all managed to exceed the accomplishments of their forebears, but they lagged behind their white contemporaries.

What is not so easy for outsiders to grasp is why we did not follow our parents' lead and try to seize what we could with what we had. For us, somehow, growing up in the '70s, it was different. Our parents tried to insulate us from the full brunt of racism, but they could not counteract the flood of racial messages, subtle and blatant, filtering into our psyches—messages that artists like Richard Wright, James Baldwin and Ralph Ellison have documented, ones you never get accustomed to: the look in white storekeepers' eyes when you enter; the "click" of door locks when you walk past whites sitting in their cars.

Our parents, we believed, had learned to swallow pride for survival's sake. But my more militant generation seemed less inclined to make that compromise. In a curious way, we saw *anything* that brought us into the mainstream as a copout. We came to regard the establishment as the ubiquitous, all powerful "white man" who controlled our parents' lives and, we believed, determined our fates as well.

I think once we resigned ourselves to that notion, we became a lost and angry lot.

It is difficult to write this without sounding apologetic. But I know many of us could not bear to think about a future in which we were wholly subject to the whims of whites. We could not see a way out of that. Moreover, like many African Americans, then and now, we couldn't make the connections that seem so basic in the world where I now live and work.

For instance, the concept of education as a passport to a better life was vague to us. We saw no relation between school and our reality. That's why it was so easy for my buddies to drop out in our sophomore year. One day, as a group of us were walking to class, someone casually suggested we quit. I did not. (After all, I reasoned, you could find girls in school.) But one by one, the others tossed their books into the trash, just like that.

Still, there were plenty of role models in the neighborhood who were not our parents—teachers, postal workers and a smattering of professionals. But even those we respected seemed unable to articulate, or expose us to, choices they had not experienced themselves.

Besides, they were unappealing to us as heroes. They couldn't stand up to the white man. They didn't fulfill our notions about manhood.

Instead, we revered the guys on the streets, the thugs who were brazen and belligerent. They wore their hats backwards, left their belt buckles unfastened and shoelaces untied. They shunned the white establishment and worshipped violence.

In our eyes, they were real men. We studied their bouncy walk, known as the Pimp, and the slick, lyrical way they talked. Manhood became a measure of who could fight fiercest, shoot hoops best or get the most girls into bed. Our self-perceptions were reflected in the nicknames some of us took on: Dirty Stink, Whiskey Bottle, Bimbo, White Mouse, Turkey Buzzard, Rat Man, Scobie-D, Gruesome, Frank Nitty, Sweet Wolf, Black Sam, Sack Eye.

Our defiance may have stemmed partly from youthful rebellion, but it came mostly from rage at a world we sensed did not welcome us. And we knew there were countless others out there just like us, armed and on edge, and often all it took was an accidental brush against a coat sleeve or a misunderstood look to trigger a brawl or a shooting.

When your life in your own mind has no value, it becomes frighteningly easy to try to take another's life.

When I think about how to explain the carnage among young blacks in our cities—and how to stop it—I think about my hometown. In Portsmouth, black males are assumed to have three post–high school options: the naval shipyard, the military or college. All of us knew that working in the system carried a price: humiliation on some level. Among us was the lingering fear that the racially integrated work world, with its relentless psychological assaults, was in some ways more perilous than life in the rough-and-tumble streets.

At least in the streets, the playing field is level and the rules don't change.

Even among those of us who opted for college, there was the feeling that it was a place to stall. "We didn't know what to do or what we could do," Calvin Roberts, an old school friend told me recently. "We were in uncharted waters. Nobody we knew had been there, and we didn't know what to expect."

Perhaps for the first time in this nation's history, blacks began searching on a large scale for alternatives, and one option, of course, was the drug trade, the urban answer to capitalism. "The drug trade is one of the few places where young, uneducated blacks can say, 'I am the boss. This is *my* corporation,'" says Portsmouth Commonwealth Attorney Johnny Morrison, who has prosecuted some of his former friends for peddling drugs.

Contrary to some assumptions, there is no lack of work ethic in the drug trade. My best friend in school parlayed $20 into a successful drug operation. By the time we were both 18, he had employed a few people, bought a gold tooth and paid cash for a Buick Electra 225 (a deuce-and-a-quarter in street parlance). College students couldn't do that.

My friend didn't get caught, but others who were selling drugs, burglarizing and robbing did. I was one of them.

Often, during my teenage years, I felt like Bigger Thomas, the protagonist in Richard Wright's "Native Son"—propelled down a destructive road over which I had no control.

Seven months after being placed on probation for shooting a man, my journey ended: Nutbrain, Charlie Gregg and myself were caught after holding up a McDonald's. I was the gunman in the late night robbery, and I came so frighteningly close to pulling the trigger when the store manager tried to flee that my fingers moistened.

We actually got away with the money—about $2,000, I think—and were driving down the highway when several police cruisers surrounded us. After being searched, handcuffed and shoved into the back seat of the police car, I remember staring out the window and thinking that my life, at age 20, was over. How, I wondered, had it come to this? I had the strange, sudden wish that I could go back in time, perhaps to the year of my third-grade spelling bee, when I felt so full of hope.

In a weird way, I also felt relieved, as if I had been saved from something potentially worse. I truly had expected a more tragic fate: to go down in a shootout with police like Prairie Dog, a cross-town hood; to be caught by surprise one day, like Charles Lee, a neighborhood kid who was shot to death while burglarizing a home. When I read stories today in which shooting is involved, I think back to the moment when two lives could have been destroyed if I had put the slightest pressure on a trigger.

I realize that skeptics will say that nothing so concentrates the mind as getting caught. But in fact, that is exactly what happened. I realized that something in my life had gone terribly wrong. Prison was my wake-up call.

For nearly three years, I was forced to nurture my spirit and ponder all that had gone on before. A job in the prison library exposed me to a world of black literature that helped me understand who I was and why prison had become—literally—a rite of passage for so many of us. I sobbed when I read "Native Son" because it captured all those conflicting feelings—Bigger's restless anger, hopelessness, his tough facade among blacks and his morbid fear of whites—that I had often sensed in myself but was unable to express.

Malcolm X's autobiography helped me understand the devastating effects of self-hatred and introduced me to a universal principle: that if you change your self-perception, you can change your behavior. I concluded that if Malcolm X, who also went to prison, could pull his life out of the toilet, then maybe I could too.

My new life is still a struggle, harsher in some ways than the one I left. At times I feel suspended in a kind of netherworld, belonging fully to neither the streets nor the establishment.

I have come to believe two things that might seem contradictory: that some of our worst childhood fears *were* true—the establishment is teeming with racism. Yet I also believe whites are as befuddled about race as we are, and they're as scared of us as we are of them. Many of them are seeking solutions, just like us.

I am torn by a different kind of anger now: I resent suggestions that blacks enjoy being "righteous victims." And when people ask, "What is wrong with black men?" it makes me want to lash out. When I hear that question, I am reminded of something once said by Malcolm X: "I have no mercy or compassion in me for a society that will crush people and then penalize them for not being able to stand up under the weight."

Sometimes I wonder how I endured when so many others were crushed. I was not special. And when I hear the numbing statistics about black men, I often think of guys I grew up with who were smarter and more talented than me, but who will never realize their potential. Nutbrain, a mastermind in the ways of the streets, had the kind of raw intellect that probably could not be gauged in achievement tests. Shane, who often breezed effortlessly through tests in school, could have done anything he wanted with his life had he known what to do.

Now he has no choices.

When Shane was caught in a police manhunt a couple of years ago, I considered volunteering as a character witness, but dismissed the notion because I knew there was no way to tell a jury what I was unable to articulate to a judge at my own trial: How could I explain our anger and alienation from the rest of the world? Where was our common language?

Most people, I'm sure, would regard Shane's fate with the same detachment I feel when reading crime reports about people I don't know. But I hurt for Shane, who will likely spend the rest of his days behind bars and who must live with the agony of having taken a life. I hurt more for Shane's mother, who has now seen two of her four sons go to prison. A divorcee, she now delivers newspapers in Cavalier Manor.

I saw her recently after she tossed a paper onto my parents' doorstep. Her hair had grayed considerably. We hugged and chatted. She seemed proud that I had turned my life around, but I felt guilty and wondered again why I got a second chance and her sons did not.

After an awkward silence, I got Shane's prison address and said goodbye. I wrote to him but got no reply.

For those who'd like answers, I have no pithy social formulas to end black-on-black violence. But I do know that I see a younger, meaner generation out there now—more lost and alienated than we were—and placing even less value on life. We were at least touched by role models; this new bunch is totally estranged from the black mainstream. Crack has taken the drug game to a more lethal level and given young blacks far more economic incentive to opt for the streets.

I've come to fear that of the many things a black man can die from, the first may be rage—his own or someone else's.

For that reason, I seldom stick around when I stop on the block. One day not long ago, I spotted a few familiar faces hanging out at the old haunt, the local convenience store. I wheeled into the parking lot, strode over and high-fived the guys I knew. Within moments, I sensed that I was in danger.

I felt the hostile stares from those I didn't know. I was frightened by these younger guys, who now controlled my former turf. I eased back to my car and left, because I knew this: that if they saw the world as I once did, they believed they had nothing to lose, including life itself.

It made me wanna holler, and throw up both my hands.

Printed in the United States
32451LVS00001B/142

9 780380 766321